YOUR MOST COMPREHENSIVE AND
REVEALING INDIVIDUAL FORECAST

SUPER HOROSCOPE

TAURUS

19 98

April 21 - May 20

BERKLEY BOOKS, NEW YORK

The publishers regret that they cannot answer
individual letters requesting personal horoscope information.

1998 SUPER HOROSCOPE TAURUS

PRINTING HISTORY
BERKLEY TRADE EDITION / AUGUST 1997

The Putnam Berkley World Wide Web address is
http://www.berkley.com

ISBN: 0-425-15887-X

CONTENTS

THE CUSP-BORN TAURUS

Are you *really* a Taurus? If your birthday falls during the fourth week of April, at the beginning of Taurus, will you still retain the traits of Aries, the sign of the Zodiac before Taurus? And what if you were born late in May—are you more Gemini than Taurus? Many people born at the edge, or cusp, of a sign have difficulty determining exactly what sign they are. If you are one of these people, here's how you can figure it out, once and for all.

Consult the cusp table on the facing page, then locate the year of your birth. The table will tell you the precise days on which the Sun entered and left your sign for the year of your birth. In that way you can determine if you are a true Taurus—or whether you are an Aries or a Gemini—according to the variations in cusp dates from year to year (see also page 17).

If you were born at the beginning or end of Taurus, yours is a lifetime reflecting a process of subtle transformation. Your life on Earth will symbolize a significant change in consciousness, for you are either about to enter a whole new way of living or are leaving one behind.

If you were born toward the end of April, you may want to read the horoscope book for Aries as well as for Taurus. The investment might be strangely revealing, for Aries contains the secret to many of your complexities and unexpressed assets and liabilities.

But this is the very irony of an Aries-Taurus cusp. The more fixed you become, the less able you are to seek out adventure, take chances, gamble—and win. Your natural tendency is to acquire, build, and collect. The more you possess, the more permanent your status in life; thus, the less able you are to simply pick up and go back to zero. Fulfillment comes through loyalty, constancy, and success in the material world.

If you were born during the third week of May, you may want to see the Gemini horoscope book as well as Taurus, for without Gemini your assets are often too stable, too fixed. Gemini provides you with fluidity and gets you moving.

You are a blend of stability and mobility—rich, raw material— with a dexterity of mind and body. Even around a fixed and constant center, change is always taking place. No matter how you hang on, there will be a series of changes, experiences, new people, new faces, places, facts, and events.

You are conservative with the very definite hint of an open mind, the blend of hardheaded realism and freewheeling experimentalism, earthy, tactile sensuality, and bold participation in life's joys.

THE CUSPS OF TAURUS

DATES SUN ENTERS TAURUS (LEAVES ARIES)

April 20 every year from 1900 to 2000, except for the following:

April 19			April 21
1948	1972	1988	1903
52	76	89	07
56	80	92	11
60	81	93	19
64	84	96	
68	85	97	

DATES SUN LEAVES TAURUS (ENTERS GEMINI)

May 21 every year from 1900 to 2000, except for the following:

May 20			May 22
1948	1972	1988	1903
52	76	89	07
56	80	92	11
60	81	93	19
64	84	96	
68	85	97	

THE ASCENDANT: TAURUS RISING

Could you be a "double" Taurus? That is, could you have Taurus as your Rising sign as well as your Sun sign? The tables on pages 8–9 will tell you Taurus what your Rising sign happens to be. Just find the hour of your birth, then find the day of your birth, and you will see which sign of the Zodiac is your Ascendant, as the Rising sign is called. The Ascendant is called that because it is the sign rising on the eastern horizon at the time of your birth. For a more detailed discussion of the Rising sign and the twelve houses of the Zodiac, see pages 17–20.

The Ascendant, or Rising sign, is placed on the 1st house in a horoscope, of which there are twelve houses. The 1st house represents your response to the environment—your unique response. Call it identity, personality, ego, self-image, facade, come-on, body-mind-spirit—whatever term best conveys to you the meaning of the you that acts and reacts in the world. It is a you that is always changing, discovering a new you. Your identity started with birth and early environment, over which you had little conscious control, and continues to experience, to adjust, to express itself. The 1st house also represents how others see you. Has anyone ever guessed your sign to be your Rising sign? People may respond to that personality, that facade, that body type governed by your Rising sign.

Your Ascendant, or Rising sign, modifies your basic Sun sign personality, and it affects the way you act out the daily predictions for your Sun sign. If your Rising sign is indeed Taurus, what follows is a description of its effects on your horoscope. If your Rising sign is not Taurus, but some other sign of the Zodiac, you may wish to read the horoscope book for that sign as well.

With Taurus on the Ascendant, that is, in your 1st house, the planet rising in the 1st house is Venus, ruler of Taurus. Venus confers an intuitive, creative mind, and a liking for ease and luxury. Venus here gives you a sociable nature—loyal, lovable, and loving. But there are contradictions! Like the Bull, the zodiacal symbol of Taurus, you strike contrasting poses. In repose, you can be seen sweetly, peaceably smelling the flowers. Enraged, you trample the very turf that supports you. A passionate, selfish, demanding streak overcomes the mild, gentle, docile mood.

You have a well-developed need for people. Personal relationships are important to you, often centering around your love life. Bestowed with ample good looks and sensual appeal, you do not lack for admirers. In fact, you are sought after, often chased. Though generally loyal and steadfast, and capable of success in marriage, you may, however, have an irresistible urge for secret affairs, which arouse other people's jealousy and antagonism. There is also the danger that you can be caught between a fierce possessiveness and a thoughtless desire to acquire popularity in an indiscriminating way.

You have an even greater need for money. For you with Taurus Rising, money symbolizes the successful self. You intend to earn money in a steady, practical way, especially one that is time-honored and contains few risks. But you tend to spend money lavishly, when your comfort and edification demand it. You like sparkle and glitter, ornamentation, and nourishment. Food, clothes, "things" can become extravagances you cannot afford. Only when threats to your personal security loom do you jealously guard your money. You may also confuse money and love, using the one to get the other and vice versa.

You have a strong creative drive, tending toward the arts and crafts. Your self-expression is best achieved by creating sensations that are pleasing to the eye and to the body in general. You are, however, capable of sustained efforts of the mind, for you are both patient and intuitive. For you, the creator, one problem lies in being too fixed in your vision, too proud to ask for help, and too self-centered to think you need it. If you get bogged down, you abandon your undertakings for a lazy, self-indulgent spell. You also keep a too tenacious hold on your creations.

Because you are basically cautious, what you create or build is usually very sound. Success through stability is your motto. Your efforts, focused in a relationship or in a product, have a tempering, personalizing influence. Sometimes you shy away from group efforts if they stress generalities or nonpersonal goals. In a setting where intimacy is discouraged, your drive is inhibited. On the other hand, you have deep compassion and an unselfish need to serve others. When an activity or cause sponsors both personal satisfaction and kindly justice, you will work for it laboriously. Otherwise, you prefer the pursuit of heady living, sometimes alone, sometimes with a partner.

For Taurus Rising, two key words are sense and sensibility. Weave them together into a rich, thick tapestry, rather than raveling them in bits and pieces of pleasure.

RISING SIGNS FOR TAURUS

Hour of Birth*	Day of Birth		
	April 20–25	April 26–29	April 30–May 4
Midnight	Capricorn	Capricorn	Capricorn
1 AM	Capricorn	Aquarius	Aquarius
2 AM	Aquarius	Aquarius	Aquarius; Pisces 5/4
3 AM	Pisces	Pisces	Pisces
4 AM	Pisces; Aries 4/22	Aries	Aries
5 AM	Aries	Taurus	Taurus
6 AM	Taurus	Taurus	Taurus; Gemini 5/4
7 AM	Gemini	Gemini	Gemini
8 AM	Gemini	Gemini	Gemini; Cancer 5/2
9 AM	Cancer	Cancer	Cancer
10 AM	Cancer	Cancer	Cancer
11 AM	Cancer; Leo 4/22	Leo	Leo
Noon	Leo	Leo	Leo
1 PM	Leo	Leo	Virgo
2 PM	Virgo	Virgo	Virgo
3 PM	Virgo	Virgo	Virgo
4 PM	Virgo; Libra 4/23	Libra	Libra
5 PM	Libra	Libra	Libra
6 PM	Libra	Libra; Scorpio 4/29	Scorpio
7 PM	Scorpio	Scorpio	Scorpio
8 PM	Scorpio	Scorpio	Scorpio
9 PM	Scorpio; Sagittarius 4/23	Sagittarius	Sagittarius
10 PM	Sagittarius	Sagittarius	Sagittarius
11 PM	Sagittarius	Sagittarius; Capricorn 4/27	Capricorn

*See note on facing page.

Hour of Birth*	Day of Birth		
	May 5–10	May 11–15	May 16–21
Midnight	Capricorn	Aquarius	Aquarius
1 AM	Aquarius	Aquarius	Aquarius; Pisces 5/18
2 AM	Pisces	Pisces	Pisces
3 AM	Pisces; Aries 5/6	Aries	Aries
4 AM	Aries	Taurus	Taurus
5 AM	Taurus	Taurus	Taurus; Gemini 5/19
6 AM	Gemini	Gemini	Gemini
7 AM	Gemini	Gemini	Gemini; Cancer 5/18
8 AM	Cancer	Cancer	Cancer
9 AM	Cancer	Cancer	Cancer
10 AM	Cancer; Leo 5/8	Leo	Leo
11 AM	Leo	Leo	Leo
Noon	Leo	Leo	Virgo
1 PM	Virgo	Virgo	Virgo
2 PM	Virgo	Virgo	Virgo
3 PM	Virgo; Libra 5/8	Libra	Libra
4 PM	Libra	Libra	Libra
5 PM	Libra	Scorpio	Scorpio
6 PM	Scorpio	Scorpio	Scorpio
7 PM	Scorpio	Scorpio	Scorpio
8 PM	Scorpio; Sagittarius 5/8	Sagittarius	Sagittarius
9 PM	Sagittarius	Sagittarius	Sagittarius
10 PM	Sagittarius	Sagittarius; Capricorn 5/12	Capricorn
11 PM	Capricorn	Capricorn	Capricorn

*Hour of birth given here is for Standard Time in any time zone. If your hour of birth was recorded in Daylight Saving Time, subtract one hour from it and consult that hour in the table above. For example, if you were born at 6 AM D.S.T., see 5 AM above.

THE PLACE OF ASTROLOGY IN TODAY'S WORLD

Does astrology have a place in the fast-moving, ultra-scientific world we live in today? Can it be justified in a sophisticated society whose outriders are already preparing to step off the moon into the deep space of the planets themselves? Or is it just a hangover of ancient superstition, a psychological dummy for neurotics and dreamers of every historical age?

These are the kind of questions that any inquiring person can be expected to ask when they approach a subject like astrology which goes beyond, but never excludes, the materialistic side of life.

The simple, single answer is that astrology works. It works for many millions of people in the western world alone. In the United States there are 10 million followers and in Europe, an estimated 25 million. America has more than 4000 practicing astrologers, Europe nearly three times as many. Even down-under Australia has its hundreds of thousands of adherents. In the eastern countries, astrology has enormous followings, again, because it has been proved to work. In India, for example, brides and grooms for centuries have been chosen on the basis of their astrological compatibility.

Astrology today is more vital than ever before, more practicable because all over the world the media devotes much space and time to it, more valid because science itself is confirming the precepts of astrological knowledge with every new exciting step. The ordinary person who daily applies astrology intelligently does not have to wonder whether it is true nor believe in it blindly. He can see it working for himself. And, if he can use it—and this book is designed to help the reader to do just that—he can make living a far richer experience, and become a more developed personality and a better person.

Astrology and Relationships

Astrology is the science of relationships. It is not just a study of planetary influences on man and his environment. It is the study of man himself.

We are at the center of our personal universe, of all our relationships. And our happiness or sadness depends on how we act, how we relate to the people and things that surround us. The emotions that we generate have a distinct effect—for better or worse—on the world around us. Our friends and our enemies will confirm this. Just look in the mirror the next time you are angry. In other words, each of us is a kind of sun or planet or star radiating our feelings on the environment around us. Our influence on our personal universe, whether loving, helpful, or destructive, varies with our changing moods, expressed through our individual character.

Our personal "radiations" are potent in the way they affect our moods and our ability to control them. But we usually are able to throw off our emotion in some sort of action—we have a good cry, walk it off, or tell someone our troubles—before it can build up too far and make us physically ill. Astrology helps us to understand the universal forces working on us, and through this understanding, we can become more properly adjusted to our surroundings so that we find ourselves coping where others may flounder.

The Challenge of Love

The challenge of love lies in recognizing the difference between infatuation, emotion, sex, and, sometimes, the intentional deceit of the other person. Mankind, with its record of broken marriages, despair, and disillusionment, is obviously not very good at making these distinctions.

Can astrology help?

Yes. In the same way that advance knowledge can usually help in any human situation. And there is probably no situation as human, as poignant, as pathetic and universal, as the failure of man's love.

Love, of course, is not just between man and woman. It involves love of children, parents, home, and friends. But the big problems usually involve the choice of partner.

Astrology has established degrees of compatibility that exist between people born under the various signs of the Zodiac. Because people are individuals, there are numerous variations and modifications. So the astrologer, when approached on mate and marriage matters, makes allowances for them. But the fact remains that some groups of people are suited for each other and some are not, and astrology has expressed this in terms of characteristics we all can study and use as a personal guide.

No matter how much enjoyment and pleasure we find in the different aspects of each other's character, if it is not an overall compatibility, the chances of our finding fulfillment or enduring happiness in each other are pretty hopeless. And astrology can help us to find someone compatible.

Astrology and Science

Closely related to our emotions is the "other side" of our personal universe, our physical welfare. Our body, of course, is largely influenced by things around us over which we have very little control. The phone rings, we hear it. The train runs late. We snag our stocking or cut our face shaving. Our body is under a constant bombardment of events that influence our daily lives to varying degrees.

The question that arises from all this is, what makes each of us act so that we have to involve other people and keep the ball of activity and evolution rolling? This is the question that both science and astrology are involved with. The scientists have attacked it from different angles: anthropology, the study of human evolution as body, mind and response to environment; anatomy, the study of bodily structure; psychology, the science of the human mind; and so on. These studies have produced very impressive classifications and valuable information, but because the approach to the problem is fragmented, so is the result. They remain "branches" of science. Science generally studies effects. It keeps turning up wonderful answers but no lasting solutions. Astrology, on the other hand, approaches the question from the broader viewpoint. Astrology began its inquiry with the totality of human experience and saw it as an effect. It then looked to find the cause, or at least the prime movers, and during thousands of years of observation of man and his *universal* environment came up with the extraordinary principle of planetary influence—or astrology, which, from the Greek, means the science of the stars.

Modern science, as we shall see, has confirmed much of astrology's foundations—most of it unintentionally, some of it reluctantly, but still, indisputably.

It is not difficult to imagine that there must be a connection between outer space and Earth. Even today, scientists are not too sure how our Earth was created, but it is generally agreed that it is only a tiny part of the universe. And as a part of the universe, people on Earth see and feel the influence of heavenly bodies in almost every aspect of our existence. There is no doubt that the Sun has the greatest influence on life on this planet. Without it there would be no life, for without it there would be no warmth, no division into day and night, no cycles of time or season at all. This is clear and easy to see. The influence of the Moon, on the other hand, is more subtle, though no less definite.

There are many ways in which the influence of the Moon manifests itself here on Earth, both on human and animal life. It is a well-known fact, for instance, that the large movements of water on our planet—that is the ebb and flow of the tides—are caused by the Moon's gravitational pull. Since this is so, it follows that these water movements do not occur only in the oceans, but that all bodies of water are affected, even down to the tiniest puddle.

The human body, too, which consists of about 70 percent water, falls within the scope of this lunar influence. For example the menstrual cycle of most women corresponds to the 28-day lunar month; the period of pregnancy in humans is 273 days, or equal to nine lunar months. Similarly, many illnesses reach a crisis at the change of the Moon, and statistics in many countries have shown that the crime rate is highest at the time of the Full Moon. Even human sexual desire has been associated with the phases of the Moon. But it is in the movement of the tides that we get the clearest demonstration of planetary influence, which leads to the irresistible correspondence between the so-called metaphysical and the physical.

Tide tables are prepared years in advance by calculating the future positions of the Moon. Science has known for a long time that the Moon is the main cause of tidal action. But only in the last few years has it begun to realize the possible extent of this influence on mankind. To begin with, the ocean tides do not rise and fall as we might imagine from our personal observations of them. The Moon as it orbits around Earth sets up a circular wave of attraction which pulls the oceans of the world after it, broadly in an east to west direction. This influence is like a phantom wave crest, a loop of power stretching from pole to pole which passes over and around the Earth like an invisible shadow. It travels with equal effect across the land masses and, as scientists were recently amazed to observe, caused oysters placed in the dark in the middle of the United States where there is no sea to open their shells to receive the nonexistent tide. If the land-locked oysters react to this invisible signal, what effect does it have on us who not so long ago in evolutionary time came out of the sea and still have its salt in our blood and sweat?

Less well known is the fact that the Moon is also the primary force behind the circulation of blood in human beings and animals, and the movement of sap in trees and plants. Agriculturists have established that the Moon has a distinct influence on crops, which explains why for centuries people have planted according to Moon cycles. The habits of many animals, too, are directed by the movement of the Moon. Migratory birds, for instance, depart only at or near the time of the Full Moon. And certain sea creatures, eels in particular, move only in accordance with certain phases of the Moon.

Know Thyself—Why?

In today's fast-changing world, everyone still longs to know what the future holds. It is the one thing that everyone has in common: rich and poor, famous and infamous, all are deeply concerned about tomorrow.

But the key to the future, as every historian knows, lies in the past. This is as true of individual people as it is of nations. You cannot understand your future without first understanding your past, which is simply another way of saying that you must first of all know yourself.

The motto "know thyself" seems obvious enough nowadays, but it was originally put forward as the foundation of wisdom by the ancient Greek philosophers. It was then adopted by the "mystery religions" of the ancient Middle East, Greece, Rome, and is still used in all genuine schools of mind training or mystical discipline, both in those of the East, based on yoga, and those of the West. So it is universally accepted now, and has been through the ages.

But how do you go about discovering what sort of person you are? The first step is usually classification into some sort of system of types. Astrology did this long before the birth of Christ. Psychology has also done it. So has modern medicine, in its way.

One system classifies people according to the source of the impulses they respond to most readily: the muscles, leading to direct bodily action; the digestive organs, resulting in emotion; or the brain and nerves, giving rise to thinking. Another such system says that character is determined by the endocrine glands, and gives us such labels as "pituitary," "thyroid," and "hyperthyroid" types. These different systems are neither contradictory nor mutually exclusive. In fact, they are very often different ways of saying the same thing.

Very popular, useful classifications were devised by Carl Jung, the eminent disciple of Freud. Jung observed among the different faculties of the mind, four which have a predominant influence on character. These four faculties exist in all of us without exception, but not in perfect balance. So when we say, for instance, that someone is a "thinking type," it means that in any situation he or she tries to be rational. Emotion, which may be the opposite of thinking, will be his or her weakest function. This thinking type can be sensible and reasonable, or calculating and unsympathetic. The emotional type, on the other hand, can often be recognized by exaggerated language—everything is either marvelous or terrible—and in extreme cases they even invent dramas and quarrels out of nothing just to make life more interesting.

The other two faculties are intuition and physical sensation. The sensation type does not only care for food and drink, nice clothes and furniture; he or she is also interested in all forms of physical experience. Many scientists are sensation types as are athletes and nature-lovers. Like sensation, intuition is a form of perception and we all possess it. But it works through that part of the mind which is not under conscious control—consequently it sees meanings and connections which are not obvious to thought or emotion. Inventors and original thinkers are always intuitive, but so, too, are superstitious people who see meanings where none exist.

Thus, sensation tells us what is going on in the world, feeling (that is, emotion) tells us how important it is to ourselves, thinking enables us to interpret it and work out what we should do about it, and intuition tells us what it means to ourselves and others. All four faculties are essential, and all are present in every one of us. But some people are guided chiefly by one, others by another. In addition, Jung also observed a division of the human personality into the extrovert and the introvert, which cuts across these four types.

A disadvantage of all these systems of classification is that one cannot tell very easily where to place oneself. Some people are reluctant to admit that they act to please their emotions. So they deceive themselves for years by trying to belong to whichever type they think is the "best." Of course, there is no best; each has its faults and each has its good points.

The advantage of the signs of the Zodiac is that they simplify classification. Not only that, but your date of birth is personal—it is unarguably yours. What better way to know yourself than by going back as far as possible to the very moment of your birth? And this is precisely what your horoscope is all about, as we shall see in the next section.

WHAT IS A HOROSCOPE?

If you had been able to take a picture of the skies at the moment of your birth, that photograph would be your horoscope. Lacking such a snapshot, it is still possible to recreate the picture—and this is at the basis of the astrologer's art. In other words, your horoscope is a representation of the skies with the planets in the exact positions they occupied at the time you were born.

The year of birth tells an astrologer the positions of the distant, slow-moving planets Jupiter, Saturn, Uranus, Neptune, and Pluto. The month of birth indicates the Sun sign, or birth sign as it is commonly called, as well as indicating the positions of the rapidly moving planets Venus, Mercury, and Mars. The day and time of birth will locate the position of our Moon. And the moment—the exact hour and minute—of birth determines the houses through what is called the Ascendant, or Rising sign.

With this information the astrologer consults various tables to calculate the specific positions of the Sun, Moon, and other planets relative to your birthplace at the moment you were born. Then he or she locates them by means of the Zodiac.

The Zodiac

The Zodiac is a band of stars (constellations) in the skies, centered on the Sun's apparent path around the Earth, and is divided into twelve equal segments, or signs. What we are actually dividing up is the Earth's path around the Sun. But from our point of view here on Earth, it seems as if the Sun is making a great circle around our planet in the sky, so we say it is the Sun's apparent path. This twelvefold division, the Zodiac, is a reference system for the astrologer. At any given moment the planets—and in astrology both the Sun and Moon are considered to be planets—can all be located at a specific point along this path.

Now where in all this are you, the subject of the horoscope? Your character is largely determined by the sign the Sun is in. So that is where the astrologer looks first in your horoscope, at your Sun sign.

The Sun Sign and the Cusp

There are twelve signs in the Zodiac, and the Sun spends approximately one month in each sign. But because of the motion of the Earth around the Sun—the Sun's apparent motion—the dates when the Sun enters and leaves each sign may change from year to year. Some people born near the cusp, or edge, of a sign have difficulty determining which is their Sun sign. But in this book a Table of Cusps is provided for the years 1900 to 2000 (page 5) so you can find out what your true Sun sign is.

Here are the twelve signs of the Zodiac, their ancient zodiacal symbol, and the dates when the Sun enters and leaves each sign for the year 1998. Remember, these dates may change from year to year.

ARIES	Ram	March 20–April 20
TAURUS	Bull	April 20–May 21
GEMINI	Twins	May 21–June 21
CANCER	Crab	June 21–July 22
LEO	Lion	July 22–August 23
VIRGO	Virgin	August 23–September 23
LIBRA	Scales	September 23–October 23
SCORPIO	Scorpion	October 23–November 22
SAGITTARIUS	Archer	November 22–December 21
CAPRICORN	Sea Goat	December 21–January 20
AQUARIUS	Water Bearer	January 20–February 18
PISCES	Fish	February 18–March 20

It is possible to draw significant conclusions and make meaningful predictions based simply on the Sun sign of a person. There are many people who have been amazed at the accuracy of the description of their own character based only on the Sun sign. But an astrologer needs more information than just your Sun sign to interpret the photograph that is your horoscope.

The Rising Sign and the Zodiacal Houses

An astrologer needs the exact time and place of your birth in order to construct and interpret your horoscope. The illustration on the next page shows the flat chart, or natural wheel, an astrologer uses. Note the inner circle of the wheel labeled 1 through 12. These 12 divisions are known as the houses of the Zodiac.

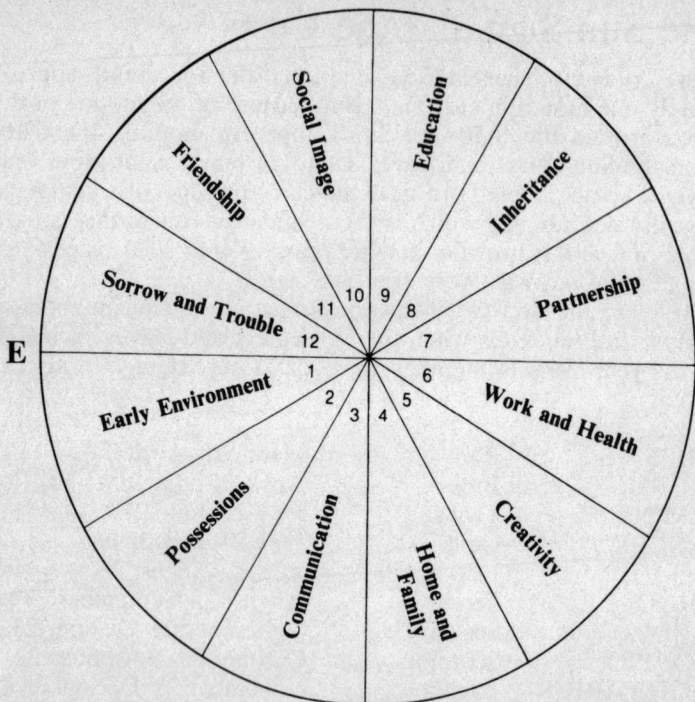

The 1st house always starts from the position marked E, which corresponds to the eastern horizon. The rest of the houses 2 through 12 follow around in a "counterclockwise" direction. The point where each house starts is known as a cusp, or edge.

The cusp, or edge, of the 1st house (point E) is where an astrologer would place your Rising sign, the Ascendant. And, as already noted, the exact time of your birth determines your Rising sign. Let's see how this works.

As the Earth rotates on its axis once every 24 hours, each one of the twelve signs of the Zodiac appears to be "rising" on the horizon, with a new one appearing about every 2 hours. Actually it is the turning of the Earth that exposes each sign to view, but in our astrological work we are discussing apparent motion. This Rising sign marks the Ascendant, and it colors the whole orientation of a horoscope. It indicates the sign governing the 1st house of the chart, and will thus determine which signs will govern all the other houses.

To visualize this idea, imagine two color wheels with twelve divisions superimposed upon each other. For just as the Zodiac is divided into twelve constellations that we identify as the signs, another twelvefold division is used to denote the houses. Now imagine one wheel (the signs) moving slowly while the other wheel (the houses) remains still. This analogy may help you see how the signs keep shifting the "color" of the houses as the Rising sign continues to change every two hours. To simplify things, a Table of Rising Signs has been provided (pages 8–9) for your specific Sun sign.

Once your Rising sign has been placed on the cusp of the 1st house, the signs that govern the rest of the 11 houses can be placed on the chart. In any individual's horoscope the signs do not necessarily correspond with the houses. For example, it could be that a sign covers part of two adjacent houses. It is the interpretation of such variations in an individual's horoscope that marks the professional astrologer.

But to gain a workable understanding of astrology, it is not necessary to go into great detail. In fact, we just need a description of the houses and their meanings, as is shown in the illustration above and in the table below.

THE 12 HOUSES OF THE ZODIAC

1st	Individuality, body appearance, general outlook on life	Personality house
2nd	Finance, possessions, ethical principles, gain or loss	Money house
3rd	Relatives, communication, short journeys, writing, education	Relatives house
4th	Family and home, parental ties, land and property, security	Home house
5th	Pleasure, children, creativity, entertainment, risk	Pleasure house
6th	Health, harvest, hygiene, work and service, employees	Health house
7th	Marriage and divorce, the law, partnerships and alliances	Marriage house
8th	Inheritance, secret deals, sex, death, regeneration	Inheritance house
9th	Travel, sports, study, philosophy and religion	Travel house
10th	Career, social standing, success and honor	Business house
11th	Friendship, social life, hopes and wishes	Friends house
12th	Troubles, illness, secret enemies, hidden agendas	Trouble house

The Planets in the Houses

An astrologer, knowing the exact time and place of your birth, will use tables of planetary motion in order to locate the planets in your horoscope chart. He or she will determine which planet or planets are in which sign and in which house. It is not uncommon, in an individual's horoscope, for there to be two or more planets in the same sign and in the same house.

The characteristics of the planets modify the influence of the Sun according to their natures and strengths.

Sun: Source of life. Basic temperament according to the Sun sign. The conscious will. Human potential.

Moon: Emotions. Moods. Customs. Habits. Changeable. Adaptive. Nurturing.

Mercury: Communication. Intellect. Reasoning power. Curiosity. Short travels.

Venus: Love. Delight. Charm. Harmony. Balance. Art. Beautiful possessions.

Mars: Energy. Initiative. War. Anger. Adventure. Courage. Daring. Impulse.

Jupiter: Luck. Optimism. Generous. Expansive. Opportunities. Protection.

Saturn: Pessimism. Privation. Obstacles. Delay. Hard work. Research. Lasting rewards after long struggle.

Uranus: Fashion. Electricity. Revolution. Independence. Freedom. Sudden changes. Modern science.

Neptune: Sensationalism. Theater. Dreams. Inspiration. Illusion. Deception.

Pluto: Creation and destruction. Total transformation. Lust for power. Strong obsessions.

Superimpose the characteristics of the planets on the functions of the house in which they appear. Express the result through the character of the Sun sign, and you will get the basic idea.

Of course, many other considerations have been taken into account in producing the carefully worked out predictions in this book: the aspects of the planets to each other; their strength according to position and sign; whether they are in a house of exaltation or decline; whether they are natural enemies or not; whether a planet occupies its own sign; the position of a planet in relation to its own house or sign; whether the sign is male or female; whether the sign is a fire, earth, water, or air sign. These are only a few of the colors on the astrologer's pallet which he or she must mix with the inspiration of the artist and the accuracy of the mathematician.

How To Use These Predictions

A person reading the predictions in this book should understand that they are produced from the daily position of the planets for a group of people and are not, of course, individually specialized. To get the full benefit of them our readers should relate the predictions to their own character and circumstances, coordinate them, and draw their own conclusions from them.

If you are a serious observer of your own life, you should find a definite pattern emerging that will be a helpful and reliable guide.

The point is that we always retain our free will. The stars indicate certain directional tendencies but we are not compelled to follow. We can do or not do, and wisdom must make the choice.

We all have our good and bad days. Sometimes they extend into cycles of weeks. It is therefore advisable to study daily predictions in a span ranging from the day before to several days ahead.

Daily predictions should be taken very generally. The word "difficult" does not necessarily indicate a whole day of obstruction or inconvenience. It is a warning to you to be cautious. Your caution will often see you around the difficulty before you are involved. This is the correct use of astrology.

In another section (pages 78–84), detailed information is given about the influence of the Moon as it passes through each of the twelve signs of the Zodiac. There are instructions on how to use the Moon Tables (pages 85–92), which provide Moon Sign Dates throughout the year as well as the Moon's role in health and daily affairs. This information should be used in conjunction with the daily forecasts to give a fuller picture of the astrological trends.

HISTORY OF ASTROLOGY

The origins of astrology have been lost far back in history, but we do know that reference is made to it as far back as the first written records of the human race. It is not hard to see why. Even in primitive times, people must have looked for an explanation for the various happenings in their lives. They must have wanted to know why people were different from one another. And in their search they turned to the regular movements of the Sun, Moon, and stars to see if they could provide an answer.

It is interesting to note that as soon as man learned to use his tools in any type of design, or his mind in any kind of calculation, he turned his attention to the heavens. Ancient cave dwellings reveal dim crescents and circles representative of the Sun and Moon, rulers of day and night. Mesopotamia and the civilization of Chaldea, in itself the foundation of those of Babylonia and Assyria, show a complete picture of astronomical observation and well-developed astrological interpretation.

Humanity has a natural instinct for order. The study of anthropology reveals that primitive people—even as far back as prehistoric times—were striving to achieve a certain order in their lives. They tried to organize the apparent chaos of the universe. They had the desire to attach meaning to things. This demand for order has persisted throughout the history of man. So that observing the regularity of the heavenly bodies made it logical that primitive peoples should turn heavenward in their search for an understanding of the world in which they found themselves so random and alone.

And they did find a significance in the movements of the stars. Shepherds tending their flocks, for instance, observed that when the cluster of stars now known as the constellation Aries was in sight, it was the time of fertility and they associated it with the Ram. And they noticed that the growth of plants and plant life corresponded with different phases of the Moon, so that certain times were favorable for the planting of crops, and other times were not. In this way, there grew up a tradition of seasons and causes connected with the passage of the Sun through the twelve signs of the Zodiac.

Astrology was valued so highly that the king was kept informed of the daily and monthly changes in the heavenly bodies, and the results of astrological studies regarding events of the future. Head astrologers were clearly men of great rank and position, and the office was said to be a hereditary one.

Omens were taken, not only from eclipses and conjunctions of the Moon or Sun with one of the planets, but also from storms and earthquakes. In the eastern civilizations, particularly, the reverence inspired by astrology appears to have remained unbroken since the very earliest days. In ancient China, astrology, astronomy, and religion went hand in hand. The astrologer, who was also an astronomer, was part of the official government service and had his own corner in the Imperial Palace. The duties of the Imperial astrologer, whose office was one of the most important in the land, were clearly defined, as this extract from early records shows:

> This exalted gentleman must concern himself with the stars in the heavens, keeping a record of the changes and movements of the Planets, the Sun and the Moon, in order to examine the movements of the terrestrial world with the object of prognosticating good and bad fortune. He divides the territories of the nine regions of the empire in accordance with their dependence on particular celestial bodies. All the fiefs and principalities are connected with the stars and from this their prosperity or misfortune should be ascertained. He makes prognostications according to the twelve years of the Jupiter cycle of good and evil of the terrestrial world. From the colors of the five kinds of clouds, he determines the coming of floods or droughts, abundance or famine. From the twelve winds, he draws conclusions about the state of harmony of heaven and earth, and takes note of good and bad signs that result from their accord or disaccord. In general, he concerns himself with five kinds of phenomena so as to warn the Emperor to come to the aid of the government and to allow for variations in the ceremonies according to their circumstances.

The Chinese were also keen observers of the fixed stars, giving them such unusual names as Ghost Vehicle, Sun of Imperial Concubine, Imperial Prince, Pivot of Heaven, Twinkling Brilliance, Weaving Girl. But, great astrologers though they may have been, the Chinese lacked one aspect of mathematics that the Greeks applied to astrology—deductive geometry. Deductive geometry was the basis of much classical astrology in and after the time of the Greeks, and this explains the different methods of prognostication used in the East and West.

Down through the ages the astrologer's art has depended, not so much on the uncovering of new facts, though this is important, as on the interpretation of the facts already known. This is the essence of the astrologer's skill.

But why should the signs of the Zodiac have any effect at all on the formation of human character? It is easy to see why people thought they did, and even now we constantly use astrological expressions in our everyday speech. The thoughts of "lucky star," "ill-fated," "star-crossed," "mooning around," are interwoven into the very structure of our language.

Wherever the concept of the Zodiac is understood and used, it could well appear to have an influence on the human character. Does this mean, then, that the human race, in whose civilization the idea of the twelve signs of the Zodiac has long been embedded, is divided into only twelve types? Can we honestly believe that it is really as simple as that? If so, there must be pretty wide ranges of variation within each type. And if, to explain the variation, we call in heredity and environment, experiences in early childhood, the thyroid and other glands, and also the four functions of the mind together with extroversion and introversion, then one begins to wonder if the original classification was worth making at all. No sensible person believes that his favorite system explains everything. But even so, he will not find the system much use at all if it does not even save him the trouble of bothering with the others.

In the same way, if we were to put every person under only one sign of the Zodiac, the system becomes too rigid and unlike life. Besides, it was never intended to be used like that. It may be convenient to have only twelve types, but we know that in practice there is every possible gradation between aggressiveness and timidity, or between conscientiousness and laziness. How, then, do we account for this?

A person born under any given Sun sign can be mainly influenced by one or two of the other signs that appear in their individual horoscope. For instance, famous persons born under the sign of Gemini include Henry VIII, whom nothing and no one could have induced to abdicate, and Edward VIII, who did just that. Obviously, then, the sign Gemini does not fully explain the complete character of either of them.

Again, under the opposite sign, Sagittarius, were both Stalin, who was totally consumed with the notion of power, and Charles V, who freely gave up an empire because he preferred to go into a monastery. And we find under Scorpio many uncompromising characters such as Luther, de Gaulle, Indira Gandhi, and Montgomery, but also Petain, a successful commander whose name later became synonymous with collaboration.

A single sign is therefore obviously inadequate to explain the differences between people; it can only explain resemblances, such as the combativeness of the Scorpio group, or the far-reaching devotion of Charles V and Stalin to their respective ideals—the Christian heaven and the Communist utopia.

But very few people have only one sign in their horoscope chart. In addition to the month of birth, the day and, even more, the hour to the nearest minute if possible, ought to be considered. Without this, it is impossible to have an actual horoscope, for the word horoscope literally means "a consideration of the hour."

The month of birth tells you only which sign of the Zodiac was occupied by the Sun. The day and hour tell you what sign was occupied by the Moon. And the minute tells you which sign was rising on the eastern horizon. This is called the Ascendant, and, as some astrologers believe, it is supposed to be the most important thing in the whole horoscope.

The Sun is said to signify one's heart, that is to say, one's deepest desires and inmost nature. This is quite different from the Moon, which signifies one's superficial way of behaving. When the ancient Romans referred to the Emperor Augustus as a Capricorn, they meant that he had the Moon in Capricorn. Or, to take another example, a modern astrologer would call Disraeli a Scorpion because he had Scorpio Rising, but most people would call him Sagittarius because he had the Sun there. The Romans would have called him Leo because his Moon was in Leo.

So if one does not seem to fit one's birth month, it is always worthwhile reading the other signs, for one may have been born at a time when any of them were rising or occupied by the Moon. It also seems to be the case that the influence of the Sun develops as life goes on, so that the month of birth is easier to guess in people over the age of forty. The young are supposed to be influenced mainly by their Ascendant, the Rising sign, which characterizes the body and physical personality as a whole.

It is nonsense to assume that all people born at a certain time will exhibit the same characteristics, or that they will even behave in the same manner. It is quite obvious that, from the very moment of its birth, a child is subject to the effects of its environment, and that this in turn will influence its character and heritage to a decisive extent. Also to be taken into account are education and economic conditions, which play a very important part in the formation of one's character as well.

People have, in general, certain character traits and qualities which, according to their environment, develop in either a positive or a negative manner. Therefore, selfishness (inherent selfishness, that is) might emerge as unselfishness; kindness and consideration as cruelty and lack of consideration toward others. In the same way, a naturally constructive person may, through frustration, become destructive, and so on. The latent characteristics with which people are born can, therefore, through environment and good or bad training, become something that would appear to be its opposite, and so give the lie to the astrologer's description of their character. But this is not the case. The true character is still there, but it is buried deep beneath these external superficialities.

Careful study of the character traits of various signs of the Zodiac are of immeasurable help, and can render beneficial service to the intelligent person. Undoubtedly, the reader will already have discovered that, while he is able to get on very well with some people, he just "cannot stand" others. The causes sometimes seem inexplicable. At times there is intense dislike, at other times immediate sympathy. And there is, too, the phenomenon of love at first sight, which is also apparently inexplicable. People appear to be either sympathetic or unsympathetic toward each other for no apparent reason.

Now if we look at this in the light of the Zodiac, we find that people born under different signs are either compatible or incompatible with each other. In other words, there are good and bad interrelating factors among the various signs. This does not, of course, mean that humanity can be divided into groups of hostile camps. It would be quite wrong to be hostile or indifferent toward people who happen to be born under an incompatible sign. There is no reason why everybody should not, or cannot, learn to control and adjust their feelings and actions, especially after they are aware of the positive qualities of other people by studying their character analyses, among other things.

Every person born under a certain sign has both positive and negative qualities, which are developed more or less according to our free will. Nobody is entirely good or entirely bad, and it is up to each of us to learn to control ourselves on the one hand and at the same time to endeavor to learn about ourselves and others.

It cannot be emphasized often enough that it is free will that determines whether we will make really good use of our talents and abilities. Using our free will, we can either overcome our failings or allow them to rule us. Our free will enables us to exert sufficient willpower to control our failings so that they do not harm ourselves or others.

Astrology can reveal our inclinations and tendencies. Astrology can tell us about ourselves so that we are able to use our free will to overcome our shortcomings. In this way astrology helps us do our best to become needed and valuable members of society as well as helpmates to our family and our friends. Astrology also can save us a great deal of unhappiness and remorse.

Yet it may seem absurd that an ancient philosophy could be a prop to modern men and women. But below the materialistic surface of modern life, there are hidden streams of feeling and thought. Symbology is reappearing as a study worthy of the scholar; the psychosomatic factor in illness has passed from the writings of the crank to those of the specialist; spiritual healing in all its forms is no longer a pious hope but an accepted phenomenon. And it is into this context that we consider astrology, in the sense that it is an analysis of human types.

Astrology and medicine had a long journey together, and only parted company a couple of centuries ago. There still remain in medical language such astrological terms as "saturnine," "choleric," and "mercurial," used in the diagnosis of physical tendencies. The herbalist, for long the handyman of the medical profession, has been dominated by astrology since the days of the Greeks. Certain herbs traditionally respond to certain planetary influences, and diseases must therefore be treated to ensure harmony between the medicine and the disease.

But the stars are expected to foretell and not only to diagnose. Astrological forecasting has been remarkably accurate, but often it is wide of the mark. The brave person who cares to predict world events takes dangerous chances. Individual forecasting is less clear cut; it can be a help or a disillusionment. Then we come to the nagging question: if it is possible to foreknow, is it right to foretell? This is a point of ethics on which it is hard to pronounce judgment. The doctor faces the same dilemma if he finds that symptoms of a mortal disease are present in his patient and that he can only prognosticate a steady decline. How much to tell an individual in a crisis is a problem that has perplexed many distinguished scholars. Honest and conscientious astrologers in this modern world, where so many people are seeking guidance, face the same problem.

Five hundred years ago it was customary to call in a learned man who was an astrologer who was probably also a doctor and a philosopher. By his knowledge of astrology, his study of planetary influences, he felt himself qualified to guide those in distress. The world has moved forward at a fantastic rate since then, and yet people are still uncertain of themselves. At first sight it seems fantastic in the light of modern thinking that they turn to the most ancient of all studies, and get someone to calculate a horoscope for them. But is it *really* so fantastic if you take a second look? For astrology is concerned with tomorrow, with survival. And in a world such as ours, tomorrow and survival are the keywords for the twenty-first century.

ASTROLOGICAL BRIDGE TO THE 21st CENTURY

As the last decade of the twentieth century comes to a close, planetary aspects for its final years connect you with the future. Major changes completed in 1995 and 1996 give rise to new planetary cycles that form the bridge to the twenty-first century and new horizons. The years 1996 through 1999 and into the year 2000 reveal hidden paths and personal hints for achieving your potential, for making the most of your message from the planets.

All the major planets begin new cycles in the late 1990s. Jupiter, planet of good fortune, transits four zodiacal signs from 1996 through 1999 and goes through a complete cycle in each of the elements earth, air, fire, and water. Jupiter is in Capricorn, then in Aquarius, next in Pisces, and finally in Aries as the century turns. With the dawning of the twenty-first century, each new yearly Jupiter cycle follows the natural progression of the Zodiac, from Aries in 2000, then Taurus in 2001, next Gemini in 2002, and so on through Pisces in 2011. The beneficent planet Jupiter promotes your professional and educational goals while urging informed choice and deliberation. Jupiter sharpens your focus and hones your skills. And while safeguarding good luck, Jupiter can turn unusual risks into achievable aims.

Saturn, planet of reason and responsibility, has begun a new cycle in the spring of 1996 when it entered fiery Aries. Saturn in Aries through March 1999 heightens a longing for independence. Your movements are freed from everyday restrictions, allowing you to travel, to explore, to act on a variety of choices. With Saturn in Aries you get set to blaze a new trail. Saturn enters earthy Taurus in March 1999 for a three-year stay over the turn of the century into the year 2002. Saturn in Taurus inspires industry and affection. Practicality, perseverance, and planning can reverse setbacks and minimize risk. Saturn in Taurus lends beauty, order, and structure to your life. In order to take advantage of opportunity through responsibility, to persevere against adversity, look to beautiful planet Saturn.

Uranus, planet of innovation and surprise, started an important new cycle in January of 1996. At that time Uranus entered its natural home in airy Aquarius. Uranus in Aquarius into the year 2003 has a profound effect on your personality and the lens through which you see the world. A basic change in the way you project yourself is just one impact of Uranus in Aquarius. More significantly, a whole new consciousness is evolving. Winds of change blowing your way emphasize movement and freedom. Uranus in Aquarius poses involvement in the larger community beyond self, family, friends, lovers, associates. Radical ideas and progressive thought signal a journey of liberation. As the century turns, follow Uranus on the path of humanitarianism. While you carve a prestigious niche in public life, while you preach social reform and justice, you will be striving to make the world a better place for all people.

Neptune, planet of vision and mystery, is in earthy Capricorn until late 1998. Neptune in Capricorn excites creativity while restraining fanciful thinking. Wise use of resources helps you build persona and prestige. Then Neptune enters airy Aquarius during November 1998 and is there into the year 2011. Neptune in Aquarius, the sign of the Water Bearer, represents two sides of the coin of wisdom: inspiration and reason. Here Neptune stirs powerful currents bearing a rich and varied harvest, the fertile breeding ground for idealistic aims and practical considerations. Neptune's fine intuition tunes in to your dreams, your imagination, your spirituality. You can never turn your back on the mysteries of life. Uranus and Neptune, the planets of enlightenment and renewed idealism both in the sign of Aquarius, give you glimpses into the future, letting you peek through secret doorways into the twenty-first century.

Pluto, planet of beginnings and endings, has completed one cycle of growth November 1995 in the sign of Scorpio. Pluto in Scorpio marked a long period of experimentation and rejuvenation. Then Pluto entered the fiery sign of Sagittarius on November 10, 1995 and is there into the year 2007. Pluto in Sagittarius during its long stay of twelve years can create significant change. The great power of Pluto in Sagittarius may already be starting its transformation of your character and lifestyle. Pluto in Sagittarius takes you on a new journey of exploration and learning. The awakening you experience on intellectual and artistic levels heralds a new cycle of growth. Uncompromising Pluto, seeker of truth, challenges your identity, persona, and self-expression. Uncovering the real you, Pluto holds the key to understanding and meaningful communication. Pluto in Sagittarius can be the guiding light illuminating the first decade of the twenty-first century. Good luck is riding on the waves of change.

THE SIGNS OF THE ZODIAC

Dominant Characteristics

Aries: March 21–April 20

The Positive Side of Aries

The Aries has many positive points to his character. People born under this first sign of the Zodiac are often quite strong and enthusiastic. On the whole, they are forward-looking people who are not easily discouraged by temporary setbacks. They know what they want out of life and they go out after it. Their personalities are strong. Others are usually quite impressed by the Ram's way of doing things. Quite often they are sources of inspiration for others traveling the same route. Aries men and women have a special zest for life that can be contagious; for others, they are a fine example of how life should be lived.

The Aries person usually has a quick and active mind. He is imaginative and inventive. He enjoys keeping busy and active. He generally gets along well with all kinds of people. He is interested in mankind, as a whole. He likes to be challenged. Some would say he thrives on opposition, for it is when he is set against that he often does his best. Getting over or around obstacles is a challenge he generally enjoys. All in all, Aries is quite positive and young-thinking. He likes to keep abreast of new things that are happening in the world. Aries are often fond of speed. They like things to be done quickly, and this sometimes aggravates their slower colleagues and associates.

The Aries man or woman always seems to remain young. Their whole approach to life is youthful and optimistic. They never say die, no matter what the odds. They may have an occasional setback, but it is not long before they are back on their feet again.

The Negative Side of Aries

Everybody has his less positive qualities—and Aries is no exception. Sometimes the Aries man or woman is not very tactful in communicating with others; in his hurry to get things done he is apt to be a little callous or inconsiderate. Sensitive people are likely to find him somewhat sharp-tongued in some situations. Often in his eagerness to get the show on the road, he misses the mark altogether and cannot achieve his aims.

At times Aries can be too impulsive. He can occasionally be stubborn and refuse to listen to reason. If things do not move quickly enough to suit the Aries man or woman, he or she is apt to become rather nervous or irritable. The uncultivated Aries is not unfamiliar with moments of doubt and fear. He is capable of being destructive if he does not get his way. He can overcome some of his emotional problems by steadily trying to express himself as he really is, but this requires effort.

Taurus: April 21–May 20

The Positive Side of Taurus

The Taurus person is known for his ability to concentrate and for his tenacity. These are perhaps his strongest qualities. The Taurus man or woman generally has very little trouble in getting along with others; it's his nature to be helpful toward people in need. He can always be depended on by his friends, especially those in trouble.

Taurus generally achieves what he wants through his ability to persevere. He never leaves anything unfinished but works on something until it has been completed. People can usually take him at his word; he is honest and forthright in most of his dealings. The Taurus person has a good chance to make a success of his life because of his many positive qualities. The Taurus who aims high seldom falls short of his mark. He learns well by experience. He is thorough and does not believe in shortcuts of any kind. The Bull's thoroughness pays off in the end, for through his deliberateness he learns how to rely on himself and what he has learned. The Taurus person tries to get along with others, as a rule. He is not overly critical and likes people to be themselves. He is a tolerant person and enjoys peace and harmony—especially in his home life.

Taurus is usually cautious in all that he does. He is not a person who believes in taking unnecessary risks. Before adopting any one line of action, he will weigh all of the pros and cons. The Taurus person is steadfast. Once his mind is made up it seldom changes. The person born under this sign usually is a good family person—reliable and loving.

The Negative Side of Taurus

Sometimes the Taurus man or woman is a bit too stubborn. He won't listen to other points of view if his mind is set on something. To others, this can be quite annoying. Taurus also does not like to be told what to do. He becomes rather angry if others think him not too bright. He does not like to be told he is wrong, even when he is. He dislikes being contradicted.

Some people who are born under this sign are very suspicious of others—even of those persons close to them. They find it difficult to trust people fully. They are often afraid of being deceived or taken advantage of. The Bull often finds it difficult to forget or forgive. His love of material things sometimes makes him rather avaricious and petty.

Gemini: May 21–June 20

The Positive Side of Gemini

The person born under this sign of the Heavenly Twins is usually quite bright and quick-witted. Some of them are capable of doing many different things. The Gemini person very often has many different interests. He keeps an open mind and is always anxious to learn new things.

Gemini is often an analytical person. He is a person who enjoys making use of his intellect. He is governed more by his mind than by his emotions. He is a person who is not confined to one view; he can often understand both sides to a problem or question. He knows how to reason, how to make rapid decisions if need be.

He is an adaptable person and can make himself at home almost anywhere. There are all kinds of situations he can adapt to. He is a person who seldom doubts himself; he is sure of his talents and his ability to think and reason. Gemini is generally most satisfied

when he is in a situation where he can make use of his intellect. Never short of imagination, he often has strong talents for invention. He is rather a modern person when it comes to life; Gemini almost always moves along with the times—perhaps that is why he remains so youthful throughout most of his life.

Literature and art appeal to the person born under this sign. Creativity in almost any form will interest and intrigue the Gemini man or woman.

The Gemini is often quite charming. A good talker, he often is the center of attraction at any gathering. People find it easy to like a person born under this sign because he can appear easy-going and usually has a good sense of humor.

The Negative Side of Gemini

Sometimes the Gemini person tries to do too many things at one time—and as a result, winds up finishing nothing. Some Twins are easily distracted and find it rather difficult to concentrate on one thing for too long a time. Sometimes they give in to trifling fancies and find it rather boring to become too serious about any one thing. Some of them are never dependable, no matter what they promise.

Although the Gemini man or woman often appears to be well-versed on many subjects, this is sometimes just a veneer. His knowledge may be only superficial, but because he speaks so well he gives people the impression of erudition. Some Geminis are sharp-tongued and inconsiderate; they think only of themselves and their own pleasure.

Cancer: June 21–July 20

The Positive Side of Cancer

The Moon Child's most positive point is his understanding nature. On the whole, he is a loving and sympathetic person. He would never go out of his way to hurt anyone. The Cancer man or woman is often very kind and tender; they give what they can to others. They hate to see others suffering and will do what they can to help someone in less fortunate circumstances than themselves. They are often very concerned about the world. Their interest in people generally goes beyond that of just their own families and close friends; they have a deep sense of community and respect humanitarian values. The Moon Child means what he says, as a rule; he is honest about his feelings.

The Cancer man or woman is a person who knows the art of patience. When something seems difficult, he is willing to wait until the situation becomes manageable again. He is a person who knows how to bide his time. Cancer knows how to concentrate on one thing at a time. When he has made his mind up he generally sticks with what he does, seeing it through to the end.

Cancer is a person who loves his home. He enjoys being surrounded by familiar things and the people he loves. Of all the signs, Cancer is the most maternal. Even the men born under this sign often have a motherly or protective quality about them. They like to take care of people in their family—to see that they are well loved and well provided for. They are usually loyal and faithful. Family ties mean a lot to the Cancer man or woman. Parents and in-laws are respected and loved. Young Cancer responds very well to adults who show faith in him. The Moon Child has a strong sense of tradition. He is very sensitive to the moods of others.

The Negative Side of Cancer

Sometimes Cancer finds it rather hard to face life. It becomes too much for him. He can be a little timid and retiring, when things don't go too well. When unfortunate things happen, he is apt to just shrug and say, "Whatever will be will be." He can be fatalistic to a fault. The uncultivated Cancer is a bit lazy. He doesn't have very much ambition. Anything that seems a bit difficult he'll gladly leave to others. He may be lacking in initiative. Too sensitive, when he feels he's been injured, he'll crawl back into his shell and nurse his imaginary wounds. The immature Moon Child often is given to crying when the smallest thing goes wrong.

Some Cancers find it difficult to enjoy themselves in environments outside their homes. They make heavy demands on others, and need to be constantly reassured that they are loved. Lacking such reassurance, they may resort to sulking in silence.

Leo: July 21–August 21

The Positive Side of Leo

Often Leos make good leaders. They seem to be good organizers and administrators. Usually they are quite popular with others. Whatever group it is that they belong to, the Leo man or woman is almost sure to be or become the leader. Loyalty, one of the Lion's noblest traits, enables him or her to maintain this leadership position.

Leo is generous most of the time. It is his best characteristic. He or she likes to give gifts and presents. In making others happy, the Leo person becomes happy himself. He likes to splurge when spending money on others. In some instances it may seem that the Lion's generosity knows no boundaries. A hospitable person, the Leo man or woman is very fond of welcoming people to his house and entertaining them. He is never short of company.

Leo has plenty of energy and drive. He enjoys working toward some specific goal. When he applies himself correctly, he gets what he wants most often. The Leo person is almost never unsure of himself. He has plenty of confidence and aplomb. He is a person who is direct in almost everything he does. He has a quick mind and can make a decision in a very short time.

He usually sets a good example for others because of his ambitious manner and positive ways. He knows how to stick to something once he's started. Although Leo may be good at making a joke, he is not superficial or glib. He is a loving person, kind and thoughtful.

There is generally nothing small or petty about the Leo man or woman. He does what he can for those who are deserving. He is a person others can rely upon at all times. He means what he says. An honest person, generally speaking, he is a friend who is valued and sought out.

The Negative Side of Leo

Leo, however, does have his faults. At times, he can be just a bit too arrogant. He thinks that no one deserves a leadership position except him. Only he is capable of doing things well. His opinion of himself is often much too high. Because of his conceit, he is

sometimes rather unpopular with a good many people. Some Leos are too materialistic; they can only think in terms of money and profit.

Some Leos enjoy lording it over others—at home or at their place of business. What is more, they feel they have the right to. Egocentric to an impossible degree, this sort of Leo cares little about how others think or feel. He can be rude and cutting.

Virgo: August 22–September 22

The Positive Side of Virgo

The person born under the sign of Virgo is generally a busy person. He knows how to arrange and organize things. He is a good planner. Above all, he is practical and is not afraid of hard work.

Often called the sign of the Harvester, Virgo knows how to attain what he desires. He sticks with something until it is finished. He never shirks his duties, and can always be depended upon. The Virgo person can be thoroughly trusted at all times.

The man or woman born under this sign tries to do everything to perfection. He doesn't believe in doing anything halfway. He always aims for the top. He is the sort of a person who is always learning and constantly striving to better himself—not because he wants more money or glory, but because it gives him a feeling of accomplishment.

The Virgo man or woman is a very observant person. He is sensitive to how others feel, and can see things below the surface of a situation. He usually puts this talent to constructive use.

It is not difficult for the Virgo to be open and earnest. He believes in putting his cards on the table. He is never secretive or underhanded. He's as good as his word. The Virgo person is generally plainspoken and down to earth. He has no trouble in expressing himself.

The Virgo person likes to keep up to date on new developments in his particular field. Well-informed, generally, he sometimes has a keen interest in the arts or literature. What he knows, he knows well. His ability to use his critical faculties is well-developed and sometimes startles others because of its accuracy.

Virgos adhere to a moderate way of life; they avoid excesses. Virgo is a responsible person and enjoys being of service.

The Negative Side of Virgo

Sometimes a Virgo person is too critical. He thinks that only he can do something the way it should be done. Whatever anyone else does is inferior. He can be rather annoying in the way he quibbles over insignificant details. In telling others how things should be done, he can be rather tactless and mean.

Some Virgos seem rather emotionless and cool. They feel emotional involvement is beneath them. They are sometimes too tidy, too neat. With money they can be rather miserly. Some Virgos try to force their opinions and ideas on others.

Libra: September 23–October 22

The Positive Side of Libra

Libras love harmony. It is one of their most outstanding character traits. They are interested in achieving balance; they admire beauty and grace in things as well as in people. Generally speaking, they are kind and considerate people. Libras are usually very sympathetic. They go out of their way not to hurt another person's feelings. They are outgoing and do what they can to help those in need.

People born under the sign of Libra almost always make good friends. They are loyal and amiable. They enjoy the company of others. Many of them are rather moderate in their views; they believe in keeping an open mind, however, and weighing both sides of an issue fairly before making a decision.

Alert and intelligent, Libra, often known as the Lawgiver, is always fair-minded and tries to put himself in the position of the other person. They are against injustice; quite often they take up for the underdog. In most of their social dealings, they try to be tactful and kind. They dislike discord and bickering, and most Libras strive for peace and harmony in all their relationships.

The Libra man or woman has a keen sense of beauty. They appreciate handsome furnishings and clothes. Many of them are artistically inclined. Their taste is usually impeccable. They know how to use color. Their homes are almost always attractively arranged and inviting. They enjoy entertaining people and see to it that their guests always feel at home and welcome.

Libra gets along with almost everyone. He is well-liked and socially much in demand.

The Negative Side of Libra

Some people born under this sign tend to be rather insincere. So eager are they to achieve harmony in all relationships that they will even go so far as to lie. Many of them are escapists. They find facing the truth an ordeal and prefer living in a world of make-believe.

In a serious argument, some Libras give in rather easily even when they know they are right. Arguing, even about something they believe in, is too unsettling for some of them.

Libras sometimes care too much for material things. They enjoy possessions and luxuries. Some are vain and tend to be jealous.

Scorpio: October 23–November 22

The Positive Side of Scorpio

The Scorpio man or woman generally knows what he or she wants out of life. He is a determined person. He sees something through to the end. Scorpio is quite sincere, and seldom says anything he doesn't mean. When he sets a goal for himself he tries to go about achieving it in a very direct way.

The Scorpion is brave and courageous. They are not afraid of hard work. Obstacles do not frighten them. They forge ahead until they achieve what they set out for. The Scorpio man or woman has a strong will.

Although Scorpio may seem rather fixed and determined, inside he is often quite tender and loving. He can care very much for others. He believes in sincerity in all relationships. His feelings about someone tend to last; they are profound and not superficial.

The Scorpio person is someone who adheres to his principles no matter what happens. He will not be deterred from a path he believes to be right.

Because of his many positive strengths, the Scorpion can often achieve happiness for himself and for those that he loves.

He is a constructive person by nature. He often has a deep understanding of people and of life, in general. He is perceptive and unafraid. Obstacles often seem to spur him on. He is a positive person who enjoys winning. He has many strengths and resources; challenge of any sort often brings out the best in him.

The Negative Side of Scorpio

The Scorpio person is sometimes hypersensitive. Often he imagines injury when there is none. He feels that others do not bother to recognize him for his true worth. Sometimes he is given to excessive boasting in order to compensate for what he feels is neglect.

Scorpio can be proud, arrogant, and competitive. They can be sly when they put their minds to it and they enjoy outwitting persons or institutions noted for their cleverness.

Their tactics for getting what they want are sometimes devious and ruthless. They don't care too much about what others may think. If they feel others have done them an injustice, they will do their best to seek revenge. The Scorpion often has a sudden, violent temper; and this person's interest in sex is sometimes quite unbalanced or excessive.

Sagittarius: November 23–December 20

The Positive Side of Sagittarius

People born under this sign are honest and forthright. Their approach to life is earnest and open. Sagittarius is often quite adult in his way of seeing things. They are broad-minded and tolerant people. When dealing with others the person born under the sign of the Archer is almost always open and forthright. He doesn't believe in deceit or pretension. His standards are high. People who associate with Sagittarius generally admire and respect his tolerant viewpoint.

The Archer trusts others easily and expects them to trust him. He is never suspicious or envious and almost always thinks well of others. People always enjoy his company because he is so friendly and easygoing. The Sagittarius man or woman is often good-humored. He can always be depended upon by his friends, family, and co-workers.

The person born under this sign of the Zodiac likes a good joke every now and then. Sagittarius is eager for fun and laughs, which makes him very popular with others.

A lively person, he enjoys sports and outdoor life. The Archer is fond of animals. Intelligent and interesting, he can begin an

animated conversation with ease. He likes exchanging ideas and discussing various views.

He is not selfish or proud. If someone proposes an idea or plan that is better than his, he will immediately adopt it. Imaginative yet practical, he knows how to put ideas into practice.

The Archer enjoys sport and games, and it doesn't matter if he wins or loses. He is a forgiving person, and never sulks over something that has not worked out in his favor.

He is seldom critical, and is almost always generous.

The Negative Side of Sagittarius

Some Sagittarius are restless. They take foolish risks and seldom learn from the mistakes they make. They don't have heads for money and are often mismanaging their finances. Some of them devote much of their time to gambling.

Some are too outspoken and tactless, always putting their feet in their mouths. They hurt others carelessly by being honest at the wrong time. Sometimes they make promises which they don't keep. They don't stick close enough to their plans and go from one failure to another. They are undisciplined and waste a lot of energy.

Capricorn: December 21–January 19

The Positive Side of Capricorn

The person born under the sign of Capricorn, known variously as the Mountain Goat or Sea Goat, is usually very stable and patient. He sticks to whatever tasks he has and sees them through. He can always be relied upon and he is not averse to work.

An honest person, Capricorn is generally serious about whatever he does. He does not take his duties lightly. He is a practical person and believes in keeping his feet on the ground.

Quite often the person born under this sign is ambitious and knows how to get what he wants out of life. The Goat forges ahead and never gives up his goal. When he is determined about something, he almost always wins. He is a good worker—a hard worker. Although things may not come easy to him, he will not complain, but continue working until his chores are finished.

He is usually good at business matters and knows the value of money. He is not a spendthrift and knows how to put something away for a rainy day; he dislikes waste and unnecessary loss.

Capricorn knows how to make use of his self-control. He can apply himself to almost anything once he puts his mind to it. His ability to concentrate sometimes astounds others. He is diligent and does well when involved in detail work.

The Capricorn man or woman is charitable, generally speaking, and will do what is possible to help others less fortunate. As a friend, he is loyal and trustworthy. He never shirks his duties or responsibilities. He is self-reliant and never expects too much of the other fellow. He does what he can on his own. If someone does him a good turn, then he will do his best to return the favor.

The Negative Side of Capricorn

Like everyone, Capricorn, too, has faults. At times, the Goat can be overcritical of others. He expects others to live up to his own high standards. He thinks highly of himself and tends to look down on others.

His interest in material things may be exaggerated. The Capricorn man or woman thinks too much about getting on in the world and having something to show for it. He may even be a little greedy.

He sometimes thinks he knows what's best for everyone. He is too bossy. He is always trying to organize and correct others. He may be a little narrow in his thinking.

Aquarius: January 20–February 18

The Positive Side of Aquarius

The Aquarius man or woman is usually very honest and forthright. These are his two greatest qualities. His standards for himself are generally very high. He can always be relied upon by others. His word is his bond.

Aquarius is perhaps the most tolerant of all the Zodiac personalities. He respects other people's beliefs and feels that everyone is entitled to his own approach to life.

He would never do anything to injure another's feelings. He is never unkind or cruel. Always considerate of others, the Water

Bearer is always willing to help a person in need. He feels a very strong tie between himself and all the other members of mankind.

The person born under this sign, called the Water Bearer, is almost always an individualist. He does not believe in teaming up with the masses, but prefers going his own way. His ideas about life and mankind are often quite advanced. There is a saying to the effect that the average Aquarius is fifty years ahead of his time.

Aquarius is community-minded. The problems of the world concern him greatly. He is interested in helping others no matter what part of the globe they live in. He is truly a humanitarian sort. He likes to be of service to others.

Giving, considerate, and without prejudice, Aquarius have no trouble getting along with others.

The Negative Side of Aquarius

Aquarius may be too much of a dreamer. He makes plans but seldom carries them out. He is rather unrealistic. His imagination has a tendency to run away with him. Because many of his plans are impractical, he is always in some sort of a dither.

Others may not approve of him at all times because of his unconventional behavior. He may be a bit eccentric. Sometimes he is so busy with his own thoughts that he loses touch with the realities of existence.

Some Aquarius feel they are more clever and intelligent than others. They seldom admit to their own faults, even when they are quite apparent. Some become rather fanatic in their views. Their criticism of others is sometimes destructive and negative.

Pisces: February 19–March 20

The Positive Side of Pisces

Known as the sign of the Fishes, Pisces has a sympathetic nature. Kindly, he is often dedicated in the way he goes about helping others. The sick and the troubled often turn to him for advice and assistance. Possessing keen intuition, Pisces can easily understand people's deepest problems.

He is very broad-minded and does not criticize others for their faults. He knows how to accept people for what they are. On the whole, he is a trustworthy and earnest person. He is loyal to his friends and will do what he can to help them in time of need. Generous and good-natured, he is a lover of peace; he is often willing to help others solve their differences. People who have taken a wrong turn in life often interest him and he will do what he can to persuade them to rehabilitate themselves.

He has a strong intuitive sense and most of the time he knows how to make it work for him. Pisces is unusually perceptive and often knows what is bothering someone before that person, himself, is aware of it. The Pisces man or woman is an idealistic person, basically, and is interested in making the world a better place in which to live. Pisces believes that everyone should help each other. He is willing to do more than his share in order to achieve cooperation with others.

The person born under this sign often is talented in music or art. He is a receptive person; he is able to take the ups and downs of life with philosophic calm.

The Negative Side of Pisces

Some Pisces are often depressed; their outlook on life is rather glum. They may feel that they have been given a bad deal in life and that others are always taking unfair advantage of them. Pisces sometimes feel that the world is a cold and cruel place. The Fishes can be easily discouraged. The Pisces man or woman may even withdraw from the harshness of reality into a secret shell of his own where he dreams and idles away a good deal of his time.

Pisces can be lazy. He lets things happen without giving the least bit of resistance. He drifts along, whether on the high road or on the low. He can be lacking in willpower.

Some Pisces people seek escape through drugs or alcohol. When temptation comes along they find it hard to resist. In matters of sex, they can be rather permissive.

Sun Sign Personalities

ARIES: Hans Christian Andersen, Pearl Bailey, Marlon Brando, Wernher Von Braun, Charlie Chaplin, Joan Crawford, Da Vinci, Bette Davis, Doris Day, W. C. Fields, Alec Guinness, Adolf Hitler, William Holden, Thomas Jefferson, Nikita Khrushchev, Elton John, Arturo Toscanini, J. P. Morgan, Paul Robeson, Gloria Steinem, Sarah Vaughn, Vincent van Gogh, Tennessee Williams

TAURUS: Fred Astaire, Charlote Brontë, Carol Burnett, Irving Berlin, Bing Crosby, Salvador Dali, Tchaikovsky, Queen Elizabeth II, Duke Ellington, Ella Fitzgerald, Henry Fonda, Sigmund Freud, Orson Welles, Joe Louis, Lenin, Karl Marx, Golda Meir, Eva Peron, Bertrand Russell, Shakespeare, Kate Smith, Benjamin Spock, Barbra Streisand, Shirley Temple, Harry Truman

GEMINI: Mikhail Baryshnikov, Ruth Benedict, Josephine Baker, Carlos Chavez, Walt Whitman, Bob Dylan, Ralph Waldo Emerson, Judy Garland, Paul Gauguin, Allen Ginsberg, Benny Goodman, Bob Hope, Burl Ives, John F. Kennedy, Peggy Lee, Marilyn Monroe, Joe Namath, Cole Porter, Laurence Olivier, Harriet Beecher Stowe, Queen Victoria, John Wayne, Frank Lloyd Wright

CANCER: "Dear Abby," Lizzie Borden, David Brinkley, Yul Brynner, Pearl Buck, Marc Chagall, Jack Dempsey, Babe Didrikson, Mary Baker Eddy, Henry VIII, John Glenn, Ernest Hemingway, Lena Horne, Oscar Hammerstein, Helen Keller, Ann Landers, George Orwell, Nancy Reagan, Rembrandt, Richard Rodgers, Ginger Rogers, Rubens, Jean-Paul Sartre, O. J. Simpson

LEO: Neil Armstrong, James Baldwin, Lucille Ball, Emily Brontë, Wilt Chamberlain, Julia Child, William J. Clinton, Cecil B. De Mille, Ogden Nash, Amelia Earhart, Edna Ferber, Arthur Goldberg, Alfred Hitchcock, Mick Jagger, George Meany, Annie Oakley, George Bernard Shaw, Napoleon, Jacqueline Onassis, Henry Ford, Francis Scott Key, Andy Warhol, Mae West, Orville Wright

VIRGO: Ingrid Bergman, Warren Burger, Maurice Chevalier, Agatha Christie, Sean Connery, Lafayette, Peter Falk, Greta Garbo, Althea Gibson, Arthur Godfrey, Goethe, Buddy Hackett, Michael Jackson, Lyndon Johnson, D. H. Lawrence, Sophia Loren, Grandma Moses, Arnold Palmer, Queen Elizabeth I, Walter Reuther, Peter Sellers, Lily Tomlin, George Wallace

LIBRA: Brigitte Bardot, Art Buchwald, Truman Capote, Dwight D. Eisenhower, William Faulkner, F. Scott Fitzgerald, Gandhi, George Gershwin, Micky Mantle, Helen Hayes, Vladimir Horowitz, Doris Lessing, Martina Navratalova, Eugene O'Neill, Luciano Pavarotti, Emily Post, Eleanor Roosevelt, Bruce Springsteen, Margaret Thatcher, Gore Vidal, Barbara Walters, Oscar Wilde

SCORPIO: Vivien Leigh, Richard Burton, Art Carney, Johnny Carson, Billy Graham, Grace Kelly, Walter Cronkite, Marie Curie, Charles de Gaulle, Linda Evans, Indira Gandhi, Theodore Roosevelt, Rock Hudson, Katherine Hepburn, Robert F. Kennedy, Billie Jean King, Martin Luther, Georgia O'Keeffe, Pablo Picasso, Jonas Salk, Alan Shepard, Robert Louis Stevenson

SAGITTARIUS: Jane Austen, Louisa May Alcott, Woody Allen, Beethoven, Willy Brandt, Mary Martin, William F. Buckley, Maria Callas, Winston Churchill, Noel Coward, Emily Dickinson, Walt Disney, Benjamin Disraeli, James Doolittle, Kirk Douglas, Chet Huntley, Jane Fonda, Chris Evert Lloyd, Margaret Mead, Charles Schulz, John Milton, Frank Sinatra, Steven Spielberg

CAPRICORN: Muhammad Ali, Isaac Asimov, Pablo Casals, Dizzy Dean, Marlene Dietrich, James Farmer, Ava Gardner, Barry Goldwater, Cary Grant, J. Edgar Hoover, Howard Hughes, Joan of Arc, Gypsy Rose Lee, Martin Luther King, Jr., Rudyard Kipling, Mao Tse-tung, Richard Nixon, Gamal Nasser, Louis Pasteur, Albert Schweitzer, Stalin, Benjamin Franklin, Elvis Presley

AQUARIUS: Marian Anderson, Susan B. Anthony, Jack Benny, Charles Darwin, Charles Dickens, Thomas Edison, John Barrymore, Clark Gable, Jascha Heifetz, Abraham Lincoln, John McEnroe, Yehudi Menuhin, Mozart, Jack Nicklaus, Ronald Reagan, Jackie Robinson, Norman Rockwell, Franklin D. Roosevelt, Gertrude Stein, Charles Lindbergh, Margaret Truman

PISCES: Edward Albee, Harry Belafonte, Alexander Graham Bell, Chopin, Adelle Davis, Albert Einstein, Golda Meir, Jackie Gleason, Winslow Homer, Edward M. Kennedy, Victor Hugo, Mike Mansfield, Michelangelo, Edna St. Vincent Millay, Liza Minelli, John Steinbeck, Linus Pauling, Ravel, Renoir, Diana Ross, William Shirer, Elizabeth Taylor, George Washington

The Signs and Their Key Words

		POSITIVE	NEGATIVE
ARIES	self	courage, initiative, pioneer instinct	brash rudeness, selfish impetuosity
TAURUS	money	endurance, loyalty, wealth	obstinacy, gluttony
GEMINI	mind	versatility	capriciousness, unreliability
CANCER	family	sympathy, homing instinct	clannishness, childishness
LEO	children	love, authority, integrity	egotism, force
VIRGO	work	purity, industry, analysis	faultfinding, cynicism
LIBRA	marriage	harmony, justice	vacillation, superficiality
SCORPIO	sex	survival, regeneration	vengeance, discord
SAGITTARIUS	travel	optimism, higher learning	lawlessness
CAPRICORN	career	depth	narrowness, gloom
AQUARIUS	friends	human fellowship, genius	perverse unpredictability
PISCES	confine-ment	spiritual love, universality	diffusion, escapism

The Elements and Qualities of The Signs

Every sign has both an *element* and a *quality* associated with it. The element indicates the basic makeup of the sign, and the quality describes the kind of activity associated with each.

Element	Sign	Quality	Sign
FIRE	ARIES	CARDINAL....	ARIES
	LEO		LIBRA
	SAGITTARIUS		CANCER
			CAPRICORN
EARTH....	TAURUS		
	VIRGO		
	CAPRICORN	FIXED	TAURUS
			LEO
			SCORPIO
AIR.........	GEMINI		AQUARIUS
	LIBRA		
	AQUARIUS		
		MUTABLE	GEMINI
WATER....	CANCER		VIRGO
	SCORPIO		SAGITTARIUS
	PISCES		PISCES

Signs can be grouped together according to their element and quality. Signs of the same element share many basic traits in common. They tend to form stable configurations and ultimately harmonious relationships. Signs of the same quality are often less harmonious, but they share many dynamic potentials for growth as well as profound fulfillment.

Further discussion of each of these sign groupings is provided on the following pages.

The Fire Signs

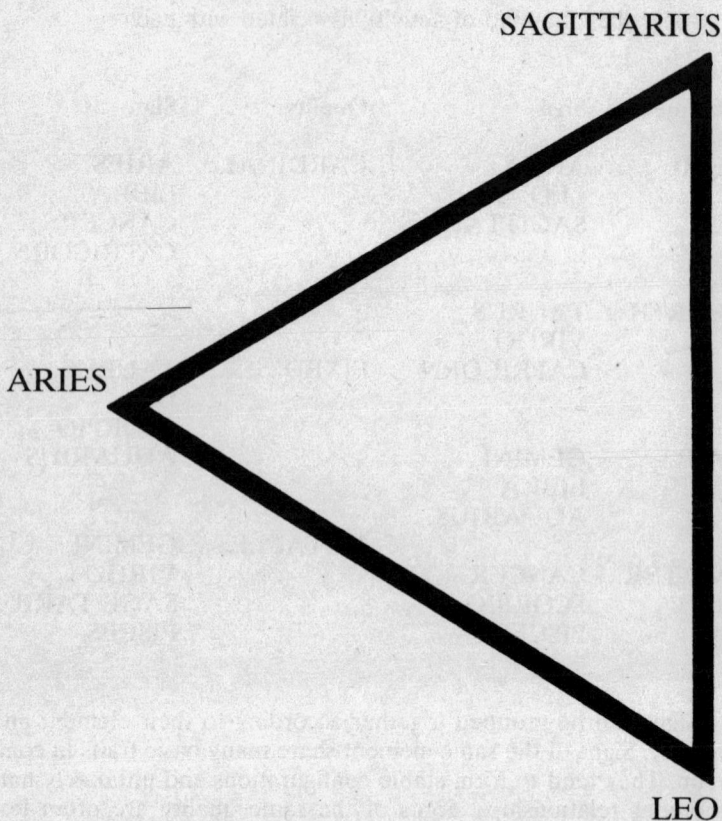

SAGITTARIUS

ARIES

LEO

This is the fire group. On the whole these are emotional, volatile types, quick to anger, quick to forgive. They are adventurous, powerful people and act as a source of inspiration for everyone. They spark into action with immediate exuberant impulses. They are intelligent, self-involved, creative, and idealistic. They all share a certain vibrancy and glow that outwardly reflects an inner flame and passion for living.

The Earth Signs

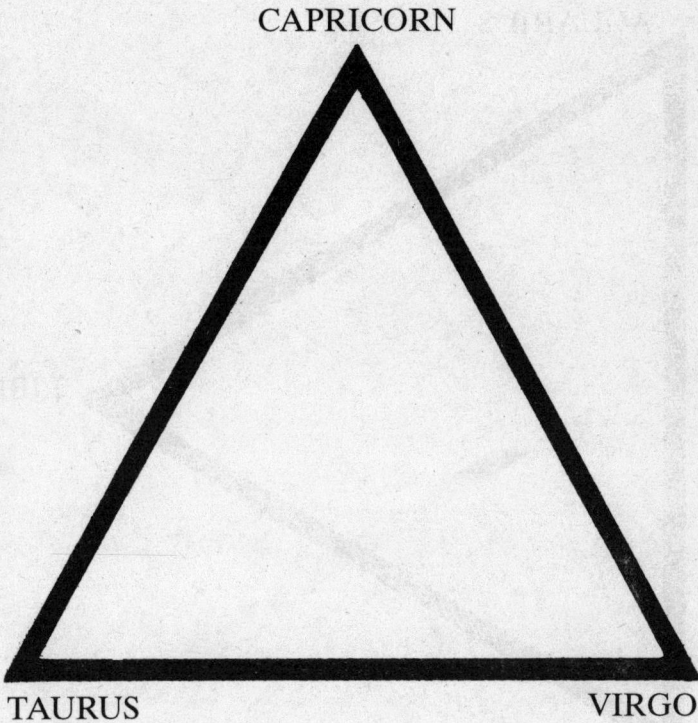

CAPRICORN

TAURUS   VIRGO

This is the earth group. They are in constant touch with the material world and tend to be conservative. Although they are all capable of spartan self-discipline, they are earthy, sensual people who are stimulated by the tangible, elegant, and luxurious. The thread of their lives is always practical, but they do fantasize and are often attracted to dark, mysterious, emotional people. They are like great cliffs overhanging the sea, forever married to the ocean but always resisting erosion from the dark, emotional forces that thunder at their feet.

The Air Signs

AQUARIUS

LIBRA

GEMINI

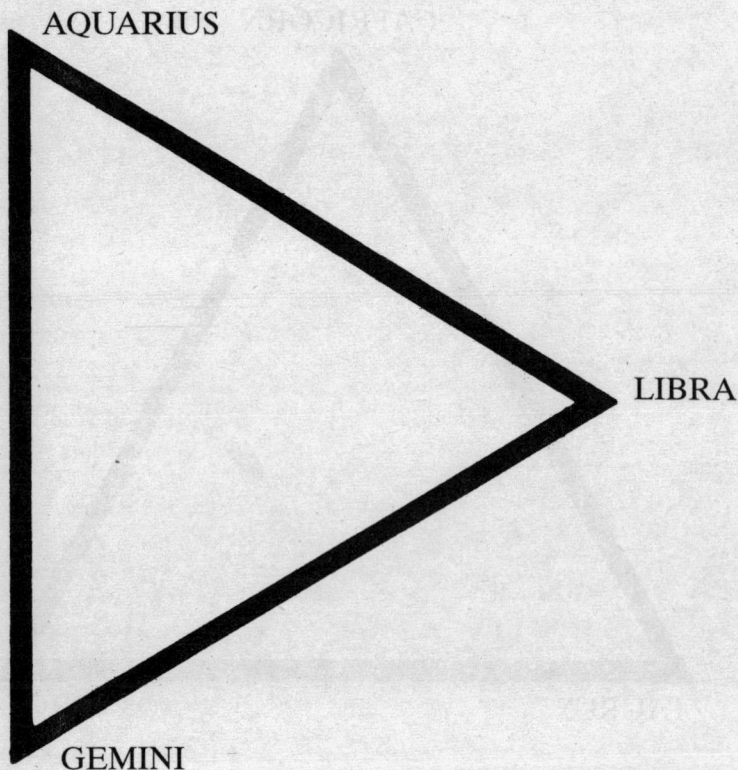

This is the air group. They are light, mental creatures desirous of contact, communication, and relationship. They are involved with people and the forming of ties on many levels. Original thinkers, they are the bearers of human news. Their language is their sense of word, color, style, and beauty. They provide an atmosphere suitable and pleasant for living. They add change and versatility to the scene, and it is through them that we can explore new territory of human intelligence and experience.

The Water Signs

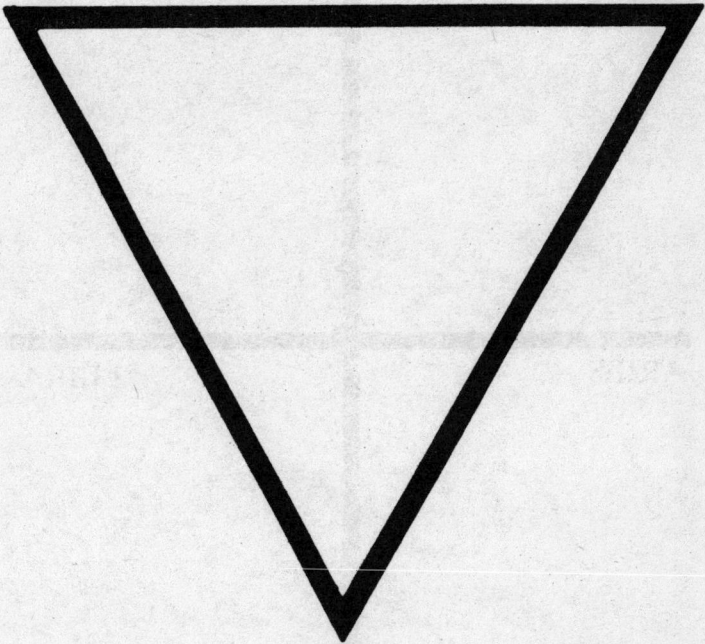

PISCES   SCORPIO

CANCER

This is the water group. Through the water people, we are all joined together on emotional, nonverbal levels. They are silent, mysterious types whose magic hypnotizes even the most determined realist. They have uncanny perceptions about people and are as rich as the oceans when it comes to feeling, emotion, or imagination. They are sensitive, mystical creatures with memories that go back beyond time. Through water, life is sustained. These people have the potential for the depths of darkness or the heights of mysticism and art.

The Cardinal Signs

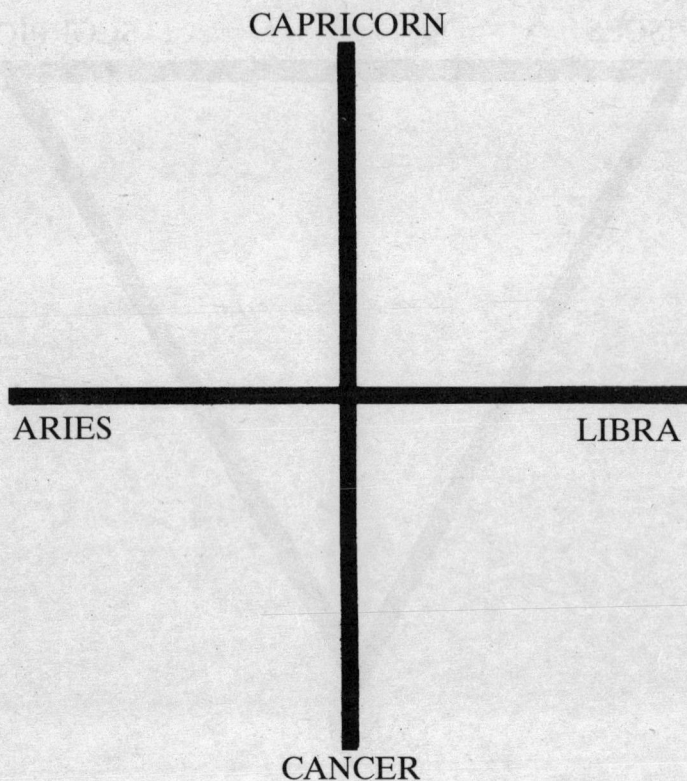

```
                    CAPRICORN
                        |
                        |
                        |
                        |
                        |
                        |
     ARIES  ————————————+———————————— LIBRA
                        |
                        |
                        |
                        |
                        |
                        |
                     CANCER
```

Put together, this is a clear-cut picture of dynamism, activity, tremendous stress, and remarkable achievement. These people know the meaning of great change since their lives are often characterized by significant crises and major successes. This combination is like a simultaneous storm of summer, fall, winter, and spring. The danger is chaotic diffusion of energy; the potential is irrepressible growth and victory.

The Fixed Signs

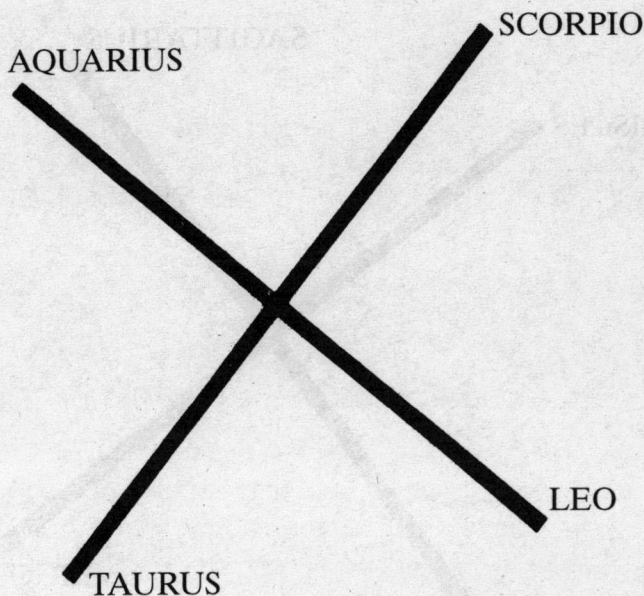

SCORPIO

AQUARIUS

LEO

TAURUS

Fixed signs are always establishing themselves in a given place or area of experience. Like explorers who arrive and plant a flag, these people claim a position from which they do not enjoy being deposed. They are staunch, stalwart, upright, trusty, honorable people, although their obstinacy is well-known. Their contribution is fixity, and they are the angels who support our visible world.

The Mutable Signs

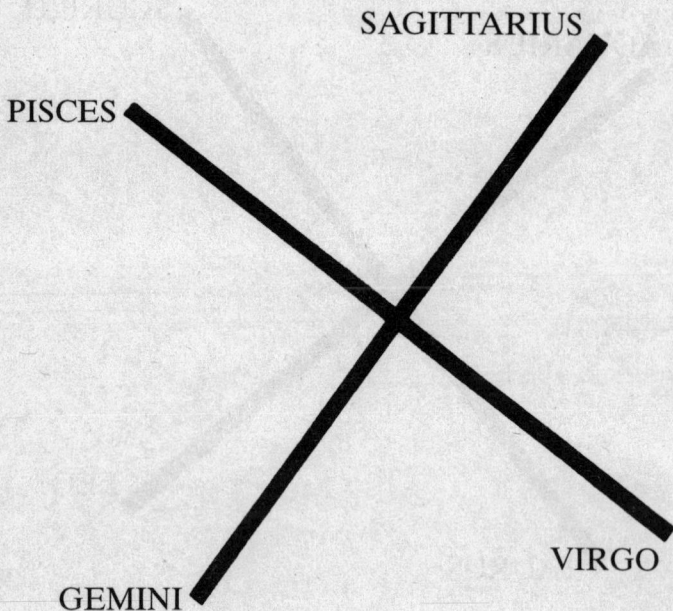

SAGITTARIUS

PISCES

VIRGO

GEMINI

Mutable people are versatile, sensitive, intelligent, nervous, and deeply curious about life. They are the translators of all energy. They often carry out or complete tasks initiated by others. Combinations of these signs have highly developed minds; they are imaginative and jumpy and think and talk a lot. At worst their lives are a Tower of Babel. At best they are adaptable and ready creatures who can assimilate one kind of experience and enjoy it while anticipating coming changes.

THE PLANETS
OF THE SOLAR SYSTEM

This section describes the planets of the solar system. In astrology, both the Sun and the Moon are considered to be planets. Because of the Moon's influence in our day-to-day lives, the Moon is described in a separate section following this one.

The Planets and the Signs
They Rule

The signs of the Zodiac are linked to the planets in the following way. Each sign is governed or ruled by one or more planets. No matter where the planets are located in the sky at any given moment, they still rule their respective signs, and when they travel through the signs they rule, they have special dignity and their effects are stronger.

Following is a list of the planets and the signs they rule. After looking at the list, read the definitions of the planets and see if you can determine how the planet ruling *your* Sun sign has affected your life.

SIGNS	RULING PLANETS
Aries	Mars, Pluto
Taurus	Venus
Gemini	Mercury
Cancer	Moon
Leo	Sun
Virgo	Mercury
Libra	Venus
Scorpio	Mars, Pluto
Sagittarius	Jupiter
Capricorn	Saturn
Aquarius	Saturn, Uranus
Pisces	Jupiter, Neptune

Characteristics of the Planets

The following pages give the meaning and characteristics of the planets of the solar system. They all travel around the Sun at different speeds and different distances. Taken with the Sun, they all distribute individual intelligence and ability throughout the entire chart.

The planets modify the influence of the Sun in a chart according to their own particular natures, strengths, and positions. Their positions must be calculated for each year and day, and their function and expression in a horoscope will change as they move from one area of the Zodiac to another.

We start with a description of the sun.

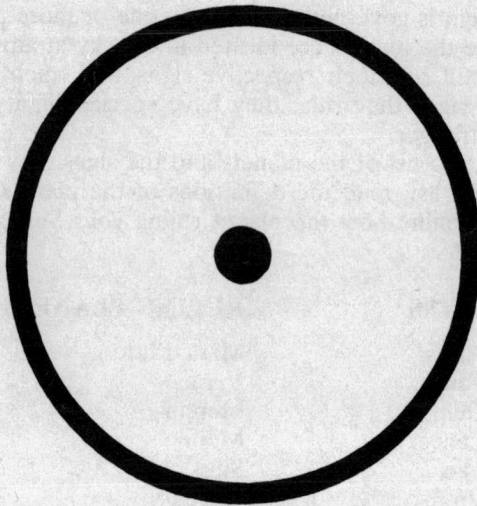

THE SUN

SUN

This is the center of existence. Around this flaming sphere all the planets revolve in endless orbits. Our star is constantly sending out its beams of light and energy without which no life on Earth would be possible. In astrology it symbolizes everything we are trying to become, the center around which all of our activity in life will always revolve. It is the symbol of our basic nature and describes the natural and constant thread that runs through everything that we do from birth to death on this planet.

To early astrologers, the Sun seemed to be another planet because it crossed the heavens every day, just like the rest of the bodies in the sky.

It is the only star near enough to be seen well—it is, in fact, a dwarf star. Approximately 860,000 miles in diameter, it is about ten times as wide as the giant planet Jupiter. The next nearest star is nearly 300,000 times as far away, and if the Sun were located as far away as most of the bright stars, it would be too faint to be seen without a telescope.

Everything in the horoscope ultimately revolves around this singular body. Although other forces may be prominent in the charts of some individuals, still the Sun is the total nucleus of being and symbolizes the complete potential of every human being alive. It is vitality and the life force. Your whole essence comes from the position of the Sun.

You are always trying to express the Sun according to its position by house and sign. Possibility for all development is found in the Sun, and it marks the fundamental character of your personal radiations all around you.

It is the symbol of strength, vigor, wisdom, dignity, ardor, and generosity, and the ability for a person to function as a mature individual. It is also a creative force in society. It is consciousness of the gift of life.

The underdeveloped solar nature is arrogant, pushy, undependable, and proud, and is constantly using force.

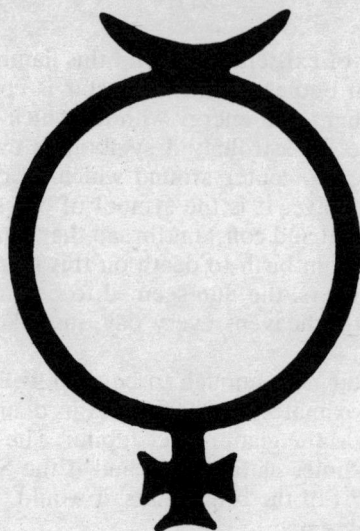

MERCURY

Mercury is the planet closest to the Sun. It races around our star, gathering information and translating it to the rest of the system. Mercury represents your capacity to understand the desires of your own will and to translate those desires into action.

In other words it is the planet of mind and the power of communication. Through Mercury we develop an ability to think, write, speak, and observe—to become aware of the world around us. It colors our attitudes and vision of the world, as well as our capacity to communicate our inner responses to the outside world. Some people who have serious disabilities in their power of verbal communication have often wrongly been described as people lacking intelligence.

Although this planet (and its position in the horoscope) indicates your power to communicate your thoughts and perceptions to the world, intelligence is something deeper. Intelligence is distributed throughout all the planets. It is the relationship of the planets to each other that truly describes what we call intelligence. Mercury rules speaking, language, mathematics, draft and design, students, messengers, young people, offices, teachers, and any pursuits where the mind of man has wings.

VENUS

Venus is beauty. It symbolizes the harmony and radiance of a rare and elusive quality: beauty itself. It is refinement and delicacy, softness and charm. In astrology it indicates grace, balance, and the aesthetic sense. Where Venus is we see beauty, a gentle drawing in of energy and the need for satisfaction and completion. It is a special touch that finishes off rough edges. It is sensitivity, and affection, and it is always the place for that other elusive phenomenon: love. Venus describes our sense of what is beautiful and loving. Poorly developed, it is vulgar, tasteless, and self-indulgent. But its ideal is the flame of spiritual love—Aphrodite, goddess of love, and the sweetness and power of personal beauty.

MARS

Mars is raw, crude energy. The planet next to Earth but outward from the Sun is a fiery red sphere that charges through the horoscope with force and fury. It represents the way you reach out for new adventure and new experience. It is energy and drive, initiative, courage, and daring. It is the power to start something and see it through. It can be thoughtless, cruel and wild, angry and hostile, causing cuts, burns, scalds, and wounds. It can stab its way through a chart, or it can be the symbol of healthy spirited adventure, well-channeled constructive power to begin and keep up the drive. If you have trouble starting things, if you lack the get-up-and-go to start the ball rolling, if you lack aggressiveness and self-confidence, chances are there's another planet influencing your Mars. Mars rules soldiers, butchers, surgeons, salesmen—any field that requires daring, bold skill, operational technique, or self-promotion.

JUPITER

This is the largest planet of the solar system. Scientists have recently learned that Jupiter reflects more light than it receives from the Sun. In a sense it is like a star itself. In astrology it rules good luck and good cheer, health, wealth, optimism, happiness, success, and joy. It is the symbol of opportunity and always opens the way for new possibilities in your life. It rules exuberance, enthusiasm, wisdom, knowledge, generosity, and all forms of expansion in general. It rules actors, statesmen, clerics, professional people, religion, publishing, and the distribution of many people over large areas.

Sometimes Jupiter makes you think you deserve everything, and you become sloppy, wasteful, careless and rude, prodigal and lawless, in the illusion that nothing can ever go wrong. Then there is the danger of overconfidence, exaggeration, undependability, and overindulgence.

Jupiter is the minimization of limitation and the emphasis on spirituality and potential. It is the thirst for knowledge and higher learning.

SATURN

Saturn circles our system in dark splendor with its mysterious rings, forcing us to be awakened to whatever we have neglected in the past. It will present real puzzles and problems to be solved, causing delays, obstacles, and hindrances. By doing so, Saturn stirs our own sensitivity to those areas where we are laziest.

Here we must patiently develop *method*, and only through painstaking effort can our ends be achieved. It brings order to a horoscope and imposes reason just where we are feeling least reasonable. By creating limitations and boundary, Saturn shows the consequences of being human and demands that we accept the changing cycles inevitable in human life. Saturn rules time, old age, and sobriety. It can bring depression, gloom, jealousy, and greed, or serious acceptance of responsibilities out of which success will develop. With Saturn there is nothing to do but face facts. It rules laborers, stones, granite, rocks, and crystals of all kinds.

THE OUTER PLANETS:
URANUS, NEPTUNE, PLUTO

Uranus, Neptune, Pluto are the outer planets. They liberate human beings from cultural conditioning, and in that sense are the lawbreakers. In early times it was thought that Saturn was the last planet of the system—the outer limit beyond which we could never go. The discovery of the next three planets ushered in new phases of human history, revolution, and technology.

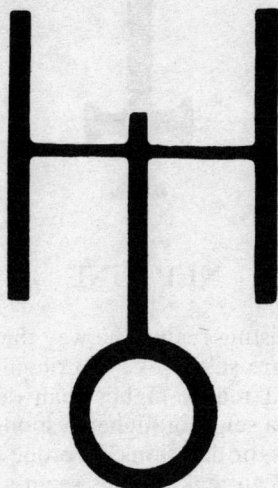

URANUS

Uranus rules unexpected change, upheaval, revolution. It is the symbol of total independence and asserts the freedom of an individual from all restriction and restraint. It is a breakthrough planet and indicates talent, originality, and genius in a horoscope. It usually causes last-minute reversals and changes of plan, unwanted separations, accidents, catastrophes, and eccentric behavior. It can add irrational rebelliousness and perverse bohemianism to a personality or a streak of unaffected brilliance in science and art. It rules technology, aviation, and all forms of electrical and electronic advancement. It governs great leaps forward and topsy-turvy situations, and *always* turns things around at the last minute. Its effects are difficult to predict, since it rules sudden last-minute decisions and events that come like lightning out of the blue.

NEPTUNE

Neptune dissolves existing reality the way the sea erodes the cliffs beside it. Its effects are subtle like the ringing of a buoy's bell in the fog. It suggests a reality higher than definition can usually describe. It awakens a sense of higher responsibility often causing guilt, worry, anxieties, or delusions. Neptune is associated with all forms of escape and can make things seem a certain way so convincingly that you are absolutely sure of something that eventually turns out to be quite different.

It is the planet of illusion and therefore governs the invisible realms that lie beyond our ordinary minds, beyond our simple factual ability to prove what is "real." Treachery, deceit, disillusionment, and disappointment are linked to Neptune. It describes a vague reality that promises eternity and the divine, yet in a manner so complex that we cannot really fathom it at all. At its worst Neptune is a cheap intoxicant; at its best it is the poetry, music, and inspiration of the higher planes of spiritual love. It has dominion over movies, photographs, and much of the arts.

PLUTO

Pluto lies at the outpost of our system and therefore rules finality in a horoscope—the final closing of chapters in your life, the passing of major milestones and points of development from which there is no return. It is a final wipeout, a closeout, an evacuation. It is a distant, subtle but powerful catalyst in all transformations that occur. It creates, destroys, then recreates. Sometimes Pluto starts its influence with a minor event or insignificant incident that might even go unnoticed. Slowly but surely, little by little, everything changes, until at last there has been a total transformation in the area of your life where Pluto has been operating. It rules mass thinking and the trends that society first rejects, then adopts, and finally outgrows.

Pluto rules the dead and the underworld—all the powerful forces of creation and destruction that go on all the time beneath, around, and above us. It can bring a lust for power with strong obsessions.

It is the planet that rules the metamorphosis of the caterpillar into a butterfly, for it symbolizes the capacity to change totally and forever a person's lifestyle, way of thought, and behavior.

THE MOON IN EACH SIGN

The Moon is the nearest planet to the Earth. It exerts more observable influence on us from day to day than any other planet. The effect is very personal, very intimate, and if we are not aware of how it works it can make us quite unstable in our ideas. And the annoying thing is that at these times we often see our own instability but can do nothing about it. A knowledge of what can be expected may help considerably. We can then be prepared to stand strong against the Moon's negative influences and use its positive ones to help us to get ahead. Who has not heard of going with the tide?

The Moon reflects, has no light of its own. It reflects the Sun—the life giver—in the form of vital movement. The Moon controls the tides, the blood rhythm, the movement of sap in trees and plants. Its nature is inconstancy and change so it signifies our moods, our superficial behavior—walking, talking, and especially thinking. Being a true reflector of other forces, the Moon is cold, watery like the surface of a still lake, brilliant and scintillating at times, but easily ruffled and disturbed by the winds of change.

The Moon takes about 27⅓ days to make a complete transit of the Zodiac. It spends just over 2¼ days in each sign. During that time it reflects the qualities, energies, and characteristics of the sign and, to a degree, the planet which rules the sign. When the Moon in its transit occupies a sign incompatible with our own birth sign, we can expect to feel a vague uneasiness; perhaps a touch of irritableness. We should not be discouraged nor let the feeling get us down, or, worse still, allow ourselves to take the discomfort out on others. Try to remember that the Moon has to change signs within 55 hours and, provided you are not physically ill, your mood will probably change with it. It is amazing how frequently depression lifts with the shift in the Moon's position. And, of course, when the Moon is transiting a sign compatible or sympathetic to yours, you will probably feel some sort of stimulation or just be plain happy to be alive.

In the horoscope, the Moon is such a powerful indicator that competent astrologers often use the sign it occupied at birth as the birth sign of the person. This is done particularly when the Sun is on the cusp, or edge, of two signs. Most experienced astrologers, however, coordinate both Sun and Moon signs by reading and confirming from one to the other and secure a far more accurate and personalized analysis.

For these reasons, the Moon tables which follow this section (see pages 86–92) are of great importance to the individual. They show the days and the exact times the Moon will enter each sign of the Zodiac for the year. Remember, you have to adjust the indicated times to local time. The corrections, already calculated for most of the main cities, are at the beginning of the tables. What follows now is a guide to the influences that will be reflected to the Earth by the Moon while it transits each of the twelve signs. The influence is at its peak about 26 hours after the Moon enters a sign. As you read the daily forecast, check the Moon sign for any given day and glance back at this guide.

MOON IN ARIES
This is a time for action, for reaching out beyond the usual self-imposed limitations and faint-hearted cautions. If you have plans in your head or on your desk, put them into practice. New ventures, applications, new jobs, new starts of any kind—all have a good chance of success. This is the period when original and dynamic impulses are being reflected onto Earth. Such energies are extremely vital and favor the pursuit of pleasure and adventure in practically every form. Sick people should feel an improvement. Those who are well will probably find themselves exuding confidence and optimism. People fond of physical exercise should find their bodies growing with tone and well-being. Boldness, strength, determination should characterize most of your activities with a readiness to face up to old challenges. Yesterday's problems may seem petty and exaggerated—so deal with them. Strike out alone. Self-reliance will attract others to you. This is a good time for making friends. Business and marriage partners are more likely to be impressed with the man and woman of action. Opposition will be overcome or thrown aside with much less effort than usual. CAUTION: Be dominant but not domineering.

MOON IN TAURUS
The spontaneous, action-packed person of yesterday gives way to the cautious, diligent, hardworking "thinker." In this period ideas will probably be concentrated on ways of improving finances. A great deal of time may be spent figuring out and going over schemes and plans. It is the right time to be careful with detail.

People will find themselves working longer than usual at their desks. Or devoting more time to serious thought about the future. A strong desire to put order into business and financial arrangements may cause extra work. Loved ones may complain of being neglected and may fail to appreciate that your efforts are for their ultimate benefit. Your desire for system may extend to criticism of arrangements in the home and lead to minor upsets. Health may be affected through overwork. Try to secure a reasonable amount of rest and relaxation, although the tendency will be to "keep going" despite good advice. Work done conscientiously in this period should result in a solid contribution to your future security. CAUTION: Try not to be as serious with people as the work you are engaged in.

MOON IN GEMINI
The humdrum of routine and too much work should suddenly end. You are likely to find yourself in an expansive, quicksilver world of change and self-expression. Urges to write, to paint, to experience the freedom of some sort of artistic outpouring, may be very strong. Take full advantage of them. You may find yourself finishing something you began and put aside long ago. Or embarking on something new which could easily be prompted by a chance meeting, a new acquaintance, or even an advertisement. There may be a yearning for a change of scenery, the feeling to visit another country (not too far away), or at least to get away for a few days. This may result in short, quick journeys. Or, if you are planning a single visit, there may be some unexpected changes or detours on the way. Familiar activities will seem to give little satisfaction unless they contain a fresh element of excitement or expectation. The inclination will be toward untried pursuits, particularly those that allow you to express your inner nature. The accent is on new faces, new places. CAUTION: Do not be too quick to commit yourself emotionally.

MOON IN CANCER
Feelings of uncertainty and vague insecurity are likely to cause problems while the Moon is in Cancer. Thoughts may turn frequently to the warmth of the home and the comfort of loved ones. Nostalgic impulses could cause you to bring out old photographs and letters and reflect on the days when your life seemed to be much more rewarding and less demanding. The love and understanding of parents and family may be important, and, if it is not forthcoming, you may have to fight against bouts of self-pity. The cordiality of friends and the thought of good times with them that are sure to be repeated will help to restore you to a happier frame

of mind. The desire to be alone may follow minor setbacks or rebuffs at this time, but solitude is unlikely to help. Better to get on the telephone or visit someone. This period often causes peculiar dreams and upsurges of imaginative thinking which can be helpful to authors of occult and mystical works. Preoccupation with the personal world of simple human needs can overshadow any material strivings. CAUTION: Do not spend too much time thinking—seek the company of loved ones or close friends.

MOON IN LEO

New horizons of exciting and rather extravagant activity open up. This is the time for exhilarating entertainment, glamorous and lavish parties, and expensive shopping sprees. Any merrymaking that relies upon your generosity as a host has every chance of being a spectacular success. You should find yourself right in the center of the fun, either as the life of the party or simply as a person whom happy people like to be with. Romance thrives in this heady atmosphere and friendships are likely to explode unexpectedly into serious attachments. Children and younger people should be attracted to you and you may find yourself organizing a picnic or a visit to a fun-fair, the movies, or the beach. The sunny company and vitality of youthful companions should help you to find some unsuspected energy. In career, you could find an opening for promotion or advancement. This should be the time to make a direct approach. The period favors those engaged in original research. CAUTION: Bask in popularity, not in flattery.

MOON IN VIRGO

Off comes the party cap and out steps the busy, practical worker. He wants to get his personal affairs straight, to rearrange them, if necessary, for more efficiency, so he will have more time for more work. He clears up his correspondence, pays outstanding bills, makes numerous phone calls. He is likely to make inquiries, or sign up for some new insurance and put money into gilt-edged investment. Thoughts probably revolve around the need for future security—to tie up loose ends and clear the decks. There may be a tendency to be "finicky," to interfere in the routine of others, particularly friends and family members. The motive may be a genuine desire to help with suggestions for updating or streamlining their affairs, but these will probably not be welcomed. Sympathy may be felt for less fortunate sections of the community and a flurry of some sort of voluntary service is likely. This may be accompanied by strong feelings of responsibility on several fronts and health may suffer from extra efforts made. CAUTION: Everyone may not want your help or advice.

MOON IN LIBRA

These are days of harmony and agreement and you should find yourself at peace with most others. Relationships tend to be smooth and sweet-flowing. Friends may become closer and bonds deepen in mutual understanding. Hopes will be shared. Progress by cooperation could be the secret of success in every sphere. In business, established partnerships may flourish and new ones get off to a good start. Acquaintances could discover similar interests that lead to congenial discussions and rewarding exchanges of some sort. Love, as a unifying force, reaches its optimum. Marriage partners should find accord. Those who wed at this time face the prospect of a happy union. Cooperation and tolerance are felt to be stronger than dissension and impatience. The argumentative are not quite so loud in their bellowings, nor as inflexible in their attitudes. In the home, there should be a greater recognition of the other point of view and a readiness to put the wishes of the group before selfish insistence. This is a favorable time to join an art group. CAUTION: Do not be too independent—let others help you if they want to.

MOON IN SCORPIO

Driving impulses to make money and to economize are likely to cause upsets all around. No area of expenditure is likely to be spared the ax, including the household budget. This is a time when the desire to cut down on extravagance can become near fanatical. Care must be exercised to try to keep the aim in reasonable perspective. Others may not feel the same urgent need to save and may retaliate. There is a danger that possessions of sentimental value will be sold to realize cash for investment. Buying and selling of stock for quick profit is also likely. The attention turns to organizing, reorganizing, tidying up at home and at work. Neglected jobs could suddenly be done with great bursts of energy. The desire for solitude may intervene. Self-searching thoughts could disturb. The sense of invisible and mysterious energies in play could cause some excitability. The reassurance of loves ones may help. CAUTION: Be kind to the people you love.

MOON IN SAGITTARIUS

These are days when you are likely to be stirred and elevated by discussions and reflections of a religious and philosophical nature. Ideas of faraway places may cause unusual response and excitement. A decision may be made to visit someone overseas, perhaps a person whose influence was important to your earlier character development. There could be a strong resolution to get away from present intellectual patterns, to learn new subjects, and to meet more interesting people. The superficial may be rejected in all its forms. An impatience with old ideas and unimaginative contacts could lead to a change of companions and interests. There may be an upsurge of religious feeling and metaphysical inquiry. Even a new insight into the significance of astrology and other occult studies is likely under the curious stimulus of the Moon in Sagittarius. Physically, you may express this need for fundamental change by spending more time outdoors: sports, gardening, long walks appeal. CAUTION: Try to channel any restlessness into worthwhile study.

MOON IN CAPRICORN

Life in these hours may seem to pivot around the importance of gaining prestige and honor in the career, as well as maintaining a spotless reputation. Ambitious urges may be excessive and could be accompanied by quite acquisitive drives for money. Effort should be directed along strictly ethical lines where there is no possibility of reproach or scandal. All endeavors are likely to be characterized by great earnestness, and an air of authority and purpose which should impress those who are looking for leadership or reliability. The desire to conform to accepted standards may extend to sharp criticism of family members. Frivolity and unconventional actions are unlikely to amuse while the Moon is in Capricorn. Moderation and seriousness are the orders of the day. Achievement and recognition in this period could come through community work or organizing for the benefit of some amateur group. CAUTION: Dignity and esteem are not always self-awarded.

MOON IN AQUARIUS

Moon in Aquarius is in the second last sign of the Zodiac where ideas can become disturbingly fine and subtle. The result is often a mental "no-man's land" where imagination cannot be trusted with the same certitude as other times. The dangers for the individual are the extremes of optimism and pessimism. Unless the imagination is held in check, situations are likely to be misread, and rosy conclusions drawn where they do not exist. Consequences for the unwary can be costly in career and business. Best to think twice and not speak or act until you think again. Pessimism can be a cruel self-inflicted penalty for delusion at this time. Between the two extremes are strange areas of self-deception which, for example, can make the selfish person think he is actually being generous. Eerie dreams which resemble the reality and even seem to continue into the waking state are also possible. CAUTION: Look for the fact and not just for the image in your mind.

MOON IN PISCES

Everything seems to come to the surface now. Memory may be crystal clear, throwing up long-forgotten information which could be valuable in the career or business. Flashes of clairvoyance and intuition are possible along with sudden realizations of one's own nature, which may be used for self-improvement. A talent, never before suspected, may be discovered. Qualities not evident before in friends and marriage partners are likely to be noticed. As this is a period in which the truth seems to emerge, the discovery of false characteristics is likely to lead to disenchantment or a shift in attachments. However, when qualities are accepted, it should lead to happiness and deeper feeling. Surprise solutions could bob up for old problems. There may be a public announcement of the solving of a crime or mystery. People with secrets may find someone has "guessed" correctly. The secrets of the soul or the inner self also tend to reveal themselves. Religious and philosophical groups may make some interesting discoveries. CAUTION: Not a time for activities that depend on secrecy.

NOTE: When you read your daily forecasts, use the Moon Sign Dates that are provided in the following section of Moon Tables. Then you may want to glance back here for the Moon's influence in a given sign.

MOON TABLES

Atlanta, Boston, Detroit, Miami, Washington, Montreal,
Ottawa, Quebec, Bogota, Havana, Lima, Santiago..Same time

Chicago, New Orleans, Houston, Winnipeg, Churchill,
Mexico City.. Deduct 1 hour

Albuquerque, Denver, Phoenix, El Paso, Edmonton,
Helena .... Deduct 2 hours

Los Angeles, San Francisco, Reno, Portland,
Seattle, Vancouver .... Deduct 3 hours

Honolulu, Anchorage, Fairbanks, Kodiak .... Deduct 5 hours

Nome, Samoa, Tonga, Midway.................... Deduct 6 hours

Halifax, Bermuda, San Juan, Caracas, La Paz,
Barbados...Add 1 hour

St. John's, Brasilia, Rio de Janeiro, Sao Paulo,
Buenos Aires, Montevideo...........................Add 2 hours

Azores, Cape Verde Islands...........................Add 3 hours

Canary Islands, Madeira, Reykjavik ....Add 4 hours

London, Paris, Amsterdam, Madrid, Lisbon,
Gibraltar, Belfast, Rabat ....Add 5 hours

Frankfurt, Rome, Oslo, Stockholm, Prague,
Belgrade...Add 6 hours

Bucharest, Beirut, Tel Aviv, Athens, Istanbul, Cairo,
Alexandria, Cape Town, Johannesburg ....Add 7 hours

Moscow, Leningrad, Baghdad, Dhahran,
Addis Ababa, Nairobi, Teheran, Zanzibar.........Add 8 hours

Bombay, Calcutta, Sri Lanka..................... Add 10 ½ hours

Hong Kong, Shanghai, Manila, Peking, Perth...... Add 13 hours

Tokyo, Okinawa, Darwin, Pusan.................... Add 14 hours

Sydney, Melbourne, Port Moresby, Guam.......... Add 15 hours

Auckland, Wellington, Suva, Wake .... Add 17 hours

1998 MOON SIGN DATES—
NEW YORK TIME

JANUARY		FEBRUARY		MARCH	
Day Moon Enters		**Day Moon Enters**		**Day Moon Enters**	
1. Aquar.		1. Aries		1. Aries	
2. Pisces	4:57 am	2. Taurus	4:26 pm	2. Taurus	0:01 am
3. Pisces		3. Taurus		3. Taurus	
4. Aries	7:44 am	4. Gemini	8:10 pm	4. Gemini	2:16 am
5. Aries		5. Gemini		5. Gemini	
6. Taurus	10:53 am	6. Gemini		6. Cancer	7:28 am
7. Taurus		7. Cancer	1:58 am	7. Cancer	
8. Gemini	2:43 pm	8. Cancer		8. Leo	3:47 pm
9. Gemini		9. Leo	9:58 am	9. Leo	
10. Cancer	7:44 pm	10. Leo		10. Leo	
11. Cancer		11. Virgo	8:10 pm	11. Virgo	2:36 am
12. Cancer		12. Virgo		12. Virgo	
13. Leo	2:46 am	13. Virgo		13. Libra	2:59 pm
14. Leo		14. Libra	8:18 am	14. Libra	
15. Virgo	0:32 pm	15. Libra		15. Libra	
16. Virgo		16. Scorp.	9:14 pm	16. Scorp.	3:52 am
17. Virgo		17. Scorp.		17. Scorp.	
18. Libra	0:45 am	18. Scorp.		18. Sagitt.	3:57 pm
19. Libra		19. Sagitt.	8:57 am	19. Sagitt.	
20. Scorp.	1:35 pm	20. Sagitt.		20. Sagitt.	
21. Scorp.		21. Capric.	5:31 pm	21. Capric.	1:44 am
22. Scorp.		22. Capric.		22. Capric.	
23. Sagitt.	0:26 am	23. Aquar.	10:11 pm	23. Aquar.	8:02 am
24. Sagitt.		24. Aquar.		24. Aquar.	
25. Capric.	7:40 am	25. Pisces	11:43 pm	25. Pisces	10:44 am
26. Capric.		26. Pisces		26. Pisces	
27. Aquar.	11:28 am	27. Aries	11:43 pm	27. Aries	10:50 am
28. Aquar.		28. Aries		28. Aries	
29. Pisces	1:09 pm			29. Taurus	10:07 am
30. Pisces				30. Taurus	
31. Aries	2:22 pm			31. Gemini	10:39 am

Summer time to be considered where applicable.

1998 MOON SIGN DATES—
NEW YORK TIME

APRIL		MAY		JUNE	
Day Moon Enters		**Day Moon Enters**		**Day Moon Enters**	
1. Gemini		1. Cancer		1. Virgo	
2. Cancer	2:11 pm	2. Leo	4:50 am	2. Virgo	
3. Cancer		3. Leo		3. Libra	10:18 am
4. Leo	9:37 pm	4. Virgo	2:48 pm	4. Libra	
5. Leo		5. Virgo		5. Scorp.	11:07 pm
6. Leo		6. Virgo		6. Scorp.	
7. Virgo	8:26 am	7. Libra	3:20 am	7. Scorp.	
8. Virgo		8. Libra		8. Sagitt.	10:35 am
9. Libra	9:05 pm	9. Scorp.	4:11 pm	9. Sagitt.	
10. Libra		10. Scorp.		10. Capric.	7:51 pm
11. Libra		11. Scorp.		11. Capric.	
12. Scorp.	9:57 am	12. Sagitt.	3:49 am	12. Capric.	
13. Scorp.		13. Sagitt.		13. Aquar.	3:04 am
14. Sagitt.	9:53 pm	14. Capric.	1:40 pm	14. Aquar.	
15. Sagitt.		15. Capric.		15. Pisces	8:32 am
16. Sagitt.		16. Aquar.	9:31 pm	16. Pisces	
17. Capric.	8:06 am	17. Aquar.		17. Aries	0:24 pm
18. Capric.		18. Aquar.		18. Aries	
19. Aquar.	3:42 pm	19. Pisces	3:04 am	19. Taurus	2:48 pm
20. Aquar.		20. Pisces		20. Taurus	
21. Pisces	8:07 pm	21. Aries	6:07 am	21. Gemini	4:27 pm
22. Pisces		22. Aries		22. Gemini	
23. Aries	9:31 pm	23. Taurus	7:07 am	23. Cancer	6:40 pm
24. Aries		24. Taurus		24. Cancer	
25. Taurus	9:10 pm	25. Gemini	7:26 am	25. Leo	11:05 pm
26. Taurus		26. Gemini		26. Leo	
27. Gemini	8:56 pm	27. Cancer	8:59 am	27. Leo	
28. Gemini		28. Cancer		28. Virgo	6:55 am
29. Cancer	10:58 pm	29. Leo	1:39 pm	29. Virgo	
30. Cancer		30. Leo		30. Libra	6:06 pm
31. Virgo	10:22 pm				

Summer time to be considered where applicable.

1998 MOON SIGN DATES—
NEW YORK TIME

JULY		AUGUST		SEPTEMBER	
Day Moon Enters		**Day Moon Enters**		**Day Moon Enters**	
1. Libra		1. Scorp.		1. Capric.	
2. Libra		2. Sagitt.	2:49 am	2. Capric.	
3. Scorp.	6:46 am	3. Sagitt.		3. Aquar.	4:22 am
4. Scorp.		4. Capric.	0:19 pm	4. Aquar.	
5. Sagitt.	6:25 pm	5. Capric.		5. Pisces	7:49 am
6. Sagitt.		6. Aquar.	6:32 pm	6. Pisces	
7. Sagitt.		7. Aquar.		7. Aries	8:53 am
8. Capric.	3:28 am	8. Pisces	10:05 pm	8. Aries	
9. Capric.		9. Pisces		9. Taurus	9:17 am
10. Aquar.	9:53 am	10. Pisces		10. Taurus	
11. Aquar.		11. Aries	0:11 am	11. Gemini	10:41 am
12. Pisces	2:23 pm	12. Aries		12. Gemini	
13. Pisces		13. Taurus	2:05 am	13. Cancer	2:21 pm
14. Aries	5:46 pm	14. Taurus		14. Cancer	
15. Aries		15. Gemini	4:47 am	15. Leo	8:49 pm
16. Taurus	8:34 pm	16. Gemini		16. Leo	
17. Taurus		17. Cancer	1:56 am	17. Leo	
18. Gemini	11:19 pm	18. Cancer		18. Virgo	5:53 am
19. Gemini		19. Leo	3:02 pm	19. Virgo	
20. Gemini		20. Leo		20. Libra	4:58 pm
21. Cancer	2:44 am	21. Virgo	11:22 pm	21. Libra	
22. Cancer		22. Virgo		22. Libra	
23. Leo	7:50 am	23. Virgo		23. Scorp.	5:23 am
24. Leo		24. Libra	10:03 am	24. Scorp.	
25. Virgo	3:35 pm	25. Libra		25. Sagitt.	6:06 pm
26. Virgo		26. Scorp.	10:26 pm	26. Sagitt.	
27. Virgo		27. Scorp.		27. Sagitt.	
28. Libra	2:15 am	28. Scorp.		28. Capric.	5:31 am
29. Libra		29. Sagitt.	10:56 am	29. Capric.	
30. Scorp.	2:45 pm	30. Sagitt.		30. Aquar.	1:54 pm
31. Scorp.		31. Capric.	9:24 pm		

Summer time to be considered where applicable.

1998 MOON SIGN DATES—
NEW YORK TIME

OCTOBER Day Moon Enters		NOVEMBER Day Moon Enters		DECEMBER Day Moon Enters	
1. Aquar.		1. Aries	6:28 am	1. Taurus	
2. Pisces	6:24 pm	2. Aries		2. Gemini	4:31 pm
3. Pisces		3. Taurus	6:13 am	3. Gemini	
4. Aries	7:33 pm	4. Taurus		4. Cancer	4:29 pm
5. Aries		5. Gemini	5:12 am	5. Cancer	
6. Taurus	6:58 pm	6. Gemini		6. Leo	6:56 pm
7. Taurus		7. Cancer	5:40 am	7. Leo	
8. Gemini	6:45 pm	8. Cancer		8. Leo	
9. Gemini		9. Leo	9:34 am	9. Virgo	1:22 am
10. Cancer	8:49 pm	10. Leo		10. Virgo	
11. Cancer		11. Virgo	5:38 pm	11. Libra	11:44 am
12. Cancer		12. Virgo		12. Libra	
13. Leo	2:26 am	13. Virgo		13. Libra	
14. Leo		14. Libra	4:59 am	14. Scorp.	0:17 am
15. Virgo	11:33 am	15. Libra		15. Scorp.	
16. Virgo		16. Scorp.	5:42 pm	16. Sagitt.	0:48 pm
17. Libra	11:03 pm	17. Scorp.		17. Sagitt.	
18. Libra		18. Scorp.		18. Capric.	11:56 pm
19. Libra		19. Sagitt.	6:14 am	19. Capric.	
20. Scorp.	11:37 am	20. Sagitt.		20. Capric.	
21. Scorp.		21. Capric.	5:46 am	21. Aquar.	9:18 am
22. Scorp.		22. Capric.		22. Aquar.	
23. Sagitt.	0:17 am	23. Capric.		23. Pisces	4:46 pm
24. Sagitt.		24. Aquar.	3:44 am	24. Pisces	
25. Capric.	0:06 pm	25. Aquar.		25. Aries	10:05 pm
26. Capric.		26. Pisces	11:15 am	26. Aries	
27. Aquar.	9:45 pm	27. Pisces		27. Aries	
28. Aquar.		28. Aries	3:35 pm	28. Taurus	1:06 am
29. Aquar.		29. Aries		29. Taurus	
30. Pisces	3:59 am	30. Taurus	4:54 pm	30. Gemini	2:23 am
31. Pisces				31. Gemini	

Summer time to be considered where applicable.

1998 PHASES OF THE MOON— NEW YORK TIME

New Moon	First Quarter	Full Moon	Last Quarter
Dec. 29 ('97)	Jan. 5	Jan. 12	Jan. 20
Jan. 28	Feb. 3	Feb. 11	Feb. 19
Feb. 26	Mar. 5	Mar. 12	Mar. 21
Mar. 27	Apr. 3	Apr. 11	Apr. 19
Apr. 26	May 3	May 11	May 18
May 25	June 1	June 9	June 17
June 23	July 1	July 9	July 16
July 23	July 31	Aug. 7	Aug. 14
Aug. 21	Aug. 30	Sept. 6	Sept. 12
Sept. 20	Sept. 28	Oct. 5	Oct. 12
Oct. 20	Oct. 28	Nov. 4	Nov. 10
Nov. 18	Nov. 26	Dec. 3	Dec. 10
Dec. 18	Dec. 26	Jan. 1 ('99)	Jan. 9 ('99)

Each phase of the Moon lasts approximately seven to eight days, during which the Moon's shape gradually changes as it comes out of one phase and goes into the next.

There will be a partial solar eclipse during the New Moon phase on February 26 and August 21.

1998 FISHING GUIDE

	Good	Best
January	5-9-10-13-14-15-28	11-12-20
February	9-10-11-12-13-14	3-8
March	5-10-11-12-13-28	14-15-16-21
April	8-9-19	3-10-11-12-13-14-26
May	3-12-13-14-25	8-9-10-11-19
June	2-8-9-10-13-17	7-11-12-24
July	6-7-10-11-12-16-23	1-8-9-31
August	7-8-11-22-30	5-6-9-10-14
September	3-4-5-7-8-9-13-20-28	6
October	2-5-6-28	3-4-7-8-12-20
November	1-2-3-5-6-7-11-19-30	4-27
December	2-3-4-10-18-26	1-5-6

1998 PLANTING GUIDE

	Aboveground Crops	Root Crops
January	2-3-7-11-30	18-19-20-21-22-26
February	3-4-7-8-27	15-16-17-18-22-23
March	2-3-7-11-12-30	14-15-16-17-21-22-26
April	3-4-10-11-27-30	12-13-14-18-22-23
May	1-7-8-9-10-28	15-16-19-20-24
June	4-5-6-7-24-25	11-12-16-20
July	1-2-3-4-5-8-28-29-30-31	13-17-18-21-22
August	1-5-6-25-26-27-28	9-10-13-14-18
September	1-2-21-22-23-24-25-29	10-14-15
October	3-4-21-22-26-27-30-31	7-8-11-12-18-19
November	22-23-27	4-8-14-15-16-17-18
December	1-19-20-24-25-28-29	5-6-12-13-14-15

	Pruning	Weeds and Pests
January	21-22	13-14-15-16-17-23-24
February	17-18	12-13-20-21-24-25
March	16-17-26	19-20-24
April	13-14-22-23	15-16-20-21-24-25
May	19-20	12-13-17-18-22
June	16	10-13-14-18-22-23
July	13-21-22	11-15-16-19-20
August	9-10-18	8-11-12-15-16-20-21
September	14-15	8-12-16-17-18-19
October	11-12	6-9-10-13-14-15-16-17
November	8-17-18	6-10-11-12-13
December	5-6-14-15	7-8-9-10-17-18

MOON'S INFLUENCE OVER PLANTS

Centuries ago it was established that seeds planted when the Moon is in signs and phases called Fruitful will produce more growth than seeds planted when the Moon is in a Barren sign.

Fruitful Signs: Taurus, Cancer, Libra, Scorpio, Capricorn, Pisces
Barren Signs: Aries, Gemini, Leo, Virgo, Sagittarius, Aquarius
Dry Signs: Aries, Gemini, Sagittarius, Aquarius

Activity	Moon In
Mow lawn, trim plants	**Fruitful sign:** 1st & 2nd quarter
Plant flowers	**Fruitful sign:** 2nd quarter; best in Cancer and Libra
Prune	**Fruitful sign:** 3rd & 4th quarter
Destroy pests; spray	**Barren sign:** 4th quarter
Harvest potatoes, root crops	**Dry sign:** 3rd & 4th quarter; Taurus, Leo, and Aquarius

MOON'S INFLUENCE OVER YOUR HEALTH

ARIES   Head, brain, face, upper jaw
TAURUS   Throat, neck, lower jaw
GEMINI   Hands, arms, lungs, shoulders, nervous system
CANCER   Esophagus, stomach, breasts, womb, liver
LEO   Heart, spine
VIRGO   Intestines, liver
LIBRA   Kidneys, lower back
SCORPIO   Sex and eliminative organs
SAGITTARIUS   Hips, thighs, liver
CAPRICORN   Skin, bones, teeth, knees
AQUARIUS   Circulatory system, lower legs
PISCES   Feet, tone of being

Try to avoid work being done on that part of the body when the
Moon is in the sign governing that part.

MOON'S INFLUENCE OVER DAILY AFFAIRS

The Moon makes a complete transit of the Zodiac every 27 days
7 hours and 43 minutes. In making this transit the Moon forms
different aspects with the planets and consequently has favorable
or unfavorable bearings on affairs and events for persons according to the sign of the Zodiac under which they were born.

When the Moon is in conjunction with the Sun it is called a
New Moon; when the Moon and Sun are in opposition it is called
a Full Moon. From New Moon to Full Moon, first and second
quarter—which takes about two weeks—the Moon is increasing
or waxing. From Full Moon to New Moon, third and fourth quarter, the Moon is decreasing or waning.

Activity	Moon In
Business: buying and selling new, requiring public support	Sagittarius, Aries, Gemini, Virgo 1st and 2nd quarter
meant to be kept quiet	3rd and 4th quarter
Investigation	3rd and 4th quarter
Signing documents	1st & 2nd quarter, Cancer, Scorpio, Pisces
Advertising	2nd quarter, Sagittarius
Journeys and trips	1st & 2nd quarter, Gemini, Virgo
Renting offices, etc.	Taurus, Leo, Scorpio, Aquarius
Painting of house/apartment	3rd & 4th quarter, Taurus, Scorpio, Aquarius
Decorating	Gemini, Libra, Aquarius
Buying clothes and accessories	Taurus, Virgo
Beauty salon or barber shop visit	1st & 2nd quarter, Taurus, Leo, Libra, Scorpio, Aquarius
Weddings	1st & 2nd quarter

TAURUS

TAURUS

Character Analysis

Of all the signs of the Zodiac, Taurus is perhaps the most diligent and determined. Taurus are hard workers and stick with something once it's begun. They are thorough people and are careful to avoid making mistakes. Patient, the Bull knows how to bide his time. If something doesn't work out as scheduled, he or she will wait until the appropriate moment comes along, then forge ahead.

The person born under this sign is far from lazy. He will work hard to achieve whatever it is he desires. He is so determined that others often think of him as being unreasonably stubborn. He'll stick to a point he believes is right—nothing can force him to give up his chosen path once his mind is made up.

Taurus takes his time in whatever he does. He wants to make sure everything is done right. At times this may exasperate people who are quick about things. Still and all, a job done by a Taurus is generally a job well done. Careful, steady, and reliable, Taurus is just the opposite of high-strung. This person can take a lot upon himself. Sometimes his burdens or worries are of such proportions that others would find them impossible to carry, but somehow Taurus manages in his silent way.

Taurus may be even-tempered, but he puts up with nonsense from no one. Others had better not take advantage of his balanced disposition. If they do, they are apt to rue the day.

The Taurus man or woman plans well before taking any one line of action. He believes in being well-prepared before embarking on any one project. Others may see him as a sort of slowpoke, but he is not being slow—just sure. He is not the sort of person who would act on a whim or fancy. He wants to be certain of the ground he is standing on.

Material things make him feel comfortable and successful. Some have a definite love of luxury and the like. This may be the result of a slight feeling of inferiority. Material goods make him feel that he is doing well and that he is just as good as the next person.

Taurus is someone who can be trusted at all times. Once he has declared himself a friend, he remains so. He is loyal and considerate of others. In his circle of friends he is quite apt to be one of the successful people. Taurus admires success; he looks up to people who have made something of themselves.

On the whole, Taurus is a down-to-earth person. He is not pretentious or lofty, but direct and earnest. Things that are a bit abstract or far-fetched may not win his immediate approval. He believes in being practical. When he makes a decision, it is generally one with a lot of thought behind it.

Health

People born under this second sign of the Zodiac generally are quite fit physically. They are often gifted with healthy constitutions and can endure more than others in some circumstances. Taurus is often vigorous and strong. At times his strength may astonish others. He can put up with more pressure than most. Pain or the threat of it generally does not frighten him.

He can be proud of his good health. Even when ill, he would rather not give in to it or admit it. But when a disability becomes such that it cannot be ignored, Taurus becomes sad and depressed. For him it is a kind of insult to be ill. When he is laid up with an illness, it generally takes awhile to recover. Although his constitution is strong, when struck down by a disease, his powers for recuperation are not very great. Getting better is a slow and gradual process for the average Taurus.

Males born under this sign are often broad and stocky. They may be wide-shouldered and powerfully built. They are seldom short on muscle. As they age, they sometimes become fat.

Females born under the sign of Taurus are often attractive and charming. They are fond of pretty things and like to see to it that they look fashionable. Although they are often beautiful when young, as they grow older some of them tend to put on a little extra weight. They often have unusually attractive eyes, and their complexions are clear and healthy.

The weakest part of the Taurus body is the throat. If ever he is sick, this part of his body is often affected. Sore throats and the like are often common Taurus complaints.

Occupation

The Taurus man or woman can do a good job—no matter what the work is. They have the ability to be thorough and accurate. They never shirk their duties. They may be looked upon as being slow, especially when they begin a task; but after they are thoroughly familiar with what they are doing, they work at an even and reasonable pace. They are methodical, which counts a good deal. They are good at detail. They seldom overlook anything.

Not all Taurus are slow. Some are quick and brilliant. In many cases, it depends on the circumstances they have to deal with. In any event, they never forget anything once they have learned it. They can be quite shrewd in business matters and are often highly valued in their place of business.

The average Taurus has plenty of get-up-and-go. He is never lazy or neglectful in his work. He enjoys working and does what he can to bring about favorable results.

In business, he will generally shy away from anything that involves what seems to be an unnecessary risk. He likes the path he trods to be a sure one, one that has been well laid out. When he has to make his own way, he sees to it that he is certain of every step of the route. This may often exasperate colleagues. His plodding ways generally pay off in the end, however. In spite of this, and because of his distrust of change, he often misses out on a good business deal. His work may become humdrum and dull due to his dislike of change in routine or schedule.

The Taurus man or woman does well in a position of authority. He is a good manager and knows how to keep everything in order. Discipline is no problem. He knows what scheme to follow and sticks to it. Because his own powers of self-control are so well developed, he has no problem in managing others. Taurus is not frightened by opposition. He knows how to forge ahead with his plans and will not stop until everything comes out according to plan.

Taurus is a stickler for detail. Every little point has to be thoroughly covered before he is satisfied. Because he is a patient person, he knows how to bide his time; he is the kind of person who will wait for the right opportunity to come along, if need be. This sort of person excels in a position where he can take his time in doing things. Any job that requires thoroughness and painstaking effort is one in which a Taurus is likely to do well. They make good managers and can handle certain technical and industrial jobs. Some Taurus are gifted with the ability to draw or design and do well in the world of architecture. Many of them are quite artistic, and it depends on the proper circumstances to bring this out. In most cases, however, Taurus is content with doing work that is sure and calculated. His creative ability may not have the proper chance to surface, and it is only through cultivation that he is able to make a broad use of it.

Although many people born under this sign work in the city, they prefer the peace and quiet of remote places to the hustle and bustle of the busy metropolis. Many of them do well in the area of agriculture. They have a way with growing things. A Taurus man or woman could easily become a successful dairy or poultry farmer. They find it easy to relate to things rural or rustic. Many of them are gifted with green thumbs.

When working with others, Taurus can be relied upon. His partner if possible should be similar in nature. The Bull may become annoyed if he works with someone who is always changing his mind or schedule. He doesn't care much for surprises or sudden changes. New ideas may not appeal to him at first; he has to have time to get used to them. Generally, he likes to think of something new as being a creation of his own. And by taking his time in approaching it, he comes to see it in that light. Taurus should be gently coaxed when working with others. He will give his consent to new ideas if his colleagues are subtle enough in their presentation.

Although the Taurus man or woman may not hold an important position in the place where he works, this does not disturb him. He doesn't mind working under others—especially if they are good and able leaders or managers. Taurus is a loyal worker. He can always be depended on to complete his tasks.

The Taurus man or woman understands the value of money and appreciates the things it can do. He may not be a millionaire, but he does know how to earn and save well enough so that he can acquire those material items he feels are important. Some people born under this sign can easily acquire a greedy streak if they don't watch out. So obsessed with material gain are some Taurus that they do not take time to relax and enjoy other things that life has to offer. Money-oriented, the ambitious Taurus sometimes turns into someone who is all work and no play. It is not surprising, then, that a great many bankers and financiers are born under this sign of the Zodiac.

The Taurus person is generally straightforward and well-meaning. If someone is in need, he will not hesitate to assist them financially. Taurus as children are sometimes stingy, but as they grow up and have enough money, they become reasonably free in their use of it. Still and all, the average Taurus will never invest all the money he has in anything. He always likes to keep a good portion of it aside for that inevitable rainy day. Although he may not be interested in taking many risks, the person born under this sign is often lucky. When he does take a chance and gambles, he quite often turns out the winner.

When a Taurus puts his best foot forward, he can achieve almost anything—even though it may take a little longer than it does with most. He has many hidden strengths and positive characteristics that help him to get ahead.

Home and Family

The Taurus person is a lover of home life. He likes to be surrounded by familiar and comfortable things. He is the kind of person who calls his home his castle. Generally, the home of a Taurus radiates comfort and hospitality. The Taurus woman knows how to decorate and arrange a house so that visitors feel immediately at home upon entering. The Taurus man is more often than not a good breadwinner. He sees to it that the members of his immediate family have everything they need.

The Taurus person usually likes the peace, quiet, and beauty of the country. If possible, he will see to it that he lives there—for part of the year if not for the whole year. The Taurus housewife has her work down to an efficient routine. She is interested in keeping everything neat and orderly. She is a very good hostess and knows how to make people feel at ease.

Being well-liked is important. Taurus likes to be surrounded by good friends. He admires important people and likes to include them in his social activities if possible. When entertaining, the Taurus woman usually outdoes herself in preparing all sorts of delicious items. She is skilled in the culinary arts. If ever she is poorly entertained or fed by others, she feels upset about it.

The Taurus man or woman usually has a tastefully furnished home. But what is more important to Taurus than beauty is comfort. His house must be a place where he can feel at home.

Taurus can be strict with their children and stand for no nonsense. They are interested in seeing that their children are brought up correctly. It is important for them that the youngsters reflect the good home they come from. Compliments from others about the behavior of their children make Taurus parents happy and proud. As the children grow older, however, and reach the teenage stage, some difficulties may occur in the beginning. The Taurus mother or father may resent the sudden change in the relationship as the child tries to assert his own individuality.

Social Relationships

Taurus generally does what he can to be popular among his friends. He is loyal and caring with people who are close to him. Because he is sincere and forthright, people generally seek him out as a friend. He makes a good talker as well as a listener. People in difficulties often turn to him for advice.

The Taurus person is genuinely interested in success, and there is nothing he admires more than someone who has achieved his goal. In making friends, it seems as though a person born under this sign gravitates toward people who have made a success of themselves or people on their way up. Influential people are admired by Taurus. Being surrounded by people who have met with some success in life makes the person born under this sign feel somewhat successful too.

The Taurus person is one who generally likes to keep his family matters to himself. He resents the meddling of friends—even close friends.

He is a person who sticks to his principles, and as a result he may make an enemy or two as he goes along.

Love and Marriage

In love matters, Taurus may go through a series of flings—many of them lighthearted—before settling down with the "right" person. By nature, Taurus is serious. In love matters, his feelings run deep; but he will take steps to guard himself against disappointment if he feels the affair won't be lasting. Taurus can be romantic. As with everything, once he has made up his mind about someone, nothing will stand in his way; he'll win the object of his affection if it's the last thing he does. Other suitors don't frighten him in the least.

Younger Taurus have nothing against light romances, but as they grow older they look for stability and deep affection in a love affair. Faithful in love as they are in most things, they look for partners who are apt to feel the way they do.

The Taurus in love does not generally attempt a coy approach. More likely than not he'll be direct in expressing his feelings. Once he has won the person he loves, the average Taurus is often possessive as well as protective.

Persons born under this sign generally do well in a marriage relationship. Matters at home go well as long as he is treated fairly by his mate. If conditions at home are not to his liking, he can be biting and mean.

There is no halfway in marriage as far as Taurus is concerned; it's a matter of two people giving themselves completely. As husbands and wives, they make ideal mates in many respects. They are usually quite considerate and generous. They like looking after the other members of their families. They are very family-oriented types, and nothing pleases them more than to be able to spend time at home with their loved ones.

Romance and the Taurus Woman

The Taurus woman has a charm and beauty that are hard to define. There is something elusive about her that attracts the opposite sex—something mysterious. Needless to say, she is much sought after. Men find her a delight. She is generally easygoing, relaxed, and good-natured. Men find her a joy to be with because they can be themselves. They don't have to try to impress her by being something they are not.

Although she may have a series of romances before actually settling down, every time she falls in love it is the real thing. She is not superficial or flighty in romance. When she gives her heart, she hopes it will be forever. When she does finally find the right person, she has no trouble in being true to him for the rest of her life.

In spite of her romantic nature, the female Taurus is quite practical, too, when it comes to love. She wants a man who can take care of her. Someone on whom she can depend. Someone who can provide her with the comforts she feels she needs. Some Taurus look for men who are well-to-do or who have already achieved success. To them, the practical side of marriage is just as important as the romantic. But most Taurus women are attracted to sincere, hardworking men who are good company and faithful in the relationship. A Taurus wife sticks by the man of her choice. She will do everything in her power to give her man the spiritual support he needs in order to advance in his career.

The Taurus woman likes pretty, gentle things. They enjoy making their home a comfortable and attractive one. They are quite artistic, and their taste in furnishings is often flawless. They know how to make a house comfortable and inviting. The Taurus woman is interested in material things. They make her feel secure and loved. Her house is apt to be filled with various objects that have an important meaning for her alone.

She is even-tempered and does what she can to get along with her mate or loved one, but once she is rubbed the wrong way she can become very angry and outspoken. The considerate mate or lover, however, has no problem with his Taurus woman. When treated well, she maintains her pleasant disposition, and is a delight to be with. She is a woman who is kind and warm when she is with the man of her choice. A man who is strong, protective, and financially sound is the sort of man who can help bring out the best in a woman born under this sign. She enjoys being flattered and being paid small attentions. It is not that she is excessively demanding, but just that she likes to have evidence from time to time that she is dearly loved.

The Taurus woman is very dependable and faithful. The man who wins her is indeed lucky. She wants a complete, comfortable, and correct home life. She seldom complains. She is quite flexible and can enjoy the good times or suffer the bad times with equal grace. Although she does enjoy luxury, if difficult times come about, she will not bicker but stick beside the man she loves. For her marriage is serious business. It is very unlikely that a Taurus woman would seek a divorce unless it was absolutely necessary.

A good homemaker, the Taurus woman knows how to keep the love of her man alive once she has won him. To her, love is a way of life. She will live entirely for the purpose of making her man happy. Men seldom have reason to be dissatisfied with a Taurus mate. Their affections never stray. Taurus women are determined people. When they put their minds to making a marriage or love relationship work, it seldom fails. They'll work as hard at romance as they will at anything else they want.

As a mother, the Taurus woman does what she can to see that her children are brought up correctly. She likes her children to be polite and obedient. She can be strict when she puts her mind to it. It is important to her that the youngsters learn the right things in life—even if they don't seem to want to. She is not at all permissive as a parent. Her children must respect her and do as she says. She won't stand for insolence or disobedience. She is well-meaning in her treatment of her children. Although the children may resent her strictness as they are growing up, in later life they see that she was justified in the way she handled them.

Romance and the Taurus Man

The Taurus man is as determined in love as he is in everything else. Once he sets his mind on winning a woman, he keeps at it until he has achieved his goal.

Women find him attractive. The Taurus man has a protective way about him. He knows how to make a woman feel wanted and taken care of. Taurus men are often fatherly, so women looking for protection and unwavering affection are attracted to them. Because of their he-man physiques, and sure ways, they have no trouble in romance. The opposite sex find their particular brand of charm difficult to resist.

He can be a very romantic person. The number of romances he is likely to have before actually settling down may be many. But he is faithful. He is true to the person he loves for as long as that relationship lasts. When he finds someone suited to him, he devotes the rest of his life to making her happy.

Married life agrees with the man born under the Taurus sign. They make good, dependable husbands and excellent, concerned fathers. The Taurus man is, of course, attracted to a woman who is good-looking and charming. But the qualities that most appeal to him often lie deeper than the skin. He is not interested in glamour alone. The girl of his choice must be a good homemaker, resourceful, and loving. Someone kind and considerate is apt to touch his heartstrings more than a pretty, one-dimensional face. He is looking for a woman to settle down with for a lifetime.

Marriage is important to him because it means stability and security, two things that are most important to Taurus. He is serious about marriage. He will do his best to provide for his family in a way he feels is correct and responsible. He is not one to shirk his family responsibilities. He likes to know that the woman he has married will stand beside him in all that he does.

The Taurus man believes that only he should be boss of the family. He may listen and even accept the advice of his spouse, but he is the one who runs things. He likes to feel that he is the king in his castle.

He likes his home to be comfortable and inviting. He has a liking for soft things; he likes to be babied a little by the woman he loves. He may be a strict parent, but he feels it is for the children's own good.

Woman—Man

TAURUS WOMAN
ARIES MAN

If you are attracted to a man born under the sign of the Ram, it is not certain as to how far the relationship would go. An Aries who has made his mark in the world and is somewhat steadfast in his outlook and attitudes could be quite a catch for you. On the other hand, Aries are swift-footed and quick-minded; their industrious manner may often fail to impress you, particularly when you become aware that their get-up-and-go sometimes leads nowhere. When it comes to a fine romance, you want a nice broad shoulder to lean on; you might find a relationship with someone who doesn't like to stay put for too long a time somewhat upsetting. Then, too, the Aries man is likely to misunderstand your interest in a slow-but-sure approach to most matters. He may see you as a stick-in-the-mud. What's more, he'll tell you so if you make him aware of it too often. Aries speak their minds, sometimes at the drop of a hat.

You may find a man born under this sign too demanding. He may give you the feeling that he wants you to be at all places at the same time. Even though he realizes that this is impossible, he may grumble at you for not at least having tried. You have a barrelful of patience at your disposal, and he may try every bit of it. Whereas you're a thorough person, he may overshoot something essential to a project or a relationship due to his eagerness to quickly achieve his end.

Being married to a Ram does not mean that you'll necessarily have a secure and safe life as far as finances are concerned. Aries are not rash with cash, but they lack the sound head that you have for putting something away for that inevitable rainy day. He'll do his best to see that you're well provided for though his efforts may leave something to be desired.

Although there will be a family squabble occasionally, you, with your steady nature and love of permanence, will learn to take it in your stride and make your marriage a success.

He'll love the children. Aries make wonderful fathers. Kids take to them like ducks to water, probably because of their quick minds and zestful behavior. Sometimes Aries fathers spoil their children, and here is where you'll have to step in. But don't be too strict with youngsters, or you'll drive most of their affection over to their father. When they reach the adolescent stage and become increasingly difficult to manage, it would perhaps be better for you to take a backseat and rely on your Aries husband's sympathy and understanding of this stage of life.

TAURUS WOMAN
TAURUS MAN

Although a man born under the same sign as you may seem like a "natural," better look twice before you leap. It can also be that he resembles you too closely to be compatible. You can be pretty set in your ways. When you encounter someone with just as much willpower or stubbornness, a royal fireworks display can be the result. When two Taurus lock horns it can be a very exhausting and totally frustrating get-together. But if the man of your dreams is one born under your sign and you're sure that no other will do, then proceed with extreme caution. Even though you know yourself well—or think you do—it does not necessarily mean that you will have an easy time understanding him. Since you both are practical, you should try a rational approach to your relationship. Put all the cards on the table, discuss the matter, and decide whether to cooperate, compromise, or call it quits.

If you both have your sights set on the same goals, a life together could be just what the doctor ordered. You both are affectionate and have a deep need for affection. Being loved, understood, and appreciated is vital for your mutual well-being.

Essentially, you are both looking for peace, security, and harmony in your lives. Working toward these goals together may be a good way of eventually attaining them, especially if you are honest and tolerant of each other.

If you should marry a Taurus man, you can be sure that the wolf will stay far away from the door. They are notoriously good providers and do everything to make their families comfortable and happy. He'll appreciate the way you make a home warm and inviting. Good food, all the comforts, and a few luxuries are essential ingredients. Although he may be a big lug of a guy, he'll be fond of gentle treatment and soft things. If you puff up his pillow and tuck him in at night, he won't complain. He'll eat it up and ask for more.

In friendships, you'll both be on even footing. You both tend to seek out friends who are successful or prominent. You admire people who work hard and achieve what they set out for. It helps to reassure your way of looking at things.

Taurus parents love their children very much and never sacrifice a show of affection even when scolding them. Since you both are excellent disciplinarians bringing up children, you should try to balance your tendency to be strict with a healthy amount of pampering and spoiling.

TAURUS WOMAN
GEMINI MAN

Gemini men, in spite of their charm and dash, may make even placid Taurus nervous. Some Twins do seem to lack the common sense you set so much store in. Their tendencies to start a half-dozen projects, then toss them up in the air out of boredom, may only exasperate you. You may be inclined to interpret their jumping around from here to there as childish if not downright psychotic. Gemini will never stay put. If you should take it into your head to try and make him sit still, he will resent it strongly.

On the other hand, he's likely to think you're a slowpoke and far too interested in security and material things. He's attracted to things that sparkle and bubble—not necessarily for a long time. You are likely to seem quite dull and uninteresting—with your practical head and feet firm on the ground—to the Gemini gadabout. If you're looking for a life of security and steadiness, then Mr. Right he ain't.

Chances are you'll be taken in by his charming ways and facile wit. Few women can resist Gemini charm. But after you've seen through his live-for-today, gossamer facade, you'll be most happy to turn your attention to someone more stable, even if he is not as interesting. You want a man who's there when you need him, someone on whom you can fully rely. Keeping track of Gemini's movements will make your head spin. Still, being a Taurus, you're a patient woman who can put up with almost anything if you think it will be worth the effort.

A successful and serious-minded Gemini could make you a very happy woman, perhaps, if you gave him half the chance. Although Gemini may impress you as being scatterbrained, he generally has a good head on his shoulders and can make efficient use of it when he wants. Some of them, who have learned the art of being steadfast, have risen to great professional heights.

Once you convince yourself that not all people born under the sign of the Twins are witless grasshoppers, you won't mind dating a few to support your newborn conviction. If you do walk down the aisle with one, accept the fact that married life with him will mean taking the bitter with the sweet.

Life with a Gemini man can be more fun than a barrel of clowns. You'll never experience a dull moment. You'd better see to it, though, that you get his paycheck every payday. If you leave the budgeting and bookkeeping to him you'll wind up behind the eight ball.

The Gemini father is apt to let children walk all over him, so you'd better take charge of them most of the time.

TAURUS WOMAN
CANCER MAN

The man born under the sign of Cancer may very well be the man after your own heart. Generally, Cancers are steady people. They share the Taurus interest in security and practicality. Despite their sometimes seemingly grouchy exterior, men born under the sign of the Crab are sensitive and kind. They are almost always hard workers and are very interested in making successes of themselves in business as well as socially. Their conservative outlook on many things often agrees with yours. He'll be a man on whom you can depend come rain or come shine. He'll never shirk his responsibilities as a provider and will always see to it that his mate and family never want.

Your patience will come in handy if you decide it's a Moon Child you want for a mate. He doesn't rush headlong into romance. He wants to be sure about love as you do. After the first couple of months of dating, don't jump to the conclusion that he's about to make his "great play."

Don't let his coolness fool you, though. Underneath his starched reserve is a very warm heart. He's just not interested in showing off as far as affection is concerned. For him, affection should only be displayed for two sets of eyes—yours and his. If you really want to see him warm up to you, you'd better send your roommate off, then bolt the doors and windows—to insure him that you won't be disturbed or embarrassed. He will never step out of line—he's too much of a gentleman for that, but it is likely that in such a sealed off atmosphere, he'll pull out an engagement ring (that belonged to his grandmother) and slip it on your finger.

Speaking of relatives, you'll have to get used to the fact that Cancers are overly fond of their mothers. When he says his mother's the most wonderful woman in the world, you'd better agree with him—that is, if you want to become his wife. It's a very touchy area for him. Say one wrong word about his mother or let him suspect that your interest in her is not real, and you'd better look for husband material elsewhere.

He'll always be a faithful husband; Cancers seldom tomcat around after they've taken that vow. They take their marriage responsibilities seriously. They see to it that everything in their homes runs smoothly. Bills will always be paid promptly. He'll take out all kinds of insurance policies on his family and property. He'll see to it that when retirement time rolls around, you'll both be very well off.

The Cancer father is patient, sensitive, and understanding, always protective of his children.

TAURUS WOMAN
LEO MAN

To know a man born under the sign of the Lion is not necessarily to love him—even though the temptation may be great. When he fixes most girls with his leonine double-whammy, it causes their hearts to throb and their minds to cloud over. But with you, the sensible Bull, it takes more than a regal strut and a roar to win you. There's no denying that Leo has a way with women, even practical Taurus women. Once he's swept you off your feet it may be hard to scramble upright again. Still, you're no pushover for romantic charm if you feel there may be no security behind it. He'll wine you and dine you in the fanciest places and shower you with diamonds if he can. Still, it would be wise to find out just how long the shower's going to last before consenting to be his wife.

Lions in love are hard to ignore, let alone brush off. Your "no" will have a way of nudging him on until he feels he has you completely under his spell. Once mesmerized by this romantic powerhouse, you will most likely find yourself doing things you never dreamed of. Leos can be like vain pussycats when involved in romance; they like to be cuddled and pampered and told how wonderful they are. This may not be your cup of tea, exactly. Still when you're romancing a Leo, you'll find yourself doing all kinds of things to make him purr. Although he may be sweet and gentle when trying to win you, he'll roar if he feels he's not getting the tender love and care he feels is his due. If you keep him well supplied with affection, you can be sure his eyes will never stray and his heart will never wander.

Leo men often turn out to be leaders. They're born to lord it over others in one way or another. If he is top banana in his firm, he'll most likely do everything he can to stay on top. And if he's not number one yet, then he's working on it, and will see to it that he's sitting on the throne before long.

You'll have more security than you can use if he's in a position to support you in the manner to which he feels you should be accustomed. He's apt to be too lavish, though. Although creditors may never darken your door, handle as much of the household bookkeeping as you can to put your mind at ease.

He's a natural-born friend-maker and entertainer. At a party, he will try to attract attention. Let him. If you allow him his occasional ego trips without quibbling, your married life will be one of warmth, wealth, and contentment.

When a little Lion or Lioness comes along, this Baby Leo will be brought up like one of the landed gentry if Papa Leo has anything to say about it.

TAURUS WOMAN
VIRGO MAN

Although the Virgo man may be a fussbudget at times, his seriousness and common sense may help you overlook his tendency to be too critical about minor things.

Virgo men are often quiet, respectable types who set great store in conservative behavior and levelheadedness. He'll admire you for your practicality and tenacity, perhaps even more than for your good looks. He's seldom bowled over by glamour. When he gets his courage up, he turns to a serious and reliable girl for romance. He'll be far from a Valentino while dating. In fact, you may wind up making all the passes. Once he does get his motor running, however, he can be a warm and wonderful fellow—to the right woman.

He's gradual about love. Chances are your romance with him will most likely start out looking like an ordinary friendship. Once he's sure you're no fly-by-night flirt and have no plans of taking him for a ride, he'll open up and rain sunshine over your heart.

Virgo men tend to marry late in life. He believes in holding out until he's met the right one. He may not have many names in his little black book; in fact, he may not even have a little black book. He's not interested in playing the field; leave that to men of the more flamboyant signs. The Virgo man is so particular that he may remain romantically inactive for a long period. His girl has to be perfect or it's no go. If you find yourself feeling weak-kneed for a Virgo, do your best to convince him that perfect is not so important when it comes to love. Help him to realize that he's missing out on a great deal by not considering the near-perfect or whatever you consider yourself to be. With your surefire persever-ance, you'll make him listen to reason and he'll wind up recipro-cating your romantic interests.

The Virgo man is no block of ice. He'll respond to what he feels to be the right feminine flame. Once your love life with a Virgo starts to bubble, don't give it a chance to fall flat. You may never have a second chance at romance with him.

If you should ever separate for a while, forget about patching up. He'd prefer to let the pieces lie scattered. Once married, though, he'll stay that way—even if it hurts. He's too conscien-tious to try to back out of a legal deal.

A Virgo man is as neat as a pin. He's thumbs down on sloppy housekeeping. An ashtray with even one used cigarette is apt to make him see red. Keep everything bright, neat, and shiny. Neat-ness goes for the children, too, at least by the time he gets home from work. But Daddy's little girl or boy will never lack for in-teresting playthings and learning tools.

TAURUS WOMAN
LIBRA MAN

Taurus may find Libra men too wrapped up in a dream world ever to come down to earth. Although he may be very careful about weighing both sides of an argument, that does not mean he will ever make a decision about anything. Decisions large and small are capable of giving Libra the willies. Don't ask him why. He probably doesn't know, himself. As a lover, you—who are interested in permanence and constancy in a relationship—may find him a puzzlement. One moment he comes on hard and strong with "I love you", the next moment he's left you like yesterday's mashed potatoes. It does no good to wonder "What did I do now?" You most likely haven't done anything. It's just one of Libra's ways.

On the other hand, you'll appreciate his admiration of harmony and beauty. If you're all decked out in your fanciest gown or have a tastefully arranged bouquet on the dining room table, you'll get a ready compliment—one that's really deserved. Libras don't pass out compliments to all and sundry. Generally, he's tactful enough to remain silent if he finds something disagreeable.

He may not be as ambitious as you would like your lover or husband to be. Where you do have drive and a great interest in getting ahead, Libra is often content to drift along. It is not that he is lazy or shiftless, it's just that he places greater value on aesthetic things than he does on the material. If he's in love with you, however, he'll do anything in his power to make you happy.

You may have to give him a good nudge now and again to get him to see the light. But he'll be happy wrapped up in his artistic dreams when you're not around to remind him that the rent is almost due.

If you love your Libra don't be too harsh or impatient with him. Try to understand him. Don't let him see the stubborn side of your nature too often, or you'll scare him away. Libras are peace-loving people and hate any kind of confrontation that may lead to an argument. Some of them will do almost anything to keep the peace—even tell little white lies, if necessary.

Although you possess gobs of patience, you may find yourself losing a little of it when trying to come to grips with your Libra. He may think you're too materialistic or mercenary, but he'll have the good grace not to tell you, for fear you'll perhaps chew his head off.

If you are deeply involved with a Libra, you'd better see to it that you help him manage his money. It's for his own good. Money will never interest him as much as it should, and he does have a tendency to be too generous when he shouldn't be.

Although Libra is a gentle and understanding father, he'll see to it that he never spoils his children.

TAURUS WOMAN
SCORPIO MAN

In the astrological scheme of things Scorpio is your zodiacal mate, but also your zodiacal opposite. If your heart is set on a Scorpio, you must figure him out to stay on his good side.

Many people have a hard time understanding a Scorpio man. Few, however, are able to resist his fiery charm. When angered, he can act like a nestful of wasps, and his sting is capable of leaving an almost permanent mark. Scorpios are straight to the point. They can be as sharp as a razor blade and just as cutting.

The Scorpio man is capable of being very blunt, and he can act like a brute or a cad. His touchiness may get on your nerves after a while. If it does, you'd better tiptoe away from the scene rather than chance an explosive confrontation.

It's quite likely that he will find your slow, deliberate manner a little irritating. He may misinterpret your patience for indifference. On the other hand, you're the kind of woman who can adapt to almost any sort of situation or circumstance if you put your mind and heart to it. Scorpio men are perceptive and intelligent. In some respects, they know how to use their brains more effectively and quicker than most. They believe in winning in everything; in business, they usually achieve the position they desire through drive and intellect.

Your interest in your home is not likely to be shared by him. No matter how comfortable you've managed to make the house, it will have very little influence on him as far as making him aware of his family responsibilities. He doesn't like to be tied down, generally. He would rather be out on the battlefield of life, belting away at what he feels is a just and worthy cause, than using leisure time at home.

He is passionate in his business affairs and political interests. He is just as passionate—if not more so—in romance. Most women are easily attracted to him—and the Taurus woman is no exception, that is, at least before she knows what she might be getting into. Those who allow their hearts to be stolen by a Scorpio man soon find that they're dealing with a cauldron of seething excitement.

Scorpio likes fathering a large family. He gets along well with children and is proud of them, but often he fails to live up to his responsibilities as a parent. When he takes his fatherly duties seriously, he is adept with youngsters. Whenever you have trouble understanding the kids, Scorpio's ability to see beneath the surface of things will be invaluable.

TAURUS WOMAN
SAGITTARIUS MAN

The Taurus woman who has her cap set for a Sagittarius man may have to apply large amounts of strategy before being able to make him pop that question. When visions of the altar enter the romance, Sagittarius are apt to get cold feet. Although you may become attracted to the Archer, because of his positive, winning manner, you may find the relationship loses some of its luster when it assumes a serious hue. Sagittarius are full of bounce—perhaps too much bounce to suit you. They are often hard to pin down and dislike staying put. If ever there's a chance to be on the move, he'll latch on to it post haste. They're quick people, both in mind and spirit. And sometimes because of their zip, they make mistakes. If you have good advice to offer, he'll tell you to keep it.

Sagittarius like to rely on their own wit whenever possible. His up-and-at-'em manner about most things is likely to drive you up the wall occasionally. Your cautious, deliberate manner is likely to make him impatient. And he can be resentful if you don't accompany him on his travel or sports ventures. He can't abide a slowpoke. At times, you'll find him too breezy and kiddish. However, don't mistake his youthful demeanor for premature senility.

Sagittarius are equipped with first-class brain power and know well how to put it to use. They're often full of good ideas and drive. Generally they're very broad-minded people and are very much concerned with fair play and equality.

In romance, he's quite capable of loving you wholeheartedly while treating you like a good pal. His hail-fellow well-met manner in the arena of love is likely to scare a dainty damsel off. However, a woman who knows that his heart is in the right place won't mind his bluff, rambunctious style.

He's not much of a homebody. He's got ants in his pants and enjoys being on the move. Humdrum routine, especially at home, bores him to distraction. At the drop of a hat he may ask you to whip off your apron and dine out for a change instead. He's fond of coming up with instant surprises. He'll love to keep you guessing. His friendly, candid nature gains him many friends.

When it comes to children, you may find that you've been left holding the bag. Sagittarius feel helpless around little shavers. When children become older, he will develop a genuine interest in them.

TAURUS WOMAN
CAPRICORN MAN

A Taurus woman is often capable of bringing out the best in a Capricorn man. While other women are puzzled by his silent and slow ways, Taurus, with her patience and understanding, can lend him the confidence he perhaps needs in order to come out from behind the rock.

Quite often, the Capricorn man is not the romantic kind of lover that attracts most women. Still, behind his reserve and calm, he's a pretty warm guy. He is capable of giving his heart completely once he has found the right girl. The Taurus woman who is deliberate by nature and who believes in taking time to be sure will find her kind of man in a Capricorn. He is slow and deliberate about almost everything—even romance. He doesn't believe in flirting and would never let his heart be led on a merry chase. If you win his trust, he'll give you his heart on a platter. Quite often, it is the woman who has to take the lead when romance is in the air. As long as he knows you're making the advances in earnest he won't mind. In fact, he'll probably be grateful.

Don't think that he's all cold fish; he isn't. Although some Goats have no difficulty in expressing passion, when it comes to displaying affection, they're at sea. But with an understanding and patient Bull, he should have no trouble in learning to express himself, especially if you let him know how important affection is to you, and for the good of your relationship.

The Capricorn man is very interested in getting ahead. He's ambitious and usually knows how to apply himself well to whatever task he undertakes. He's far from a spendthrift and tends to manage his money with extreme care. But a Taurus woman with a knack for putting away money for that rainy day should have no trouble in understanding this.

The Capricorn man thinks in terms of future security. He wants to make sure that he and his wife have something to fall back on when they reach retirement age.

He'll want you to handle the household efficiently, but that's no problem for most Taurus. If he should check up on you from time to time about the price of this and the cost of that, don't let it irritate you. Once he is sure you can handle this area to his liking, he'll leave it all up to you.

Although he may be a hard man to catch when it comes to marriage, once he's made that serious step, he's quite likely to become possessive. Capricorns need to know that they have the support of their women in whatever they do, every step of the way. Your Capricorn man, because he's waited so long for for the right mate, may be considerably older than you.

Capricorn fathers never neglect their children and instinctively know what is good for them.

TAURUS WOMAN
AQUARIUS MAN

The Aquarius man in your life is perhaps the most broad-minded you have ever met. Still, you may think he is the most impractical. He's more of a dreamer than a doer. If you don't mind putting up with a man whose heart and mind are as wide as the sky but his head is almost always up in the clouds, then start dating that Aquarius man who somehow has captured your fancy. Maybe you, with your Taurus good sense, can bring him down to earth before he gets too starry-eyed.

He's no dumbbell; make no mistake about that. He can be busy making complicated and idealistic plans when he's got that out-to-lunch look in his eyes. But more than likely, he'll never execute them. After he's shared one or two of his progressive ideas with you, you may think he's a nut. But don't go jumping to any wrong conclusions. There's a saying that the Water Bearer is a half-century ahead of everybody else. If you do decide to say yes to his will-you-marry-me, you'll find out how right some of his zany whims are on your golden anniversary. Maybe the waiting will be worth it. Could be that you have an Einstein on your hands—and heart.

Life with an Aquarius won't be one of total despair for you if you learn to balance his airiness with your down-to-brass-tacks practicality. He won't gripe if you do. Being the open-minded man he is, the Water Bearer will entertain all your ideas and opinions. He may not agree with them, but he'll give them a trial airing out, anyway.

Don't tear your hair out when you find that it's almost impossible to hold a normal conversation with your Aquarius friend. He's capable of answering your how-do-you-do with a running commentary on some erudite topic. Always keep in mind that he means well. His broad-mindedness extends to your freedom and individuality, a modern idea indeed.

He'll be kind and generous as a husband and will never lower himself by quibbling over petty things. You take care of the budgeting and bookkeeping; that goes without saying. He'll be thankful that you do such a good job of tracking all the nickels and dimes that would otherwise burn a hole in his pocket.

In your relationship with a man born under Aquarius you'll have plenty of opportunities to put your legendary patience to good use. At times, you may feel like tossing in the towel and calling it quits, but try counting to ten before deciding it's the last straw.

Aquarius is a good family man. He's understanding with children and will overlook a naughty deed now and then or at least try to see it in its proper perspective.

TAURUS WOMAN
PISCES MAN

The Pisces man could be the man you've looked for high and low and thought never existed. He's terribly sensitive and terribly romantic. Still, he has a very strong individual character and is well aware that the moon is not made of green cheese. He'll be very considerate of your every wish and will do his best to see to it that your relationship is a happy one.

The Pisces man is great for showering the object of his affection with all kinds of gifts and tokens of his love.

He's just the right mixture of dreamer and realist; he's capable of pleasing most women's hearts. When it comes to earning bread and butter, the strong Pisces will do all right in the world. Quite often they are capable of rising to very high positions. Some do extremely well as writers or psychiatrists. He'll be as patient and understanding with you as you will undoubtedly be with him. One thing a Pisces man dislikes is pettiness. Anyone who delights in running another into the ground is almost immediately crossed off his list of possible mates. If you have any small grievances, don't tell him about them. He couldn't care less and will think less of you if you do.

If you fall in love with a weak Pisces man, don't give up your job before you get married. Better hang on to it a long time after the honeymoon; you may still need it. A funny thing about the man born under this sign is that he can be content almost anywhere. This is perhaps because he is inner-directed and places little value on material things. In a shack or in a palace, the Pisces man is capable of making the best of all possible adjustments. He won't kick up a fuss if the roof leaks and if the fence is in sad need of repair. He's got more important things on his mind, he'll tell you. At this point, you're quite capable of telling him to go to blazes. Still and all, the Pisces man is not shiftless or aimless, but it is important to understand that material gain is never an urgent goal for him.

Pisces men have a way with the sick and troubled. It's often his nature to offer his shoulder to anyone in the mood for a good cry. He can listen to one hard-luck story after another without seeming to tire. He often knows what's bothering a person before the person knows it himself.

As a lover, he'll be attentive. You'll never have cause to doubt his intentions or sincerity. Everything will be aboveboard in his romantic dealings with you.

Children are often delighted with the Pisces man because he spoils and pampers them no end.

Man—Woman

TAURUS MAN
ARIES WOMAN

The Aries woman may be a little too bossy and busy for you. Generally, Aries are ambitious creatures and can become impatient with people who are more thorough and deliberate than they are—especially when they feel it's taking too much time. Unlike you, the Aries woman is a fast worker. In fact, sometimes she's so fast, she forgets to look where she's going. When she stumbles or falls, it's a nice thing if you're there to grab her. She'll be grateful. Don't ever tell her "I told you so" when she errs.

Aries are proud and don't like people to naysay them. That can turn them into blocks of ice. And don't think that an Aries woman will always get tripped up in her plans because she lacks patience. Quite often they are capable of taking aim and hitting the bull's-eye. You'll be flabbergasted at times by their accuracy as well as by their ambition. On the other hand, because of your interest in being sure and safe, you're apt to spot many a mistake or flaw in your Aries friend's plans before she does.

In some respects, the Aries-Taurus relationship is like that of the tortoise and the hare. Although it may seem like plodding to the Ram, you're capable of attaining exactly what she has her sights set on. It may take longer but you generally do not make any mistakes along the way.

Taurus men are renowned lovers. With some, it's almost a way of life. When you are serious, you want your partner to be as earnest and as giving as you are. An Aries woman can be giving when she feels her partner is deserving. She needs a man she can look up to and be proud of. If the shoe fits, slip into it. If not, put your sneakers back on and tiptoe out of her sight. She can cause you plenty of heartache if you've made up your mind about her but she hasn't made up hers about you. Aries women are very demanding, or at least they can be if they feel it's worth their while. They're high-strung at times and can be difficult if they feel their independence is being restricted.

If you manage to get to first base with the Ram of your dreams, keep a pair of kid gloves in your back pocket. You'll need them for handling her. Not that she's all that touchy; it's just that your relationship will have a better chance of progressing if you handle her with tender loving care. Let her know that you like her for her brains as well as for her good looks. Don't even begin to admire a woman sitting opposite you in the bus. When your Aries date sees green, you'd better forget about a rosy future together.

Aries mothers believe in teaching their children initiative at a very early age. Unstructured play might upset your Taurus notion of tradition, but such experimentation encouraged by your Aries mate may be a perfect balance for the kids.

TAURUS MAN
TAURUS WOMAN

Although two Taurus may be able to understand each other and even love each other, it does not necessarily hold true that theirs will be a stable and pleasant relationship. The Taurus woman you are dating may be too much like you in character to ever be compatible. You can be set in your ways. When you encounter someone with just as much willpower or stubbornness, the results can be anything but pleasant.

Whenever two Bulls lock horns it can be a very exhausting and unsatisfactory get-together. However, if you are convinced that no other will do, then proceed—but with caution. Even though you know yourself well—or, at least, think you do—it does not necessarily mean that you will have an easy time understanding your Taurus mate. However, since both of you are basically practical people, you should try a rational approach to your relationship:

put your cards on the table, talk it over, then decide whether you should or could cooperate, compromise, or call it a day. If you both have your sights set on the same goal, life together could be just what the doctor ordered.

Both of you are very affectionate people and have a deep need for affection. Being loved, understood, and appreciated are very important for your well-being. You need a woman who is not stingy with her love because you're very generous with yours. In the Taurus woman you'll find someone who is attuned to your way of feeling when it comes to romance. Taurus people, although practical and somewhat deliberate in almost everything they do, are very passionate. They are capable of being very warm and loving when they feel that the relationship is an honest one and that their feelings will be reciprocated.

In home life, two Bulls should hit it off very well. Taurus wives are very good at keeping the household shipshape. They know how to market wisely, how to budget, and how to save. If you and your Taurus wife decide on a particular amount of money for housekeeping each month, you can bet your bottom dollar that she'll stick to it right up to the last penny.

You're an extremely ambitious person—all Bulls are—and your chances for a successful relationship with a Taurus woman will perhaps be better if she is a woman of some standing. It's not that you're a social climber or that you are cold and calculating when it comes to love, but you are well aware that it is just as easy to fall in love with a rich or socially prominent woman as it is with a poor one.

Both of you should be careful in bringing up your children. Taurus has a tendency to be strict. When your children grow up and become independent, they could turn against you as a result.

TAURUS MAN
GEMINI WOMAN
The Gemini woman may be too much of a flirt ever to take your honest heart too seriously. Then again, it depends on what kind of a mood she's in. Gemini women can change from hot to cold quicker than a cat can wink its eye. Chances are her fluctuations will tire you after a time, and you'll pick up your heart—if it's not already broken into small pieces—and go elsewhere.

Women born under the sign of the Twins have the talent of being able to change their moods and attitudes as frequently as they change their party dresses. They're good-time gals who like to whoop it up and burn the candle to the wick. You'll always see them at parties, surrounded by men of all types, laughing gaily or kicking up their heels at every opportunity. Wallflowers they're not. The next day you may bump into her at the library, and you'll hardly recognize her. She'll probably have five or six books under her arms—on five or six different subjects. In fact, she may even work there. Don't come on like an instant critic. She may know more about everything than you would believe possible. She is one smart lady.

You'll probably find her a dazzling and fascinating creature—for a time, at any rate—just as the majority of men do. But when it comes to being serious, sparkling Gemini may leave quite a bit to be desired. It's not that she has anything against being serious, it's just that she might find it difficult trying to be serious with you. At one moment she'll praise you for your steadfast and patient ways, the next moment she'll tell you in a cutting way that you're an impossible stick-in-the-mud.

Don't even try to fathom the depths of her mercurial soul—it's full of false bottoms. She'll resent close investigation, anyway, and will make you rue the day you ever took it into your head to try to learn more about her than she feels is necessary. Better keep the relationship fancy-free and full of fun until she gives you the go-ahead sign. Take as much of her as she's willing to give and don't ask for more. If she does take a serious interest in you and makes up her fickle mind about herself and you, then she'll come across with the goods.

There will come a time when the Gemini girl will realize that she can't spend her entire life at the ball and that the security and warmth you offer is just what she needs in order to be a happy, fulfilled woman.

Don't try to cramp her individuality; she'll never try to cramp yours.

A Gemini mother enjoys her children, which can be the truest form of love. Like them, she's often restless, adventurous, and easily bored. She will never complain about their fleeting interests because she understands the changes the youngsters will go through as they mature.

TAURUS MAN
CANCER WOMAN

The Cancer woman needs to be protected from the cold, cruel world. She'll love you for your masculine yet gentle manner; you make her feel safe and secure. You don't have to pull any he-man or heroic stunts to win her heart; that's not what interests her. She's will be impressed by your sure, steady ways—the way you have of putting your arm around her and making her feel that she's the only girl in the world. When she's feeling glum and tears begin to well up in her eyes, you have that knack of saying just the right thing. You know how to calm her fears, no matter how silly some of them may seem.

The Moon Child is inclined to have her ups and downs. You have the talent for smoothing out the ruffles in her sea of life. She'll most likely worship the ground you walk on or put you on a terribly high pedestal. Don't disappoint her if you can help it. She'll never disappoint you. She will take great pleasure in devoting the rest of her natural life to you. She'll darn your socks, mend your overalls, scrub floors, wash windows, shop, cook, and do just about anything short of murder in order to please you and to let you know that she loves you. Sounds like that legendary good old-fashioned girl, doesn't it? Contrary to popular belief, there are still a good number of them around—and many of them are Cancers.

Of all the signs in the Zodiac, the women under Cancer are the most maternal. In caring for and bringing up children, they know just how to combine the right amount of tenderness with the proper dash of discipline. A child couldn't ask for a better mother. Cancer women are sympathetic, affectionate, and patient with children.

While we're on the subject of motherhood, there's one thing you should be warned about: never be unkind to your mother-in-law. It will be the only golden rule your Cancer wife will probably expect you to live up to. No mother-in-law jokes in the presence of your mate, please. With her, they'll go over like a lead balloon. Mother is something special for her. She may be the crankiest, nosiest old bat, but if she's your wife's mother, you'd better treat her like royalty. Sometimes this may be difficult. But if you want to keep your home together and your wife happy, you'd better learn to grin and bear it.

Your Cancer wife will prove to be a whiz in the kitchen. She'll know just when you're in the mood for your favorite dish or snack, and she can whip it up in a jiffy.

Treat your Cancer wife fairly, and she'll treat you like a king.

TAURUS MAN
LEO WOMAN

The Leo woman can make most men roar like lions. If any woman in the Zodiac has that indefinable something that can make men lose their heads and find their hearts, it's the Leo woman. She's got more than her share of charm and glamour, and she knows how to put them to good use. Jealous men either lose their sanity or at least their cool when trying to woo a woman born under the sign of the Lion.

She likes to kick up her heels quite often and doesn't care who knows it. She often makes heads turn and tongues wag. You don't necessarily have to believe any of what you hear—it's most likely just jealous gossip or wishful thinking.

This vamp makes the blood rush to your head, and you momentarily forget all of the things that you thought were important and necessary in your life. When you come back down to earth and are out of her bewitching presence, you'll conclude that although this vivacious creature can make you feel pretty wonderful, she just isn't the kind of girl you'd planned to bring home to mother. Although Leo will certainly do her best to be a good wife for you, she may not live up to your idea of what your wife should be like.

If you're planning on not going as far as the altar with that Leo woman who has you flipping your lid, you'd better be financially equipped for some very expensive dating. Be prepared to shower her with expensive gifts, take her dining and dancing in the smartest nightspots in town. Promise her the moon, if you're in a position to go that far. Luxury and glamour are two things that are bound to lower a Leo's resistance. She's got expensive tastes, and you'd better cater to them if you expect to get to first base with this gal.

If you've got an important business deal to clinch and you have doubts as to whether it will go over well or not, bring your Leo partner along to that business luncheon. It will be a cinch that you'll have that contract—lock, stock, and barrel—in your pocket before the meeting is over. She won't have to say or do anything—just be there at your side. The grouchiest oil magnate can be transformed into a gushing, obedient schoolboy if there's a charm-studded Leo woman in the room.

Easygoing and friendly, the Leo mother loves to pal around with the children and proudly show them off. She can be so proud of her kids that she sometimes is blind to their faults. Yet when she wants the children to learn and to take their rightful place in society, the Leo mother is a strict but patient teacher.

TAURUS MAN
VIRGO WOMAN

The Virgo woman is particular about choosing her men friends. She's not interested in just going out with anybody. She has her own idea of what a boyfriend or prospective husband should be, and it's possible that image has something of you in it. Generally, Virgo is quiet and refined. She doesn't believe that nonsense has any place in a love affair. She's serious and will expect you to be. She's looking for a man who has both of his feet on the ground—someone who can take care of himself as well as take care of her.

She knows the value of money and how to get the most out of a dollar. She's far from being a spendthrift. Throwing money around unnerves her, even if it isn't her money that's being tossed to the winds.

She'll most likely be very shy about romancing. Even the simple act of holding hands may make her blush—on the first couple of dates. You'll have to make all the advances, which is how you feel it should be. You'll have to be careful not to make any wrong moves. She's capable of showing anyone who oversteps the boundaries of common decency the door. It may even take a long time before she'll accept that goodnight kiss. Don't give up. You're exactly the kind of man who can bring out the woman in her. There is warmth and tenderness underneath Virgo's seemingly frigid facade. It will take a patient and understanding man to bring her enjoyment of sex to full bloom.

You'll find Virgo a very sensitive partner, perhaps more sensitive than is good for her. You can help her overcome this by treating her with gentleness and affection.

When a Virgo has accepted you as a lover or mate, she won't stint on giving her love in return. With her, it's all or nothing at all. You'll be surprised at the transformation your earnest attention can bring about in this quiet kind of woman. When in love, Virgos only listen to their hearts, not to what the neighbors say.

Virgo women are honest in love once they've come to grips with it. They don't appreciate hypocrisy, particularly in romance. They believe in being honest to their hearts, so much so that once they've learned the ropes and they find that their hearts have stumbled on another fancy, they will be true to the new heart-throb and leave you standing in the rain. But if you're earnest about your interest in her, she'll know and reciprocate your affection. Do her wrong once, however, and you can be sure she'll snip the soiled ribbon of your relationship.

The Virgo mother encourages her children to develop practical skills in order to stand on their own two feet. If she is sometimes short on displays of affection, here is where you come in to demonstrate warmth and cuddling.

TAURUS MAN
LIBRA WOMAN
It is a woman's prerogative to change her mind. This is a woman born under the sign of Libra. Her changeability, in spite of its undeniable charm, could actually drive even a man of your patience up the wall. She's capable of smothering you with love and kisses one day, and the next day she's apt to avoid you like the plague. If you think you're a man of steel nerves, perhaps you can

tolerate her sometimeness without suffering too much. However, if you own up to the fact that you're only a mere mortal of flesh and blood, then you'd better try to fasten your attention on someone more constant.

But don't get the wrong idea: a love affair with a Libra is not all bad. In fact, it has an awful lot of positives. Libra women are soft, very feminine, and warm. She doesn't have to vamp in order to gain a man's attention. Her delicate presence is enough to warm the cockles of any man's heart. One smile and you're a piece of putty in the palm of her hand.

She can be fluffy and affectionate, things you like in a girl. On the other hand, her indecision about what dress to wear, what to cook for dinner, or whether or not to redo the house could make you tear your hair out. What will perhaps be more exasperating is her flat denial that she can't make a simple decision when you accuse her of this. The trouble is she wants to be fair and thinks the only way to do this is to weigh both sides of the situation before coming to a decision. A Libra can go on weighing things for days, months, or years if allowed the time.

The Libra woman likes to be surrounded with beautiful things. Money is no object when beauty is concerned. There'll always be plenty of flowers around her apartment. She'll know how to arrange them tastefully, too. Women under this sign are fond of beautiful clothes and furnishings. They'll run up bills without batting an eye, if given the chance, in order to surround themselves with luxury.

Once she's cottoned to you, the Libra woman will do everything in her power to make you happy. She'll wait on you hand and foot when you're sick, bring you breakfast in bed, and even read you the funny papers if you're too sleepy to open your eyes. She'll be very thoughtful about anything that concerns you. If anyone dares suggest you're not the grandest man in the world, your Libra wife will give him or her a good talking to.

The Libra woman, ruled by the lovely planet Venus as you are, will share with you the joys and burdens of parenthood. She works wonders in bringing up children, although you most always will come first in her affections. The Libra mother understands that youngsters need both guidance and encouragement. Her children will never lack anything that could make their lives easier and richer.

TAURUS MAN
SCORPIO WOMAN

Scorpio is the true zodiacal mate and partner for a Taurus, but is also your zodiacal opposite. The astrological link between Taurus and Scorpio draws you both together in the hopes of an ideal partnership, blessed by the stars. But the Taurus man with a placid disposition and a staid demeanor may find the woman born under the sign of Scorpio too intense and moody.

When a Scorpio woman gets upset, be prepared to run for cover. There is nothing else to do. When her temper flies, so does everything else that's not bolted down. On the other hand, when she chooses to be sweet, she can put you in a hypnotic spell of romance. She can be as hot as a tamale or as cool as a cucumber, but whatever mood she happens to be in, it's for real. She doesn't believe in poses or hypocrisy. The Scorpio woman is often seductive and sultry. Her femme fatale charm can pierce through the hardest of hearts like a laser ray. She doesn't have to look like Mata Hari—many resemble the tomboy next door—but once you've looked into those tantalizing eyes, you're a goner.

The Scorpio woman can be a whirlwind of passion, perhaps too much passion to suit even a hot-blooded Taurus. Life with a girl born under this sign will not be all smiles and smooth sailing. When prompted, she can unleash a gale of venom. If you think you can handle a woman who purrs like a pussycat when treated correctly but spits bullets once her fur is ruffled, then try your luck. Your stable and steady nature will have a calming effect on her. But never cross her, even on the smallest thing. If you do, you'll be in the doghouse.

Generally, the Scorpio woman will keep family battles within the walls of your home. When company visits, she's apt to give the impression that married life is one great big joyride. It's just her way of expressing loyalty to you, at least in front of others. She may fight you tooth and nail in the confines of your living room, but at the ball or during an evening out, she'll hang on your arm and have stars in her eyes. She doesn't consider this hypocrisy, she just believes that family quarrels are a private matter and should be kept so. She's pretty good at keeping secrets. She may even keep a few from you if she feels like it.

By nature, you're a calm and peace-loving man. You value dependability highly. A Scorpio may be too much of a pepperpot for your love diet; you might wind up a victim of chronic heartburn. She's an excitable and touchy woman. You're looking to settle down with someone whose emotions are more steady and reliable. You may find a relationship with a Scorpio too draining.

Never give your Scorpio partner reason to think you've betrayed her. She's an eye-for-an-eye woman. She's not keen on forgiveness when she feels she's been done wrong.

If you've got your sights set on a shapely Scorpio siren, you'd better be prepared to take the bitter with the sweet.

The Scorpio mother secretly idolizes her children, although she will never put them on a pedestal or set unrealistic expectations for them. She will teach her children to be courageous and steadfast. Astrologically linked, the Taurus-Scorpio couple make wonderful parents together. Both of you will share the challenges and responsibilities for bringing up gracious yet gifted youngsters.

TAURUS MAN
SAGITTARIUS WOMAN

The Sagittarius woman is hard to keep track of. First she's here, then she's there. She's a woman with a severe case of itchy feet. She'll win you over with her hale-fellow-well-met manner and breezy charm. She's constantly good-natured and almost never cross. She will strike up a palsy-walsy relationship with you, but you might not be interested in letting it go any further. She probably won't sulk if you leave it on a friendly basis. Treat her like a kid sister, and she'll love you all the more for it.

She'll probably be attracted to you because of your restful, self-assured manner. She'll need a friend like you to rely on and will most likely turn to you frequently for advice.

There's nothing malicious about the female Archer. She'll be full of bounce and good cheer. Her sunshiny disposition can be relied upon even on the rainiest of days. No matter what she'll ever say or do, you'll know that she means well. Sagittarius are often short on tact and say literally anything that comes into their heads, no matter what the occasion. Sometimes the words that tumble out of their mouths seem downright cutting and cruel. She never meant it that way, however. She is capable of losing her friends, and perhaps even yours, through a careless slip of the lip. On the other hand, you will appreciate her honesty and good intentions.

She's not a date you might be interested in marrying, but she'll certainly be a lot of fun to pal around with. Quite often, Sagittarius women are the outdoor type. They're crazy about hiking, fishing, white-water canoeing, and even mountain climbing. She's a busy little lady, and no one could ever accuse her of being a slouch. She's great company most of the time and can be more fun than a three-ring circus when treated fairly. You'll like her for her candid and direct manner. On the whole, Sagittarius are very kind and sympathetic women.

If you do wind up marrying this girl-next-door type, you'll perhaps never regret it. Still, there are certain areas of your home life that you'll have to put yourself in charge of just to keep matters on an even keel. One area is savings. Sagittarius often do not have heads for money and as a result can let it run through their fingers like sand before they realize what has happened to it.

Another area is children. She loves kids so much, she's apt to spoil them silly. If you don't step in, she'll give them all of the freedom they think they need. But the Sagittarius mother trusts her youngsters to learn from experience and know right from wrong.

TAURUS MAN
CAPRICORN WOMAN

You'll probably not have any difficulty in understanding the woman born under the sign of Capricorn. In some ways, she's just like you. She is faithful, dependable, and systematic in just about everything that she undertakes. She is concerned with security and sees to it that every penny she spends is spent wisely. She is very economical in using her time, too. She doesn't believe in whittling away her energy in a scheme that is bound not to pay off.

Ambitious themselves, they're often attracted to ambitious men—men who are interested in getting somewhere in life. If a man of this sort wins her heart, she'll stick by him and do all she can to see to it that he gets to the top. The Capricorn woman is almost always diplomatic and makes an excellent hostess. She can be very influential with your business acquaintances.

She's not the most romantic woman of the Zodiac, but she's far from being frigid when she meets the right man. She believes in true love and doesn't appreciate getting involved in flings. To her, they're just a waste of time. She's looking for a man who means business—in life as well as in love. Although she can be very affectionate with her boyfriend or mate, she tends to let her head govern her heart. That is not to say that she is a cool, calculating cucumber. On the contrary, she just feels she can be more honest about love if she consults her brains first. She'll want to size up the situation first before throwing her heart in the ring. She wants to make sure that it won't get crushed.

A Capricorn woman is concerned and proud about her family tree. Relatives are important to her, particularly if they've been able to make their mark in life. Never say a cross word about her family members. That can really go against her grain, and she won't talk to you for days on end.

She's generally thorough in whatever she undertakes: cooking, cleaning, entertaining. Capricorn women are well-mannered and gracious, no matter what their background. They seem to have it in their natures always to behave properly.

If you should marry a Capricorn, you need never worry about her going on a wild shopping spree. The Goat understands the value of money better than most women. If you turn over your paycheck to her at the end of the week, you can be sure that a good hunk of it will go into the bank and that all the bills will be paid on time.

With children, the Capricorn mother is both loving and correct. She will teach the youngsters to be polite and kind, and to honor tradition as much as you do. The Capricorn mother is very ambitious for the children. An earth sign like you, she wants the children to have every advantage and to benefit from things she perhaps lacked as a child.

TAURUS MAN
AQUARIUS WOMAN

The woman born under the sign of the Water Bearer can be odd and eccentric at times. Some say that this is the source of her mysterious charm. You may think she's nutty, and you may be fifty percent right. Aquarius women have their heads full of dreams, and stars in their eyes. By nature, they are often unconventional and have their own ideas about how the world should be run. Sometimes their ideas may seem pretty weird, but more likely than not they are just a little too progressive for their time. There's a saying that runs: the way Aquarius thinks, so will the world in fifty years.

If you find yourself falling in love with an Aquarius, you'd better fasten your safety belt. It may take some time before you really know what she's like and even then you may have nothing more to go on but a string of vague hunches. She can be like a rainbow, full of dazzling colors. She's like no other girl you've ever known. There's something about her that is definitely charming, yet elusive; you'll never be able to put your finger on it. She seems to radiate adventure and magic without even half trying. She'll most likely be the most tolerant and open-minded woman you've ever encountered.

If you find that she's too much mystery and charm for you to handle—and being a Taurus, chances are you might—just talk it out with her and say that you think it would be better if you called it quits. She'll most likely give you a peck on the cheek and say you're one hundred percent right but still there's no reason why you can't remain friends. Aquarius women are like that. And perhaps you'll both find it easier to get along in a friendship than in a romance.

It is not difficult for her to remain buddy-buddy with someone she has just broken off with. For many Aquarius, the line between friendship and romance is a fuzzy one.

She's not a jealous person and, while you're romancing her, she'll expect you not to be, either. You'll find her a free spirit most of the time. Just when you think you know her inside out, you'll discover that you don't really know her at all. She's a very sympathetic and warm person. She can be helpful to people in need of assistance and advice.

She's a chameleon and can fit in anywhere. She'll seldom be suspicious even when she has every right to be. If the man she loves slips and allows himself a little fling, chances are she'll just turn her head the other way and pretend not to notice that the gleam in his eye is not meant for her.

The Aquarius mother is generous and seldom refuses her children anything. You may feel the youngsters need a bit more discipline and practicality. But you will appreciate the Aquarius mother's wordly views, which prepare the youngsters to get along in life. Her open-minded attitude is easily transmitted to the children. They will grow up to be respectful and tolerant.

TAURUS MAN
PISCES WOMAN

The Pisces woman places great value on love and romance. She's gentle, kind, and romantic. Perhaps she's that girl you've been dreaming about all these years. Like you, she has very high ideals; she will only give her heart to a man who she feels can live up to her expectations.

Many a man dreams of an alluring Pisces woman. You are no exception. She's soft and cuddly and very domestic. She'll let you be the brains of the family; she's contented to play a behind-the-scenes role in order to help you achieve your goals. The illusion that you are the master of the household is the kind of magic that the Pisces woman is adept at creating.

She can be very ladylike and proper. Your business associates and friends will be dazzled by her warmth and femininity. Although she's a charmer, there is a lot more to her than just a pretty exterior. There is a brain ticking away behind that soft, womanly facade. You may never become aware of it—that is, until you're married to her. It's no cause for alarm, however, she'll most likely never use it against you, only to help you and possibly set you on a more sucessful path.

If she feels you're botching up your married life through careless behavior or if she feels you could be earning more money than you do, she'll tell you about it. But any wife would really.

She will never try to usurp your position as head and breadwinner of the family.

No one had better dare say one uncomplimentary word about you in her presence. It's likely to cause her to break into tears. Pisces women are usually very sensitive beings. Their reaction to adversity, frustration, or anger is just a plain, good, old-fashioned cry. They can weep buckets when inclined.

She can do wonders with a house. She is very fond of dramatic and beautiful things. There will always be plenty of fresh-cut flowers around the house. She will choose charming artwork and antiques, if they are affordable. She'll see to it that the house is decorated in a dazzling yet welcoming style.

She'll have an extra special dinner prepared for you when you come home from an important business meeting. Don't dwell on the boring details of the meeting, though. But if you need that grand vision, the big idea, to seal a contract or make a conquest, your Pisces woman is sure to confide a secret that will guarantee your success. She is canny and shrewd with money, and once you are on her wavelength you can manage the intricacies on your own.

If you are patient and kind, you can keep a Pisces woman happy for a lifetime. She, however, is not without her faults. Her sensitivity may get on your nerves after a while. You may find her lacking in practicality and good old-fashioned stoicism. You may even feel that she uses her tears as a method of getting her own way.

Treat her with tenderness, and your relationship will be an enjoyable one. Pisces women are generally fond of sweets, so keep her in chocolates (and flowers, of course) and you'll have a very happy wife. Never forget birthdays, anniversaries, and the like. These are important occasions for her. If you ever let such a thing slip your mind, you can be sure of sending her off in a huff.

Your Taurus talent for patience and gentleness can pay off in your relationship with a Pisces woman. Chances are she'll never make you sorry that you placed that band of gold on her finger.

There is usually a strong bond between a Pisces mother and her children. She'll try to give them things she never had as a child and is apt to spoil them as a result. She can deny herself in order to fill their needs. But the Pisces mother will teach her youngsters the value of service to the community while not letting them lose their individuality.

TAURUS
LUCKY NUMBERS 1998

Lucky numbers and astrology can be linked through the movements of the Moon. Each phase of the thirteen Moon cycles vibrates with a sequence of numbers for your Sign of the Zodiac over the course of the year. Using your lucky numbers is a fun system that connects you with tradition.

New Moon	First Quarter	Full Moon	Last Quarter
Dec. 29 ('97) 9 6 1 0	Jan. 5 4 8 2 9	Jan. 12 1 9 5 3	Jan. 20 4 4 8 5
Jan. 28 2 6 9 0	Feb. 3 0 7 5 5	Feb. 11 1 1 3 4	Feb. 19 7 2 8 5
Feb. 26 9 3 4 1	March 5 1 0 8 4	March 12 6 7 2 4	March 21 4 1 7 2
March 27 5 6 3 1	April 3 1 1 6 8	April 11 8 9 4 1	April 19 7 4 8 2
April 26 6 3 9 7	May 3 7 3 5 6	May 11 9 1 0 7	May 18 4 8 1 5
May 25 2 8 6 2	June 1 2 4 5 9	June 9 4 6 3 7	June 17 1 5 8 5
June 23 1 3 8 1	July 1 1 2 6 3	July 9 1 9 4 7	July 16 2 5 3 2
July 23 2 7 9 1	July 31 1 5 2 8	August 7 7 3 6 1	August 14 1 7 4 2
August 21 2 2 4 5	August 30 9 6 3 7	Sept. 6 2 1 5 8	Sept. 12 8 6 6 2
Sept. 20 2 5 6 0	Sept. 28 7 4 8 2	Oct. 5 5 3 9 7	Oct. 12 7 7 3 5
Oct. 20 5 6 4 1	Oct. 28 7 2 5 0	Nov. 4 0 6 3 1	Nov. 10 1 6 8 9
Nov. 18 9 4 4 0	Nov. 26 5 8 3 9	Dec. 3 3 6 4 9	Dec. 10 9 2 3 7
Dec. 18 7 4 6 0	Dec. 26 4 8 5 2	Jan. 1 ('99) 1 9 5 7	Jan. 9 ('99) 7 8 3 9

TAURUS
YEARLY FORECAST 1998

*Forecast for 1998 Concerning Business
and Financial Affairs, Job Prospects,
Travel, Health, Romance and Marriage
for Those Born with the Sun
in the Zodiacal Sign of Taurus.
April 21–May 20*

For those born under the influence of the Sun in the zodiacal sign
of Taurus, ruled by Venus, planet of love, beauty, and charm, this
promises to be a challenging and expansive year. There are many
opportunities to make new friends and employment-related contacts. You will find numerous opportunities to grow personally
and to expand your social circle through club and sports interests.
Any group involvement is likely to be highly productive and stimulating. Many former obstacles to your personal fulfillment are
going to be removed, although quite gradually and not overnight.
Pushing yourself beyond your current personal limits is not advised. You should benefit most by carefully balancing your priorities and scheduling plenty of rest and relaxation. Business and
professional matters may develop unexpectedly and quite quickly,
moving you closer toward a long-held goal. Opportunities exist to
move into more exciting realms. Both your experience and status
are likely to increase as a result of accepting a particularly challenging offer. Where finances are concerned, opportunities are
open to increase your earnings through a change of job or occu-
pation. Investment in property and real estate may be risky this
year. It would be wiser to conserve your resources in order to
reap the interest that can be accrued with safety of your principal.
With regard to routine occupational affairs, obstacles to achieving
your dreams may not be as hard to overcome as you imagine.
Increased job satisfaction may stem from accepting an unusual job
offer which involves a major relocation. Distant contacts should
be a significant help when it comes to establishing yourself in a

new locale. This could be a springboard from which you can greatly expand your horizons. Exceptional travel opportunities are likely in connection with your long-term career ambitions. In addition, new job possibilities can emerge from long-distance journeys. Taurus health needs an extra measure of protection this year. A good diet and plenty of exercise, as well as ample rest and relaxation, are required to keep you at your peak. Where love and romance are concerned, this is a year when the urge to settle down with your loved one is likely to be strong. On the other hand, married Taurus people may need to uproot the whole family in pursuit of a long-held dream. You and your spouse are likely to spend more time together in order to achieve mutual goals or pursue mutual hobbies. You could be busy around the home, renovating and improving in order to create more comfort for yourselves.

For professional Taurus people, this is a key year for investment and expansion. It is not in your nature to take unnecessary risks, but from January 1 to January 29 speculation tends to bring very fortunate results. Investment in employee training is apt to be beneficial in the long term, ensuring more loyal staff members. A reassessment of your basic aims may be necessary. Some of the dreams and schemes you have been harboring and nurturing for a while may have to be relinquished, but all is not lost. The ability to fulfill one very central aim is likely to more than compensate for what you have to give up. Your success this year lies in managing to combine far-reaching vision with an intuitive sense of timing. Extra good fortune in your career life between January 1 and February 4 makes that a wise time for an all-important move or decision. Be wary, however, of making large investments on impulse. Bide your time in all business-related finances. Friends, colleagues, and acquaintances who comprised your network of business contacts in the past may gradually drop off as the year develops. You are not strongly in need of their support this year. Instead, you have the opportunity to build on new associations and create a stable work base with their support. Moving to a new location can also help secure an improved base of operations. Greater investment in business expansion this year is likely to lead to increased profits. They may not be immediate, but are likely to be reaped when you most need them.

With regard to finances, this is a year when your return from past investments can be disappointing. This, combined with needing to repay existing debts, means that your expendable income is going to be limited for a large proportion of the year. Nevertheless, you should have sufficient funds to cover necessities. Keep frivolous, impetuous spending to a minimum, at least until the period between November 29 and December 31 when the desire to spoil loved ones with gifts and to attend social functions is likely to be hard to resist. Seek ways to safeguard your long-term financial situation and build financial security for the future. If there are numerous debts to repay, one overall loan could be a better option, offering a lower interest rate and manageable payments. Involvement in work of a charitable nature may not offer immediate returns, but in the longer term your endeavors could pay off substantially. Fees for membership in a club or society may be raised this year, causing you to reconsider whether it is truly worthwhile. Teamwork is your key to success. Through your network of friends and acquaintances, and through group endeavors, you can enhance your financial situation.

Routine occupational affairs are apt to be worrisome for part of the year. There are obstacles to fulfilling a special dream, but these are by no means insurmountable. Your natural Taurus determination is bound to aid you in achieving your goals. Outstanding good fortune during the period between January 1 and February 4 makes this an excellent time for responding to key opportunities which come your way. You could be offered quite an unusual role, which may involve working in a totally different environment, possibly even abroad. This could turn out to be the path to achieving one of your most important objectives. There is likely to be more than one opportunity to increase work satisfaction through a job change. Which one you accept, if any, could depend on family obligations and pressure. Foreign travel could bring some of those opportunities your way. If you decide to move in connection with work, it may take quite a while to establish yourself in the new environment. Work and hobby contacts can be a great help in this respect. Once you gain a foothold in your new community, you will settle down for a long time. The chance to broaden your horizons through work which involves travel will no doubt appeal to you. Any extra language which you speak is likely to give you an edge in securing a key job for which others are almost equally qualified.

There is both more need and more desire to travel this year. In the pursuit of your career ambitions you may be encouraged to specialize. A contact in a far-off location could direct an excellent career opening your way. Spend some time getting a feel for the lifestyle that prevails in an area that is new to you. It is also possible that a new job opportunity will come along incidentally as a result of a foreign friend or foreign travel. The period between October 8 and November 27 is especially good for taking a vacation, even if your arrangements are made at the last minute.

Where health matters are concerned, you need to take special care with regard to your diet. Wholesome eating and getting plenty of exercise can help combat a tendency to sluggishness. It is also important to get basic rest and relaxation. There is a tendency this year to drive yourself almost beyond your limits, both in terms of the time and energy you expend. Balance busy periods with less active intervals. There is no real reason for you to feel less than at your peak so long as you take the trouble to look after your basic well-being. Be strict about the number of new responsibilities you take on so that you have time to think, plan carefully, relax, and relate to friends and family members.

Where romance and marriage are concerned, this year should be especially stable and rewarding. For single Taurus men and women there is opportunity to take a romantic relationship one step further. The urge to settle down with someone you love is likely to become increasingly strong. This is a desirable option for you since as a Taurus you thrive on security. If you are still waiting and hoping to meet somebody, romance is likely to come into your life as the result of a work relationship. With a co-worker you can create a stable and highly loving personal relationship. Married Taurus people can strengthen the bonds of love by working together to achieve personal and professional ambitions. If you want to consider uprooting your family to another location, be sure to discuss this far in advance. The initial upheaval may place some strains on your relationship, but this is unlikely to be a lasting problem. This is a good year for working together at home with your loved one in order to make major improvements. Spending time together on domestic projects gives you the chance to enjoy more of each other's company in an especially creative and constructive manner. Whether married or single, you have the chance this year to make your most important relationships the basis for growth and success.

TAURUS
DAILY FORECAST

January–December 1998

JANUARY

1. THURSDAY. Good. This is a promising start to the New Year for Taurus people. Include in your resolutions for the coming twelve months some specific goals concerning your work life. If you are thinking of becoming self-employed, start researching the details. You have good reason to be feeling optimistic about the future. Do not let anyone pour cold water on your hopes and plans, no matter how ambitious your goals. The key to ultimate success lies in thinking big. Even if you were up until the wee hours you should still have the energy to party some more this evening. Social gatherings of all kinds should go with a swing, with you at the center of attention.

2. FRIDAY. Disquieting. If you are saying goodbye to one who has been staying with you or is moving away, it is sure to be a sad day. The departure can leave you feeling at loose ends. The end of the festive season may be more of a letdown than you had anticipated. Make a greater effort to shake off an attack of the blahs. It is important now to think ahead. Making plans for the future can give you a renewed sense of purpose. If you do not have to work today, make a point of taking it easy. Keep in mind that fatigue can lower your spirits. If you have to go to work, ease back into your routine as gently as possible.

3. SATURDAY. Confusing. Find time to take a look at the sales being offered by local stores. Money you received at Christmas may be burning a hole in your pocket. Treat yourself to something new, but guard against spending more of your own money than you can afford. A check on your financial situation may reveal that you have already spent more than you realize. This is unlikely to be a good time for buying on credit or opening a store account. Repayments can soon become a millstone around your neck. Avoid any social activity this evening which you suspect will be costly, despite pressure from a friend who offers to pay your way.

4. SUNDAY. Fair. Morning hours are likely to be the more enjoyable part of the day. If you have a chance to sleep later, be grateful. Treating your partner to breakfast in bed can be a fun and relaxing start to the day. If you had overnight guests during the festive period, now is a good time to put your home back in order. Domestic chores can be dispensed with quickly once you get started. This is not a favorable day for long-distance traveling. If you must use public transportation of any kind, expect some delays. Having some time to yourself should be a priority later in the day. If you are going back to work tomorrow, aim for an early night.

5. MONDAY. Variable. If this is your first day at work after the Christmas break it may be hard to get into the swing of things. Although there should be plenty on your agenda, knowing where to start can be difficult. The important thing is to be well organized. Make a list of jobs that need to be done, and put them in order of priority. In this way you can avoid wasting time and should also find it easier to concentrate. For Taurus professionals, this is a favorable time for detailing your aims and goals for the coming year. Budgets or financial projections of all kinds may need to be reappraised and reworked based on economic forecasts.

6. TUESDAY. Deceptive. You may not be in the happiest of moods this morning. Expect to be unusually sensitive to other people's careless remarks or criticisms; try not to overreact to them. Someone who comes across as interfering may be awkwardly trying to help; give them the benefit of the doubt. In the workplace this is a day for keeping a low profile. Do not confront an authority figure. You are almost sure to lose out when someone pulls rank on you. Single Taurus people need to guard against trying too hard to impress a newcomer. Your efforts are likely to backfire. Just being yourself and acting naturally is the best way to win someone's interest or affection.

7. WEDNESDAY. Changeable. For Taurus people who are unemployed this is a good day for job hunting. Avoid putting all your hopes in one interview or advertisement. It could also be a mistake to rely on the efforts of one employment agency. Your own efforts could be more productive. Buy the quality newspapers and go through the recruitment section with a fine-tooth comb. Opportunities in the educational field are especially promising and worth following up. Seriously consider the possibility of working abroad. Taurus people are well known for a love of food. If you put on weight during the Christmas vacation, this is a good time for starting a diet and an exercise regimen.

8. THURSDAY. Challenging. With the New Year well into its stride, review your resolutions. If you realize that some have already been broken, make a fresh start today. Although it is important to learn from past experiences, this is a time when you can benefit from wiping the slate clean. Do not keep mulling over past mistakes; put them firmly behind you. In the workplace you can afford to push yourself forward more assertively. Do not shy away from the praise and limelight you deserve for your achievements. You may get a chance to earn some extra money, or a raise may be more generous than you anticipated.

9. FRIDAY. Useful. This is a productive end to the working week. A business deal clinched today should prove lucrative both now and into the future. You may finally be able to wrap up a project which has been on the drawing board for some time. In work matters of all kinds this is a good time to seek out the advice of someone who has more experience than you. They may be able to give you useful pointers concerning what to do and, in particular, what to avoid. Do not struggle on alone with difficult work; help is available if you just ask for it. If you regret having recently broken off a relationship, there may be the chance of a reconciliation this evening.

10. SATURDAY. Misleading. Joint finances require some discussion. If you share a bank account with your mate or partner, together check your budgeting for the rest of the month. Some small economies now could be all that is needed to avoid incurring high-interest debt or having to dip into precious savings. Avoid spending on the strength of money due you; wait until it is definitely in the bank. Single Taurus people could be introduced to someone interesting. Find out more about them before you get carried away into fantasyland. It may be best to avoid a romance with someone who is still disentangling themselves from another relationship.

11. SUNDAY. Disconcerting. A new romance may not be going as smoothly as you had hoped. There may be other factors involved which you do not yet know about. Avoid sitting around on the off chance of a telephone call; the person you are hoping to hear from may be caught up with other matters. Keep busy with your own plans and pursuits. Whatever your social arrangements today, it is wise to have an alternative up your sleeve since there is a greater risk of being let down on short notice. Public transportation can be unreliable; allow extra time for a journey. This is not a good time to buy a secondhand car or any used appliance. Get an expert's opinion before you part with cash.

12. MONDAY. Stressful. This is unlikely to be an easy start to the working week. Taurus commuters may have a difficult journey into work. If possible, travel earlier or later than the rush hour. Administrative matters of all kinds are apt to be troublesome. You may have to spend a lot of time sorting out other people's mistakes. Someone may not get back to you with necessary information unless you pester them. Do not make too much of a colleague's bad temper; realize that they may be under a lot of pressure. Your best policy is simply to stay out of their way and pick another time for a discussion or for asking questions. Favors are unlikely to be granted.

13. TUESDAY. Variable. If you work full time you may feel that your personal life is suffering as a result. Pressures at work may mean that someone special has had to take a back seat for a while. Make sure that they do not feel they are at the bottom of your list of priorities. You can probably squeeze out more free time for yourself than you realize. Keep in mind that time can work for or against you. Plan a schedule rather than letting time slip through your fingers. If you are looking for a new home you may find a suitable place through a friend or former roommate. Make sure that you ask about hidden charges, such as trash pickup or outdoor maintenance.

14. WEDNESDAY. Mixed. All sorts of surprises are likely to be a drain on your time and energy. Try to keep your schedule flexible. A carefully worked out timetable can soon become useless when unforeseen demands are made on you. The Taurus nature is usually sure and steady. Someone who is trying to influence you may soon find that they have taken on a difficult task. Guard against letting a certain individual goad you to the point that you lose your temper. This is a day when it is important to deal with irritations or problems as they arise rather than trying to ignore them. In this way you should avoid letting resentment build up to the boiling point.

15. THURSDAY. Good. Any tension at work recently is likely to evaporate today. A colleague who has been difficult to work with may now make renewed efforts at friendliness and cooperation. This should make teamwork much more pleasant and productive. If you rely on your creative skills in your job, this promises to be a starred day. Jot down your ideas as soon as inspiration strikes. Written work of all kinds should flow more easily than usual. A lucrative commission may come your way through referral from a satisfied customer or client. Do nothing that could negatively affect your good reputation. Be willing to apologize even if you were only partly to blame.

16. FRIDAY. Pleasant. You are unlikely to be under any particular pressure. At work you can tackle the day's tasks in your own time and at your own pace. Working with children can be especially rewarding. An innocent remark from a younger person can put a fresh perspective on an issue with which you have been wrestling. You may realize that you have been taking something or someone too seriously. A lighter approach should earn you the best results both in your professional and personal life. A night out with friends could lead to a romantic encounter for single Taurus people. Enjoy indulging the flirtatious side of your nature.

17. SATURDAY. Productive. This is not a day when you are content to sit around at home. Sporting activities of all kinds are favored, whether you are participating or just sitting in the stands. Games played for the fun of it rather than solely to win may appeal to you. Put the emphasis on fun. Taurus parents should include children in as many activities as possible. Teaching a child a new skill can be memorable. If you are married enjoy real togetherness by sharing an outside interest, or hobby. Romance is in the cards for Taurus people who are unattached but ready for an emotional commitment.

18. SUNDAY. Fair. A telephone call from a friend may not be cheerful. Although you may be more than willing to listen to their problems, you could feel helpless, especially if you live far apart. Keep in mind that you cannot always fight other people's battles for them or solve their dilemmas no matter how much you would like to do so. The important thing right now is to be there with moral support. Keep long-distance calls short so that your bill stays low. This is a good day for tackling small repair jobs around the home. Even if you do not consider yourself gifted at decorating or other practical skills, you could be pleasantly surprised by the results once you try.

19. MONDAY. Frustrating. If you are trying to instigate changes of any kind in your workplace, keep your expectations realistic. The Taurus ability to hold out for as long as it takes should stand you in good stead at the moment, even if others accuse you of being much too stubborn. Try to meet others halfway; compromise should be your watchword for the day. Because you may not be in top form physically, do not bite off more than you can chew. It may be best to postpone an engagement which requires you to be at your sparkling best. Devote some time to clearing routine tasks out of the way so that you can make a fresh start soon.

20. TUESDAY. Mixed. The morning is the more productive part of the day. Meetings of all kinds should be straightforward even if you expect to run into difficulties. It should be easier to win support from those in influential or powerful positions. Taurus people who are self-employed could receive a new rush of business, but be realistic when it comes to agreeing on delivery dates or deadlines. Keep in mind that most people are willing to wait a reasonable length of time if you have what they need. Later in the day you may have to deal with some friction at home. For once it may be best to take the path of least resistance in order to restore peace.

21. WEDNESDAY. Variable. You may find that your workload is increasing more than you would like. This is a good time to create your own work schedule so that all of your projects are completed on time. Do not be tempted to skip a lecture or conference; you could miss out on some valuable information. In the business world this is a favorable time for dealings with foreign contacts. A trip may need to be arranged on short notice for negotiations which require a face-to-face meeting. For Taurus employees, changes at the management level can have a direct effect on you. Try to be open to change rather than sticking to old ways merely because they are familiar and comfortable.

22. THURSDAY. Uncertain. In any current situation where you are unsure of your legal rights, seek professional advice. A consultation fee could be money well spent. If you are involved in litigation of any kind at the moment, there should be some significant progress today. However, do not underestimate your adversaries; they may still have some tricks to pull. Do not allow yourself to be pushed into making any binding decision. If you want more time to think something over, stand your ground. In business dealings this is not a good time for being overly ambitious. Stick to what you do well. Practice new skills in private before going public with them.

23. FRIDAY. Slow. This may be a tedious end to the working week. You might not be able to make much progress with a certain project because of a lack of information or slowness on the part of colleagues. The famous Taurus capacity for patience should stand you in good stead. If you try to boss someone around you could end up making an enemy. If you are already on the wrong side of someone at work, your relationship is apt to be especially strained today. It is time for an honest heart-to-heart talk; be willing to hear out their grievances as well as air your own. A social occasion this evening may take a while to get going; try to find a way of breaking the conversational ice.

24. SATURDAY. Quiet. You should welcome a day at home. If you feel lazy, it may be best to just indulge your mood, watching television or catching up on some light reading. You may also want to spend some time putting your personal finances or paperwork in order. Check your insurance policies; some may need renewing or updating. If you do not have enough life insurance, this is a good time to assess your needs, especially if you are the main breadwinner in your family. A new romance can benefit from some quiet time together. Suggest cooking a meal at home rather than going out for the evening with friends.

25. SUNDAY. Good. This is the more sociable day of the weekend. Even if you had nothing special planned, you may be invited out by a friend, perhaps to lunch. Spontaneous outings can be the most fun. If you find yourself at loose ends take the initiative; call your friends and make some suggestions. The day also favors cultural activities, such as visiting a museum or art gallery. You will enjoy yourself most in the company of like-minded people. Discussions about politics or religion can be lively and educational. If you keep an open mind, you may find yourself rethinking some views which you have held for a long time.

26. MONDAY. Challenging. This is likely to be a difficult start to the working week. It may seem that a certain individual is deliberately blocking you; you may be the object of professional jealousy. However, this is not a good time to tackle sensitive issues. Concentrate on the work at hand and let your results speak for themselves. Go out of your way to lend a helping hand to a colleague. If you are willing to pitch in above and beyond the call of duty, you can improve your most important working relationships. For Taurus singles a romance with someone from another country or culture could be in the cards; differences between you could be the main attraction.

27. TUESDAY. Deceptive. Guard against putting your trust in the wrong people. Someone you do not yet know well may prove to be all talk and no action. Those who deserve your trust are probably those who have already shown that they merit it. Although you have already formed an opinion about someone new, now is not the time for broadcasting what you think. Keep your thoughts to yourself, even if someone tries to draw you out. This is not the time to risk becoming embroiled in idle gossip, especially in the workplace. Steer far clear of office politics. A new romantic interest may be a passing infatuation; try to keep your feet on the ground and your options open.

28. WEDNESDAY. Fortunate. This is a lucky day for starting a new job or project. You may feel you have finally discovered your true vocation. If you are bored with your present position, current conditions favor seeking a promotion. Have the confidence to aim high; someone in authority may already have more faith in you than you have in yourself. If you have climbed as high on the ladder of success as you can where you are, start looking in new directions. Someone with influence may be willing to pull some strings on your behalf. Make use of who you know as well as what you know. This evening is a good time for treating a loved one to a special night out on the town.

29. THURSDAY. Productive. Taurus energy is higher than usual this morning. You are likely to wake up early, eager to get on with the day. This is a good time for getting an early start, perhaps long before sunup. Having some uninterrupted time can be vital if you have a lot to do. Meetings of all kinds are apt to be most productive before lunchtime. You may want to continue a discussion over lunch with a colleague or associate. Later in the day is good for teamwork of all kinds, although a certain individual may have to be discouraged from taking over. Arguments can break out unless attention is paid to democratic decision making and the principle of majority rule.

30. FRIDAY. Calm. This should be an easy end to the working week. You may be able to finish up earlier than usual. If there is little for you to do, this is a good time for taking a day off so that you can enjoy a long weekend. Socially you are likely to be in demand at the moment. There should be plenty of invitations for the weekend. This is a good day for a leisurely lunch with an old friend; catch up on the latest gossip and local news. For Taurus people who are unattached, a new friendship with someone you met through an outside interest may show signs of developing into a romance. Getting to know someone as a friend first can be a definite plus.

31. SATURDAY. Easygoing. The mail may bring a card or letter from someone who is traveling or from a friend who has recently moved. You could receive an invitation to visit later in the year. This is a good day for a shopping trip with a friend. If you want to buy new clothes it can be helpful to go with someone whose taste you admire; they may prevent you from making an expensive mistake. The day favors getting together with friends. A dinner party or going out to eat at a local restaurant should be enjoyable. If you are short of money, others may pay your way willingly. You may get the chance to play matchmaker between two of your friends who hit it off on first meeting.

FEBRUARY

1. SUNDAY. Slow. If you had a late night you may need most of the day to recover. A headache or hangover may be difficult to shake. Be easy on yourself. Make an extra effort to eat right. Boost your energy level with some extra vitamins. Spend time on your own; other people's conversation or their demands on you can be wearying. An argument or misunderstanding with a loved one is a possibility. Be quick to apologize if you know you were too sensitive. Guard against brooding about criticism leveled at you; consider whether it is justified. Try not to bear a grudge over little things that on another day would hardly matter to you.

2. MONDAY. Confusing. The morning is the more productive part of the day. You can get a lot done if you are able to work in privacy and under your own steam. The early part of the day is also a favorable time for meetings of a confidential nature. A dispute of any kind in the workplace may not be as serious as you first suppose. Do not be too quick to make a grievance official; there is a good chance that you can straighten out matters yourself by having an off-the-record discussion. Negotiations can be tricky later in the day. Do not sign any document which is unclear; make sure that you understand the fine print.

3. TUESDAY. Sensitive. You may start the day with a fresh surge of confidence, but your good mood is unlikely to rub off on those around you. In fact, you could find that their negativity brings you down. A certain individual may be set on pouring cold water on your latest ideas or plans. It is important not to fall into the trap of trying to justify yourself too strenuously. Try to attach less importance to what other people might think. Have the courage of your own convictions. A job interview can be a stressful experience. It may be best not to accept a job from someone you instinctively distrust or dislike. If you are looking for new work, do not let your current employer know.

4. WEDNESDAY. Variable. This is a busy day, with your workload much greater than usual because someone in authority is delegating too much to you. Try not to allow yourself to become swamped. This might mean having to say no to extra responsibilities for the time being. Keep in mind that feeling stressed can lead you to be of no use to anyone, especially yourself. This is a good day for tackling written work or bringing your personal correspondence up to date. A close friend may need your counsel. Make time for a heart-to-heart talk, even if this means having to rearrange your day. They may be relying on your loyalty more than you realize.

5. THURSDAY. Changeable. Money owed to you may still not be forthcoming. If you are unemployed, look into any benefits to which you might be entitled, such as help with fuel bills. If a friend owes you money there is a chance that they have simply forgotten about it; a gentle reminder can prompt their repayment. Try to avoid borrowing money or anything of value from a friend; it could put a strain on your friendship. It is better to arrange a loan through a bank or credit union. Someone who always seems able to undermine your self-esteem should be kept at arm's length until your confidence returns in full measure. Get to bed early tonight.

6. FRIDAY. Quiet. You may need to spend some time on financial matters. Send out reminders for any invoices which remain unpaid from before Christmas, especially if your cash-flow situation is not too good at the moment. This is a favorable time for a meeting with your accountant or other financial adviser, who may be able to offer some tax-saving ideas. Opening a separate savings account to pay large bills could be helpful. Take the time to plan long term as far as your personal finances are concerned. An endowment policy can be a good way to provide for the future. If you want to make a special purchase later in the year, now is a good time to start saving for it.

7. SATURDAY. Happy. Someone who has been out of touch for a while may call you this morning. It is possible that this person has been dealing with a crisis which you know nothing about. Now you should be able to pick up your relationship from where you left off. Spending time with a brother, sister, or other relative can be enjoyable. If you are single, a family member could introduce you to someone interesting in their social circle. This is a good day for healing rifts of any kind. Do not let Taurus stubbornness stop you from making the first move. Strive to develop greater trust in all of your personal relationships, but guard against wearing your heart on your sleeve.

8. SUNDAY. Unsettling. Although you may feel uptight or restless, it is best not to rely too much on other people for company. There is no point pressuring someone into an outing if they clearly do not want to go; you may succeed only in creating bad feelings. Under such circumstances you will enjoy yourself more if you go alone. Allow extra time for traveling; there is a greater risk of public transportation cancellations or frustrating traffic jams. If you often drive long distances, consider signing up for an automobile road service. Be conscientious about making the usual mechanical checks before you drive anywhere, and also check oil and water levels.

9. MONDAY. Deceptive. There is a risk of oversleeping this morning. Arriving late for work can create chaos in your schedule, forcing you to pull out all the stops in order to catch up. Someone in authority may choose to make an issue out of punctuality; resolve to improve your record if you know that their complaints are aimed at you. Try to avoid tasks which require total concentration. You have a greater tendency to daydream today, or you may just find that your analytical abilities are not at their best. In your personal life guard against putting someone on a pedestal; they are sure to fall off it in the end.

10. TUESDAY. Mixed. If you are not feeling as positive as usual, take steps to cheer yourself up. This can be more productive than looking to others to raise your spirits. As a Taurus you have a love of nature. Buy some fresh flowers or a plant for your place of work. Creating a pleasant atmosphere can make a great deal of difference. Meetings of all kinds can be time consuming. You may underestimate how long it will take to resolve certain issues, but the eventual outcome should be satisfactory on all sides. If you are interviewing for a job do not be tempted to exaggerate your past achievements; honesty is your best policy.

11. WEDNESDAY. Disconcerting. It may seem that career issues are dominating your life at the moment, creating more pressure than you can comfortably cope with. It may be time to ask the boss to lighten your load if you are continually struggling to keep on top of everything. Consider whether the time is approaching for you to move on to new work responsibilities. Even though money is important to you, do not base your career moves solely on financial considerations. It can be worth taking a drop in salary in order to work in a field that is more in keeping with your true vocational interests.

12. THURSDAY. Rewarding. In business dealings this is not a time for taking an extreme gamble. However, some calculated risk taking could pay off. You may realize that sitting safely on the fence is getting you nowhere fast. Be guided by a combination of your own instincts and advice from those whose judgment has proved accurate in the past. In legal matters this can be a favorable time to appeal a decision which did not go in your favor; you stand a greater chance of winning a reversal. If you need some intellectual stimulus, sign up for a local evening school class or a correspondence course from a reputable school.

13. FRIDAY. Pleasant. This is a productive end to the workweek for Taurus people who rely on creative skills to make a living. Whatever your job, you should be able to use your artistic abilities in some useful way. This is a good time for taking a class aimed at improving your work skills. If you are single there is a greater chance of meeting someone attractive in a classroom situation. Starting off with interests in common can be a big bonus. This is a good time for buying skin care products and for investigating medical help for a recurring skin condition. The emphasis this evening should be on fun and romance.

14. SATURDAY. Starred. This is a good day for starting on home decorating or improvements. Practical jobs are likely to appeal. You can do certain tasks yourself without going to the expense of hiring a professional. If you have a spare room at home, consider renting it out; the extra cash can give you more disposable income each month. Be sure, however, to ask for references and a deposit. A night on the town can be fun this evening. Try a new restaurant or nightclub with friends or neighbors, but do not stay out too late.

15. SUNDAY. Frustrating. If you do not feel well you may be forced to cancel a social arrangement because you are not really up to it. It is likely that you are suffering from fatigue, especially if you have been burning the candle at both ends. Try to catch up on sleep. This is not a favorable time for trying to kick a bad habit such as smoking, snacking, or cracking your knuckles; your willpower is not at its best. Wait until you are in a frame of mind to make a wholehearted effort. A relationship which has been increasingly stressful may reach the breaking point; do not fight against obvious incompatibility.

16. MONDAY. Misleading. The working week gets off to a cheerful start. A meeting scheduled for this morning is likely to be straightforward. Start early to make appointments for the coming week; there is a greater chance of getting through to the real decision-makers. Telephoned requests should be productive, but do not rely on promises which are made verbally. Until you have a check and a signed contract, a customer is likely to have second thoughts or pull out at the last minute. Friction between you and your partner later in the day could spring from a misunderstanding; check out the facts and ignore rumors.

17. TUESDAY. Unsettled. Problems in a personal relationship may be weighing on your mind. Your anxiety may interfere with your work or your ability to concentrate on other matters. A superior is unlikely to be as sympathetic as you hope. This is a day when it is best not to discuss your personal life at work; a certain individual may use what you say against you at a later date. If you are currently looking for work this is not a time for being too fussy. If you accept a position which is not really what you want it may lead to other opportunities. The important thing is to get your foot in the door and a chance to prove what you are capable of doing.

18. WEDNESDAY. Good. If you are self-employed this is a good time to consider taking on a partner. Being able to share the responsibilities means that you will have more free time and less stress. Someone else's creative input can be particularly helpful if you are hoping to expand your business. Although it is in the Taurus nature to be cautious, this is a time to be bolder as far as romance is concerned. Take the initiative with someone who has sparked your interest; you are unlikely to be rejected. If someone is clearly interested in you, do not hesitate to be encouraging. A casual romance can now be put on a firmer footing. An engagement now is starred.

19. THURSDAY. Difficult. Meetings or casual discussions at work can be tricky to handle. If you are trying to push forward a new idea you are apt to encounter considerable opposition. Although you may be tempted to back down, keep in mind that it is important to have your say. Your opinion is likely to be respected even if you are ultimately outvoted. This is not a favorable day for negotiations which involve a great deal of money. Do not provide financial backing to a new venture until you have investigated it fully. What looks convincing on paper may prove to have hidden pitfalls when tested under actual conditions.

20. FRIDAY. Stressful. This is a demanding end to the working week for many Taurus employees. You can get the best results today from pure hard work. Certain tasks require dogged determination if they are going to be completed before the weekend. It is important to let others know that you do not want to be disturbed because you have urgent work to complete. In this way you should avoid interruptions which would put you behind schedule. If you need to tackle a sensitive issue with a loved one, find the right moment to open a conversation this evening. Do not let sharp words or tears deter you from saying what is on your mind.

21. SATURDAY. Enjoyable. This is a good time for going away for the weekend, maybe to visit friends or family members in another part of the country. A change of environment can be therapeutic, especially if you have been working very hard recently. If funds allow, consider a weekend break at a resort. Sightseeing or cultural activities of any kind are favored. A friend may go out of their way to do you a favor; let them know how much it is appreciated. This evening favors going out in a group to the movies or the theater. There is a good chance of getting tickets for a play or concert at the last minute, although you may have to pay top dollar.

22. SUNDAY. Fair. Inviting your loved ones or friends to spend the day with you can be fun and relaxing. However, be prepared for some sparks to fly if sports or politics is discussed. You may find yourself taking on the role of peacemaker if an argument breaks out, but guard against taking sides. Stay as neutral as possible even if you secretly know where your sympathies lie. If you are going out there is a greater chance of running into an old friend or a former romantic interest. The encounter may not be welcome. This is not a time for renewing a friendship or a romance just out of politeness; cut the meeting short without being obviously rude. Be wary of making any long-term commitment.

23. MONDAY. Satisfactory. This is likely to be a pleasant start to the workweek. The day favors studying and educational endeavors of all kinds. You may get a chance to learn about another area of your work. Tackling a brand-new project can have its frustrating moments. Realize that the learning process is often slow; do not put yourself under unnecessary pressure to begin with. Teamwork of all kinds can be helpful. Be prepared to share ideas and resources with colleagues; cooperation can bring the best results. You could be on the receiving end of a friend's generosity, probably returning a favor that you did for them last year.

24. TUESDAY. Demanding. Your usual work schedule may be disrupted. Stay flexible. Deal with tasks or problems only as they come up rather than anticipating them. You may have to make decisions in the absence of a superior; if you use your common sense you should not go far wrong. If you have been working from home you may feel that the time has come to find another work site. This is a good time for contacting a commercial real estate agent to get an idea of what is available as well as the costs involved. Try not to let work overwhelm your personal life. Canceling a social engagement is unlikely to go over very well with those you let down.

25. WEDNESDAY. Rewarding. This should be an excellent day for Taurus business men and women. A deal which is finalized now should go through smoothly. The financial rewards for past negotiations may be greater than you expect. This is also a very favorable time for starting a new business. A company merger or buyout is favored. Your professional reputation may be spreading more than you realize. New customers may come your way through recommendations from satisfied clients. For Taurus employers this is a good time for introducing a new bonus or commission plan. Providing the right incentives either for your staff or for yourself can be remarkably rewarding.

26. THURSDAY. Easygoing. You may feel that life is all work and no play at the moment. If your social life is at a low ebb, now is a good time to make a fresh start. Call friends and come up with some arrangements for the weekend. Having something to look forward to can be the best tonic for you now. Keep in mind that maintaining solid friendships requires a lot of effort. This can be worthwhile when you find yourself being automatically included in other people's lives. A personal anxiety should not be ignored. Seek the counsel of someone who has your best interests at heart and is known for telling the truth.

27. FRIDAY. Variable. You should have a lot of energy, but keep in mind the saying of more haste, less speed. Your eagerness to get certain jobs done quickly can result in making unnecessary errors. Review any written work carefully, especially if it has to be passed on to a superior. Take extra care filling out any kind of forms. Be sure to include all required information before mailing them off or handing them in. If you have to send any important paperwork through the mail, pay for a return receipt. Or you may want to use a courier service. There is a greater danger of an envelope or package going astray.

28. SATURDAY. Fortunate. This weekend is an excellent time for a reunion. A get-together with old school friends can bring back a lot of happy memories. Someone who shares your sense of humor can be great fun to be around, reminding you that laughter is the best medicine. A broken relationship can be repaired if you are both determined to settle your differences. The second time around could prove even better than the first. Married Taurus people can revitalize romance by revisiting old haunts. You may even want to plan a second honeymoon for later this year. A cruise could be especially memorable.

MARCH

1. SUNDAY. Sensitive. This promises to be a quiet day for most Taurus people. If much of your working life demands interacting with others, welcome this time to yourself. A loved one may misinterpret your quietness for moodiness. If you want to be alone, make sure that friends and family members do not take it personally. This is a good day for cleaning out drawers, closets, or the attic. Items which you no longer have any use for could be donated to a charity resale shop or a homeless shelter. However, do not be too ruthless when it comes to throwing out mementos from your childhood or from a past relationship; you may later regret the loss of these keepsakes.

2. MONDAY. Fair. Safety at home and at work is very important today. If you are an employer, make sure that safety regulations are being followed to the letter. Keep a properly equipped first-aid kit on hand. A fire drill is a good way to be certain that all escape exits are noticed as well as usable. At home consider installing a burglar or smoke alarm. Business dealings of all kinds can be tricky to handle. An unexpected turn of events may create more work for you. Meeting a deadline can be touch-and-go; do not hesitate to rope in the help of colleagues who are under less current pressure than you are.

3. TUESDAY. Good. This is an especially productive day for Taurus people who make a living from writing. There is a greater chance of being in the right place at the right time. Creative pursuits of all kinds should be rewarding, whether you are working for money or just as a hobby. Keeping a journal is a good way of resolving personal issues; a problem should become clearer once you analyze it on paper. In the workplace this is a favorable day for meetings with colleagues; a certain working relationship is going from strength to strength. Teamwork of all kinds can be fun, interesting, and more productive than you might think.

149

4. WEDNESDAY. Variable. If you are paid at the beginning of the month this is a good time for sorting out your finances. Make a budget for the rest of the month, especially if you are still trying to pay off expenses from the Christmas period. The biggest expense at the moment is apt to be your social life. Cut back on eating out or other entertainment which always proves costly. You do not have to spend a lot of money in order to enjoy yourself. If you receive a bonus at this time, resist the temptation to blow it all at once. Put some aside for that proverbial rainy day. This evening is a good time to go to the movies or rent a video.

5. THURSDAY. Mixed. Do not pay attention to idle gossip concerning someone you know. If you speak up at all, rise to their defense when they are not present to speak for themselves. Check out information of all kinds for yourself; anything which comes to you secondhand could prove incorrect or at least unreliable. Keep a close hold on your personal belongings when you are out and about. There is a greater risk of leaving something behind such as a credit card after making a purchase. If you lost something recently it could be worth checking the lost and found column in the newspaper; someone may be honest enough to be trying to return it to you. Taurus pet owners should keep a watchful eye.

6. FRIDAY. Deceptive. This is a demanding end to the working week. You may have underestimated how long certain tasks would take to complete. Be sure to keep copies of any important correspondence; you may need to refer back to your exact words sometime in the future. Do not risk putting yourself in a situation where it could be your word against someone else's. If you want to apply for a new job or a promotion, make sure that you obtain the job description first. You may discover that you are underqualified. Do not risk telling a lie or even stretching the truth while talking to someone close to you. You could be found out, and explaining yourself could be embarrassing.

7. SATURDAY. Uncertain. A promised letter may fail to turn up in today's mail. Prolonged silence from someone you have been corresponding with frequently could cause you some anxiety, but it is unlikely that you have been forgotten. Accept that this person is probably frantically busy and will contact you as soon as possible. For Taurus singles who are embarking upon a new romance, all may not be plain sailing. Guard against expecting too much too soon. If you are unrealistic you could be setting yourself up for disappointment. This is a time when it is important to maintain an independent group social life. Do not pass up invitations in hopes of getting a call from that special someone.

8. SUNDAY. Favorable. This is an especially favorable day for family get-togethers. If you have many relatives it may be possible to bring most of them together under the same roof. A cousin, niece, or nephew who has been an unknown quantity to you may now show a greater interest in getting to know you; soon you may become firm friends. The Taurus nature has a tendency to bear grudges, but this is a good time for consciously letting go of old grievances. A fresh start can be made without any need for direct confrontation or long heart-to-heart discussions. Make a point of having your camera handy so that you can update your family photograph album. Try to learn more about family history by talking with an older loved one.

9. MONDAY. Disconcerting. Looking for a new home may not be as easy as you hope. It is important not to take the wrong place out of a sense of urgency, unless it is purely on a temporary basis. Be sure to obtain good references from a previous landlord or mortgage lender. If you find yourself up against competition from other prospective tenants or buyers, proof of your good credit history and other information could swing the decision in your favor. A friend who has always been reliable in the past may act out of character today. Being let down by someone you trust can be crushing, but try to give them the benefit of the doubt.

10. TUESDAY. Calm. If possible, arrange to be at home for at least part of the day. You may need to catch up with domestic chores or just relish a day away from the incessant pressure of work deadlines. If you normally work from home, this should be a productive day with fewer interruptions than usual. This means that it will be easier to completely concentrate on a difficult task. If you feel stressed, try out relaxation techniques such as yoga or meditation. If you need to discuss a personal issue, seek out someone who knows you really well. Their intuition should prove reliable and their insights helpful. However, do not expect or accept financial help from them.

11. WEDNESDAY. Disquieting. If you are at home with young children you may find that your patience is on a shorter fuse than usual. Youngsters may act up if they sense they do not have your full attention. Your best approach is to avoid being cooped up inside all day. Go out to the nearest park if the weather is good, or join forces with another parent for the day; you could benefit from each other's company. Work of a creative nature may come to a grinding halt. It can be useful to put a certain project aside until inspiration strikes. If an argument with a loved one erupts this evening, try not to say anything you will later regret.

12. THURSDAY. Useful. In your business dealings this is a time when certain contacts can be useful. Someone is willing to pass on information to you which would normally be unavailable. This is a good time for resolving any difficulties within a working relationship. The key to success lies in clearer communication. Let those who work for you know that they are valued. Animosity may arise if they feel taken for granted or dismissed in any way. You could be on the receiving end of a personal confidence. Make sure that secrets revealed to you go no further. Do not jeopardize your own integrity or good reputation by spreading a rumor.

13. FRIDAY. Fortunate. This promises to be a satisfying end to the working week. You should be able to wrap up a project which has been on the go for a long time. Seeing the fruits of your labor should be rewarding. Any deal which is finalized today will probably be honored. However, put any verbal agreement into writing as soon as possible while the details are fresh in your mind. If you are in the process of buying or selling property there is a greater chance that terms of a contract will be accepted. A job interview should go better than expected. If you are currently unemployed there may be an immediate offer of work. A well-calculated risk is likely to pay off later in the year.

14. SATURDAY. Excellent. You should have lots of energy and big plans. Even if you normally sleep late on the weekends, this is a day when you are apt to wake up early or feel too restless to stay in bed. This is a good time for getting some physical exercise. If you are out of condition, consider joining a health club. A professional assessment of your current strengths and weaknesses can put you back on the road to fitness. A workout tailor-made to fit your own individual requirements could be especially helpful. In a new romance the time has come for making a commitment. Do not leave that special someone in your life wondering where they stand with you and if you envision a long-term future together.

15. SUNDAY. Slow. In contrast to yesterday, this is a quiet day. A feeling of lethargy may be difficult to shake off. If you are engaged in physical exercise of any kind, listen to your body; do not push yourself too hard or too fast. Family duties may seem burdensome to you. However, older relatives, in particular, may be counting on a visit, so avoid pulling out of arrangements at the last moment. Social engagements run the risk of being boring, but you may be able to liven things up with your own suggestions. Agree to disagree with someone whose views conflict with your own; the chances of seeing eye-to-eye on certain issues are probably minimal. Avoid any direct verbal or physical confrontation.

16. MONDAY. Optimistic. This is likely to be a cheerful start to the workweek. If you work as part of a large department, this morning is a good time to meet with your colleagues. Some changes to your usual routine are a definite possibility. You may be asked to take on a new project or responsibilities which could make your job more interesting. Do not shy away from accepting new challenges; experience gained now could be useful to you in the near future. This is also a favorable time for taking a firmer line with someone who often tries to interfere in your life. They may respond better than you think to your request for more freedom to do what seems right to you.

17. TUESDAY. Unsettling. You may be unsure how far to trust a certain individual in your work life. The Taurus nature is usually careful in most matters; your instinct that this is a time to proceed with extreme caution is probably justified. Do not give someone your trust until you can safely say that they have earned it. If a troublesome situation seems to be brewing, you need to make sure that your own conscience is clear. When it comes to challenges from a superior, your best policy is to have reasons to offer rather than excuses. Your partner is apt to be in a difficult mood; to avoid a showdown, avoid discussing future plans.

18. WEDNESDAY. Rewarding. This is a busy day. In the workplace you should be at your best when involved in teamwork of any kind. Your communication skills are better than usual. This is a good time for brainstorming; new ideas should be plentiful once you get the ball rolling. In your business dealings you can afford to be less conventional than usual. Be prepared to embrace change rather than sticking to old methods for safety's sake. If you are teaching, concentrate on activities where students work in pairs or small groups; the more interaction you can achieve, the better. A promise made to you this evening is sure to be fulfilled.

19. THURSDAY. Fair. You may regret being too talkative recently with a certain colleague or acquaintance. There could now be evidence that someone has abused your trust or not honored a promise of secrecy. An apology may not be forthcoming. Try to be philosophical rather than angry; you will have to accept that this time you have learned a lesson the hard way. It is important to resolve not to take this person into your confidence again. Single Taurus people who have a romantic interest in someone new should not be too bold just yet. Try not to wear your heart on your sleeve until you are more certain that the interest is mutual. Guard against becoming involved in a romantic triangle.

20. FRIDAY. Good. This is a satisfying end to the working week. In your business dealings, concentrate on listening rather than talking. You can learn a lot just by being observant and keeping alert for clues of how other people are reacting. This can be a favorable time for sorting out personal finances. It may be easier to secure a loan at a competitive interest rate if you need to make a large purchase. If you have various small debts, consider taking out a consolidation loan; your total repayment figure could be considerably reduced. Put this evening aside for a quiet dinner with someone special who is often in your thoughts.

21. SATURDAY. Manageable. If you have not yet decided on your summer vacation plans, give this some thought today. This is a good time for visiting a local travel agent to find out about special vacation package deals. You may be invited to go away with a group of friends; this could be an appealing change if you usually travel alone or with just one other person. Traveling of all kinds is favored today; you are unlikely to experience transportation delays. A change of scenery can be a tonic. If you feel the need for some mental stimulation, consider attending a workshop or lecture on a subject which interests you. Check books out from your local library, or spend some time in a well-stocked bookstore.

22. SUNDAY. Confusing. There could be some hostility between you and a loved one. Trying to unearth the cause of the problem may not be easy if this person has opted to give you the silent treatment rather than having the courage to be open and forthright. Do not let your imagination run riot. If you cannot identify your supposed offense, you simply have to come right out and ask. More importantly, insist on a clear answer so that you have a chance to set the record straight. In your love life this is a time when you need to judge your mate or partner by their actions rather than their words; be alert to any secretiveness on their part.

23. MONDAY. Excellent. This should be an excellent start to the working week for you. Negotiations of all kinds can be easier to handle. Take the time to listen to different opinions even though you can afford to put more faith in your own judgment rather than looking to others for specific advice. Your decision making is apt to be right on target, and your hunches are also likely to pay off. If you are self-employed this should be an especially profitable day. If your cash-flow situation has been diminishing lately, you should now be able to make a bank deposit. Grasp a chance to push ahead in your chosen career while the opportunity exists; you may never get as good an opening again.

24. TUESDAY. Demanding. In your working life you could be under more pressure than usual. You might have to cover for an absent colleague, which means that some less urgent tasks of your own have to be put on to the back burner for a while. Do not rely purely on your memory; write down messages or new ideas before they slip your mind. If you have written work to complete, find a quiet space where you will not be disturbed; you will need all your powers of concentration. If you are studying toward a degree, spending time in the library rather than at home can be more conducive to studying.

25. WEDNESDAY. Pressured. The pressure of immediate work and responsibilities in your daily life may seem particularly demanding at the moment. This means that there is very little time for making long-term plans. If you feel trapped by your current lifestyle it may seem impossible to break out of an unsatisfying routine. The key to change lies in identifying small areas where you can start, then tackling them one at a time. A serious discussion with a partner should not be sidestepped. If you avoid communication now you could be setting the stage for growing apart. Confide your inner feelings without passing judgment on the actions of other people.

26. THURSDAY. Cheerful. If life has appeared rather bleak lately you should find that today is a lot more colorful. Colleagues can be especially helpful at this time. Certain work tasks are much easier to deal with if you cooperate to get them done. You may even find yourself with some free time on your hands. Focus on your social life. There could be several invitations for the coming weekend. Choose the one where you are apt to meet new people. If you are short of money at the moment there is a greater chance of benefiting from other people's generosity. Someone may offer to pay your way simply because he or she is eager to have your company.

27. FRIDAY. Satisfactory. This promises to be a satisfying end to the workweek. As far as work matters are concerned, you have learned a lot lately. This is a time to put your new skills to effective use. Also consider signing up for a training course with a view to improving your career prospects. You may find that your current employer is willing to subsidize you or give you the necessary time off for attending class. At a personal level you should be more at ease with yourself and the world around you. You have learned useful lessons from recent experiences and can now stop being hard on yourself. You deserve a pat on the back.

28. SATURDAY. Pleasant. Make a point of getting in touch with close friends and family members. If you have a tendency to run up large telephone bills, this is a good time to get back into the habit of letter writing. If you or a loved one has been ill recently, a turning point for the better is foreseen today. Find the time to visit someone who is hospitalized, or confined at home, especially if they are now well enough to enjoy some company. This is a favorable day for repairing a broken romance. There is a greater chance that you can smooth over your differences. Taurus singles are more likely to meet someone new at an intimate gathering of work colleagues.

29. SUNDAY. Tranquil. Observe the tradition of a day of rest today. Keep housework or other domestic chores to a minimum. Reading or listening to music can be especially relaxing. This is also a favorable day for going out to eat instead of cooking at home. If some work worries are playing on your mind, make a greater effort to forget about them until tomorrow. Otherwise you may not enjoy your leisure time as much as you should. Loved ones could find it boring if you insist on talking shop. However, someone who has worked in your field could have some useful advice to share; discuss any work-related problems with them if you get the chance. Clarification is as important as specific advice.

30. MONDAY. Mixed. This is a productive start to the working week. If you have to deal with tricky business negotiations of any kind you can rely on the power of your own Taurus personality and persuasiveness. You may also feel that luck is definitely on your side, but guard against becoming too complacent. If you are interviewing or attending an important meeting, make sure that you look your best. A sloppy appearance could count against you. Be sure to carry a little extra money in case of a sudden emergency. Do not hesitate to stand up for someone who is being unfairly treated, either at work or in your personal life.

31. TUESDAY. Frustrating. If a certain individual is becoming a thorn in your side at the moment, remind yourself that you do not have to put up with sarcasm or barbed comments. Under no circumstances should you give in to emotional blackmail. You will only end up perpetuating the problem, which could then make matters even more difficult to deal with. Now is the time for some straight talking, but guard against arguing in public. What you have to say should be just between the two of you. Unexpected expenses could strain your finances. You may have to make some personal sacrifices in order to get your bank balance back up to a comfortable level.

APRIL

1. WEDNESDAY. Exciting. If you are paid at the beginning of the month you may receive more than usual. This could be a tax rebate or a bonus. You could now be paid for overtime as well. The temptation is probably to go on a spending spree, but it is important to curtail your more extravagant impulses at the moment. By all means treat yourself to something new. However, do not blow extra cash all at once. Make sure that you check your change after making a purchase; there is a greater risk of being overcharged. In the workplace there may be plans under consideration which could improve your current working position. Be sure to stay on the good side of higher-ups.

2. THURSDAY. Demanding. You should start the day in a light-hearted mood. Today's mail can bring a chatty letter from a friend. There is a greater chance of striking up a conversation with a fellow passenger while traveling. Taurus people who are unattached could be asked to go on a blind date; meeting for lunch is a safe option. In the workplace you could soon find your good mood melting away. The pessimism of a certain individual may affect you in spite of your efforts to make light of problems. Keep your wits about you and you should be able to avoid walking straight into the arms of a troublemaker who has targeted you.

3. FRIDAY. Promising. If your local travel is on the increase, consider investing in a season ticket; you could gain considerable savings in the long run. At work you may have to spend a lot of time sorting through a backlog of administrative work. Keep your eyes peeled for small mistakes which could cause problems at a later date. This can be a testing time in a personal relationship. You may want to discuss certain issues but feel unsure about how to start the conversation. It is important to create the right atmosphere rather than just hoping for the right moment to pop up. Once you are together without outsiders it should be plain sailing.

157

4. SATURDAY. Stressful. If you are planning a shopping trip for today, try to get an extra early start. There is a greater possibility of heavy traffic or other delays in local traveling. Parking can also prove to be a headache, but you cannot afford to risk leaving your car in an unauthorized spot; you could easily be ticketed or even towed away. If you are looking for a secondhand car, obtain expert advice. Be willing to pay for an independent assessment of a vehicle before you make a deal for it. Social plans for this evening may be changed. Someone could let you down at the last moment or just not have the money to go out on the town as you had planned.

5. SUNDAY. Variable. The weekend has probably not gone according to plan so far, and today follows the same pattern. A family member may pressure you into going along with their wishes despite the fact that you would prefer to be elsewhere or doing other things. If there is no getting out of unappealing tasks or arrangements, your best policy is to join in with as much good grace as you can muster. Your personal preferences may have to wait until another time, but at least you are creating some credit for yourself. If you decide to stay home for the day, this is a good time to rearrange furniture for a better effect or hang some pictures on blank walls.

6. MONDAY. Lucky. This is a productive start to the working week. There is a greater chance of being offered a new project which you can really sink your teeth into. Job satisfaction can spur you on to greater efforts. If you are looking for work at the moment, get in touch with former contacts. You could hear of a vacancy by word of mouth and in this way get a foot in the door before the job is even advertised. There is a greater chance of success if you are applying for a promotion. Taurus singles who have been in an ongoing romantic relationship for some time may now decide to make it permanent. An engagement or wedding now is starred.

7. TUESDAY. Disquieting. Taurus people who work with children need to tap into extra reserves of energy. Join in their games and play. Plan special activities for them or an outing of some kind. Any educational work requires more ingenuity on your part to keep students interested. Discipline issues can cause anxiety for Taurus parents. Concentrate on finding the balance between firmness and kindness. This is a time when directives or strict rules are unlikely to work; try to be flexible but consistent. Do not ignore a younger person's problem if they come to you for support or advice. Try to see the situation from their point of view.

8. WEDNESDAY. Frustrating. If you rely on your creative or artistic skills in your work, you are likely to be brimming over with ideas. The amount of work you are able to produce may be irrelevant. What is important at the moment is quality, not quantity. Your best approach is to pick out one or two of your best ideas and concentrate on perfecting them. A friend who is in a new romance may not have time for you. Although it can be hard not to feel pushed aside, in time you should be able to restore your former closeness. In the meantime keep your social life as varied as possible. Joining a new club or other group can bring exciting new people into your life.

9. THURSDAY. Quiet. This should be an uneventful but pleasant day on the whole. Enjoy having a day when you are not under the usual pressure. You should be able to sort through a backlog of small tasks which had to be ignored during busier times. This is a favorable time for wining and dining a potential business client or associate. In less formal circumstances you could discover that you have many outside interests in common. Later in the day can be a good time for sports of all kinds. You will probably get the most pleasure from games which are played for fun rather than just to win. Outdoor swimming season is right around the corner. Try on last year's bathing suit, then consider whether you need to diet or tone up.

10. FRIDAY. Fair. This should be a reasonably easy end to the working week. Although you may be busy, you are unlikely to be rushed off your feet. You should be able to set your own pace. A colleague may confide some gossip or off-the-record information. Keep in mind the need for discretion; there is a greater risk of letting the cat out of the bag in a moment of carelessness. If you have an ongoing health problem of any kind, this is a good time for trying out a new treatment, perhaps in the field of alternative medicine. However, do not expect instant results. It is important to commit to a course of treatment and follow through on it as prescribed.

11. SATURDAY. Disconcerting. The past busy week at work and at home could catch up with you today. If you get a chance to sleep late, take it. Tiredness could cause an attack of the blues or irritability. Little things which normally wash over you can upset you now. Avoid spending time with anyone who is difficult to cope with at the best of times; you could easily rub each other the wrong way. If you live with family members or roommates, everyday friction is likely to come to a head. If things are not working out it could be time for you to begin looking for new living accommodations. Do not stay out too late tonight.

12. SUNDAY. Mixed. Tiredness or boredom can still be hard to shake off. For some Taurus people the weekend has probably not lived up to expectations. If you realize that you have been relying too much on one particular individual for your social life, now is the time to broaden your horizons. Having social options means that you will not be left stranded if one person lets you down. Get in touch with old friends or workmates. They may be surprised to hear from you but pleased to arrange a get-together. It is often in the Taurus nature to follow rather than initiate, but it is now up to you to do the calling and make plans.

13. MONDAY. Unsettling. Taurus people who are self-employed are apt to be stretched to the limit. Although you may be considering taking on a partner, this is not a good time for such a major decision. You could ease your workload with a partner, but there is a greater risk that you could wind up resenting someone else's involvement in your business. If you need extra help, hiring temporary staff is a better choice for the time being. In your personal life you may sense that someone is not telling you the full story. You need to wait for further information to come to light before your faith in a certain relationship is going to be totally restored.

14. TUESDAY. Calm. This promises to be a pleasant day in the workplace. If you have struggled to build a working relationship with a certain colleague, your efforts could now start to pay off. People appear to be more cooperative than usual. Make a point of joining in on all that is going on around you. If you sit on the sidelines you could end up missing out on a lot of fun. For Taurus people who are unattached this is a lucky day for romance. Someone who is attracted to you could now make their interest more obvious; it is up to you to be encouraging. Married Taurus people should set this evening aside to be alone with that special person.

15. WEDNESDAY. Deceptive. A friend may announce plans or intentions which you consider ill advised. However, this is a time when it is probably wiser to keep your misgivings to yourself. They are unlikely to thank you for any advice or words of caution if their mind is already made up. Instead, you could be accused of being a killjoy. A business client or associate may not be as honest and open as they seem. Tread carefully in negotiations of all kinds; keep your options open. Taurus employers should check references before hiring someone new. Do not allow yourself to be pressured into making decisions of any kind; time for independent reflection is essential.

16. THURSDAY. Variable. If a budget is being worked out for your job, make sure that you put forward a strong case for your own department. You have to be loud and clear in order to get what you want. Joint finances could be under extra strain. Your partner may need more cash than usual, which could mean that some of your own nonurgent needs have to be put on hold. It is important to make such sacrifices willingly. If you are grudging you could make a loved one feel guilty; instead, let them feel happy about your generosity. In the long run you always get back what you give, both materially and emotionally.

17. FRIDAY. Good. This should be a satisfying end to the working week. Deadlines of all kinds can be met comfortably, and maybe with time to spare. You should be proud of your own efficiency and good planning. Business dealings with overseas contacts are likely to prove especially lucrative. There may be an opportunity to combine a long-distance business trip with time for pleasure. This is a favorable day for tackling difficult work; some fresh insights can now get the ball rolling. There is a greater chance of being able to come to grips with a new subject or project. This evening favors cultural activities, such as a live music concert or going to the theater or opera.

18. SATURDAY. Enjoyable. This is a sociable start to the weekend. Even if you do not have any definite plans you could be invited out by friends for lunch or even a day's outing. This is a good time for joining a group or association of any kind. Your social life can be extended through your outside interests. New friendships made at this time are apt to be lasting. You can now get closer to someone who has so far been only a casual acquaintance. For Taurus people who are politically active, this should be a favorable time for discussing your views. You may also want to join in on a peaceful rally or demonstration for a cause which you feel strongly about.

19. SUNDAY. Confusing. Do not put off thinking about your long-term plans and ambitions in life. By all means seek to fulfill your hopes and wishes, but also be realistic. Practical considerations may need to be given more attention than you realize. Be sure to set your sights on achievable goals rather than building castles in the air. If you are married or engaged, discuss proposed changes in your work life with your loved one. Seek their agreement rather than presenting them with a final decision. If you are meeting new people, especially someone considerably older than you, do not try to impress. Just relax and let them see you as you are.

20. MONDAY. Fair. The working week gets off to a hectic start. If you are starting a new job or embarking upon a new project, be prepared to be thrown in at the deep end. You should find that you actually learn a great deal in this way. Do not be afraid to ask questions or seek explanations from colleagues, even if you have to ask more than once. Legal matters can be tricky this morning. Take steps to ensure that you have been properly advised; a second opinion may be worthwhile. Do not stick to a rigid timetable. This is a day when unexpected developments can throw carefully laid plans into disarray; remain as flexible as possible.

21. TUESDAY. Manageable. The early part of the day is the best time for wrapping up a business deal or negotiations of any kind. It can be a relief to clear your desk of a matter which has taken a long time to complete. Confidential meetings are also likely to be useful before lunch. Later in the day you are apt to be in demand by your colleagues or a superior. Make the most of the limited time you have to yourself for attending to your own tasks. Morale in the workplace is likely to be higher than usual. Team effort should be particularly successful. Do not be afraid to ask for favors; a friend is more than willing to help out if you just let them know what you need from them.

22. WEDNESDAY. Challenging. If you are seeking a promotion or transfer at work you cannot afford to be complacent. Competition for the position could be fiercer than you expect. Many of your colleagues are rooting for you; one of them may sing your praises to someone in a position of power. Keep alert for a certain individual who is jealous of your success. Such a person may stoop to damaging your professional or personal reputation if they get the chance, forcing you to defend yourself. A new romance can be exciting, but avoid letting it take over your whole life. You cannot afford to get too far behind with work matters or to ignore other obligations.

23. THURSDAY. Buoyant. Special events of all kinds are likely to live up to and even surpass your expectations. In the business world this is the perfect time to entertain your most important clients and contacts. The more memorable the get-together, the better. Someone who has steered a lot of business your way should be left in no doubt of your appreciation. For Taurus people embarking upon a new personal relationship, this is a time to indulge the purely romantic side of your nature. Do not shy away from the obvious even if it seems old-fashioned. Sending a bouquet of flowers or arranging a candlelit dinner can create special moments for you both to share.

24. FRIDAY. Productive. In your business dealings subtlety should be your watchword. There is nothing to be gained by going in with all guns blazing, especially if you work in sales. Let customers feel as if they are buying rather than being sold to. If you are self-employed, new business can come your way by referral from satisfied customers. In your personal life this is a favorable time for planning a surprise party or gathering for a loved one. There could be plans in the works for your own birthday, but keep quiet if someone unwittingly lets you in on the plans. Your loved one is apt to be especially attentive this evening; enjoy being spoiled and pampered.

25. SATURDAY. Stressful. You are not likely to be in the best of moods this morning. If you have been going over and over a problem in your mind, now is the time to try to solve it. Worrying alone will probably not produce an answer. An older friend or relative can be helpful. If you ask for their advice, you could be both comforted and guided by their words of wisdom. If you work on weekends this is apt to be a stressful day. You may not feel equal to the demands that are being made on you. Be quick to protest if someone clearly has unreasonable expectations. A social event this evening may fall flat; have an alternative in mind in case you decide to leave early.

26. SUNDAY. Disconcerting. Family duties and responsibilities may be greater than usual. It can be difficult not to feel penned in. A relative may expect you to change your own plans at the last moment to suit them. It is up to you to insist on having your own space and a right of refusal. This includes the right to say no to arrangements which do not appeal to you or which are simply inconvenient. Accusations of selfishness should not be taken too much to heart. Someone who is used to getting their own way will have to play second fiddle for a change; this can do your relationship more good than harm. Advance preparation for work tomorrow could pay off.

27. MONDAY. Good. This promises to be a cheerful start to the workweek. If you have some free time, go shopping for spring clothes. If your image needs updating, choose an outfit that is in the latest fashion. You may also want to go for a more modern hairstyle; a professional stylist can make the right suggestions. You could receive compliments on your appearance; notice how your confidence increases when you feel good about the way you look. First impressions are very important if you are meeting someone recently hired. There may be an opportunity to earn some extra cash later in the day. If you have a temporary job, it could now be offered to you on a permanent basis and with a raise in salary.

28. TUESDAY. Manageable. If money is owed to you, chase it down. It is up to you to be assertive; do not allow yourself to be put off with lame excuses or a sob story. If you are unemployed at the moment, make sure that you are claiming all of the benefits that you are entitled to, including retraining. If a payment does not arrive on time do not sit and wait for it; make a call to find out the reason for the delay. This is a productive day for written work of all kinds. Your Taurus imaginative powers are at their best if you have creative work to finish up. If you are single, a note or a call from an old flame may take you by surprise; getting together for lunch or dinner could be fun.

29. WEDNESDAY. Difficult. This is unlikely to be one of your better days at work. A clash with someone in authority may be unavoidable if you have honest disagreements with them. This person's idea of resolving a difficulty may simply be to pull rank on you, which could leave you seething with resentment. However, avoid taking the matter any further until you have a chance to cool down. Acting on the spur of the moment or letting your heart rule your head could have disastrous consequences. Be extra attentive to all safety precautions. There is a greater danger of being accident-prone, probably because of a lack of concentration or advance planning on your part.

30. THURSDAY. Fair. Administrative tasks of all kinds can be time consuming. If you are feeling disorganized at work, try to come up with a more efficient filing system. Being able to put your hands on the right paperwork at a moment's notice can save you a lot of time and trouble. Be sure to keep a copy of important correspondence; you may need to refer back to your exact words at some future date. Get in touch with your brother, sister, or other close relative. Be sure they know that they can bring a problem to you even if you cannot guarantee to come up with the whole answer for them. Someone may want the comfort of your company rather than the benefit of your advice.

MAY

1. FRIDAY. Changeable. Allow plenty of time for any traveling you have to do. If you have several appointments scheduled for the day, allow longer than usual gaps between them. Public transportation is likely to be slow; you might have to wait a long time for a bus or train. Make sure that you have extra cash for a cab in case you really get stuck. Be sure to look in on an elderly or disabled neighbor. Running some errands for them could be easy for you and a lifesaver for them. It is wise to confirm social arrangements for this evening because there is a greater chance of a mix-up as far as time and place and even what to wear are concerned. Do things to please and pamper yourself in your Taurus birthday month.

2. SATURDAY. Manageable. As an earth sign it is important for Taurus people to feel organized and comfortable at home. This should be a good day for putting your home in better order. A blitz on the housework or other chores can be satisfying. This is also a good time for buying houseplants or repotting old ones. Fresh flowers can bring you a lot of pleasure; treat yourself to your favorite blooms. If you have a garden, plant new bulbs or seeds which will flower in the summer months. You may not be in the mood for living it up this evening, but accept an invitation to visit a friend. Sharing takeout food and chatting can be relaxing for both of you.

3. SUNDAY. Frustrating. Sometimes there is no accounting for other people's behavior. A person you have recently started to get to know may reveal another side of their character which surprises you because it does not fit with your understanding of them. Remind yourself that everyone has a dark and a light side. Try not to take their words or actions too personally. You may be the safe target for anger not actually intended for you. Be understanding, but at the same time do not allow yourself to be used as an emotional punching bag. Do not be too accommodating in a new romance; your own desires should have equal weight.

4. MONDAY. Useful. If you have some vacation leave or personal time to take this year, today is perfect for taking a day off. A long weekend can be therapeutic, especially if you have lots of personal errands to catch up with. Just puttering around at home doing nothing in particular can be an equally good reason for a day off. If you have the option to work from home, you might decide to do so today. Self-discipline can be easier, especially if you are up against a deadline. This is also a good time for finishing off odds and ends before taking on any new work responsibilities. In this way you should feel uncluttered both mentally and physically.

5. TUESDAY. Buoyant. You should start the day feeling especially lighthearted. Your optimism is bound to rub off on those around you; you are capable of creating a good mood wherever you go today. Conditions favor creative endeavors of all kinds. Artistic work can bring you a great deal of personal satisfaction. Working with children can be most rewarding if you concentrate on activities which encourage self-expression, such as drama or finger painting. If you work in the arts, this promises to be a productive day. An audition is likely to go well. Taurus performers should find it easier to secure regular work. A contact from your past can be an invaluable ally in landing a new part.

6. WEDNESDAY. Stressful. Your day is likely to be especially busy. Even if you thrive on constant activity, this is a time when you need to guard against overdoing. Avoid getting carried away when it comes to making social arrangements; you could easily find yourself booked solid with no private time left for yourself. Make a point of scheduling specific time on your calendar which will be just for you. A new relationship may not develop as fast as you would like because of work commitments on both sides. Now is the time to plan ahead so that the relationship does not peter out before it has really begun. An after-work drink could easily turn into a night out on the town.

7. THURSDAY. Fair. Do not be surprised if you are not at your best physically. Even if you have not been burning the candle at both ends, you may have been overdoing in other ways, perhaps without realizing it. Consider whether you are taking certain work matters too seriously. Do not forget to delegate where appropriate; there is no point burdening yourself with tasks that other people are paid to do. Be extra health conscious. Avoiding foods which you know are bad for you or cutting out alcohol for a while can boost your system and give you more energy. Keep in mind that gentle exercise actually serves to combat fatigue, not to cause it.

8. FRIDAY. Variable. Make an extra effort to find work if you are currently unemployed. However, avoid putting all your hopes in one interview. Sign up with more than one employment agency. If you are responding to newspaper advertisements, be sure to read them carefully to decide if you are adequately qualified. In this way you minimize the chance of extra rejections which could eat away at your self-confidence. At home this is a favorable day for getting through as many chores as possible before the weekend starts. If you are expecting guests, plan, shop for, and maybe even prepare meals in advance. If you are eating out tonight, avoid an expensive restaurant where you could have to pay a cover charge as well as menu prices.

9. SATURDAY. Mixed. If you have a family to look after you may feel burdened by too much routine. Make sure that you get some help with housework, especially if you have teenagers who are prone to vanishing just when there are jobs to be done. Do not hesitate to exert a bit more discipline. Working Taurus parents may want to consider paying someone to clean the house or take care of the lawn. This could be a necessity rather than a luxury in order to protect the quality of your life. Other people may make you late or keep you waiting around. A change of plans this evening can be annoying at first but may turn out for the best.

10. SUNDAY. Stressful. A family gathering may not be the most relaxing of occasions. There is apt to be a lot of friction barely hidden beneath the surface. You may sense this even if you do not know about it in advance. Getting through the day without an argument could be impossible. If you are not directly involved, your best policy is to keep quiet; you could make matters worse by appearing to take sides. A relationship which has not been satisfactory for some time may reach a crisis point today, forcing you to make a final decision. Decide between making further commitments to one another or breaking it off so that you can both make a fresh start.

11. MONDAY. Unpredictable. This could be a testing start to the working week. As a Taurus you are known for your stubbornness. Today, however, you should quickly realize that cooperation and compromise are essential to successful working relationships. Guard against taking a stand regarding an issue which is relatively minor. Be willing to hear others out, or even to accept that their way of doing something may be better than yours. If team decisions create a lot of conflict, suggest putting the matter to a majority vote. If you are married, avoid making mutual social commitments without first consulting your spouse in advance. Get to bed early tonight.

12. TUESDAY. Productive. Make a point of settling any outstanding bills, especially if you have already received the final demand. If it is often difficult to find time for going to the bank, consider having your regular bills electronically paid. It can help your budget to spread the cost of recurring quarterly bills by paying them in monthly installments. A number of extra expenses may all come up at once, forcing you to juggle your finances in order to avoid going further into debt. You should have lots of energy, making this the right time to tackle physically demanding jobs which you have been putting off. Settling down at the end of the day might be more difficult than you imagine.

13. WEDNESDAY. Slow. Work matters can prove unstimulating but should be easier to cope with if you realize that it is just a temporary lull. However, if you have been bored with your job for a long time, you need to guard against getting stuck in a rut. Keep in mind that the Taurus nature tends to stay put until pushed; you may need to find a way of rousing yourself into action. It can be helpful to write down your goals, also identifying what you want to achieve and what makes you feel enthusiastic. Even consider a drop in salary if it means that you can find your true vocation. Be cautious in romance; learn more about someone before you make any type of commitment.

14. THURSDAY. Rewarding. This is a favorable day for holding business meetings or other get-togethers of all kinds. Interacting with people in your line of work could be productive. You may also make new contacts who can be helpful to you in the future. Taurus people who are unattached could meet someone new when least expecting it. This could be a work contact; having professional interests in common can be a fortunate start to a love relationship. If you are married there could be good news for your spouse, perhaps involving a promotion or a substantial pay increase. Enjoy a special night out if there is cause to celebrate.

15. FRIDAY. Sensitive. Legal matters of all kinds can be tricky to handle. Although a court decision may not go in your favor, it could still be worthwhile lodging an appeal. If you are single you may be forced to accept that a newcomer you admire does not feel as strongly as you do. They may be the type intent on playing the field while you could be ready to settle into a committed relationship. This could prove to be a recipe for unhappiness; find the strength to walk away now rather than later. Recognize that the timing is all wrong and that you deserve better. If you are recovering from a broken romance do not be too reclusive. A night out could be the stimulation you need to get back in circulation.

16. SATURDAY. Misleading. If you have not yet planned your summer vacation this is a good time for deciding where you would like to go and with whom. If you want to break with tradition, be extremely tactful when telling this to those who are usually your companions. There is a greater risk of someone taking your action very personally. Avoid making reservations at any resort or hotel without at least seeing a photograph first; in this way you can avoid disappointment. Check out information of all kinds for yourself. You cannot afford to rely on someone else's opinion; they may have their facts wrong or just have tastes that differ from yours. If you are out on the town tonight leave the car at home and go along with a friend.

17. SUNDAY. Variable. The usual Sunday routine may not appeal to you. Suggest new and different activities to your friends or family members. You may be surprised how eagerly others agree to your plans or offer attractive alternatives of their own. This is a day when you need to be active. Avoid situations where you will be cooped up indoors for a long period. Seek out the company of people who are interesting and who have the knack of making you think. Controversial subjects can spark a great deal of debate. Do not get into too heated a discussion with someone who is clearly bigoted; it is probably not worth the effort since you are unlikely to ever sway them.

18. MONDAY. Mixed. This is a demanding start to the working week for you. If you work in a managerial capacity you could be called upon to settle all sorts of problems. A staff member whose personal life is in crisis may need extra support at this time; do what you can to take the pressure off them. Guard against biting off more responsibility than you can reasonably handle. Be realistic when it comes to allotting time to certain tasks, both for today and for the week ahead. A meeting could take much longer than you anticipate. Try not to take work home with you this evening. A loved one may want your undivided attention and become resentful if you are distracted.

19. TUESDAY. Fair. A certain friend or colleague is being particularly difficult at the moment. If you suspect that they have a grievance toward you, it might be best to ask them directly. In this way you can set the record straight. This is also a time when hostilities can arise through misunderstandings. Clear, open communication is much more important than usual. Be quick to accept responsibility for errors which are clearly your fault. Others are more willing to come to your aid if you are honest. This evening is a good time for getting together with a few of your closest friends. If you are playing host, cook something quick and simple or place an order with a takeout restaurant.

20. WEDNESDAY. Successful. There is very little that you cannot deal with successfully. In business matters luck is on your side. Your Taurus intuition can be invaluable when it comes to decision making; follow a hunch even if it seems illogical on its face. A buoyant atmosphere in the workplace makes this an especially enjoyable day. A colleague is sure to be available to see you through a critical moment. Let co-workers know how much you appreciate their support, particularly if it is given without your having to ask. If you are in the mood for fun this evening, spend time with someone who shares your sense of humor and love of life.

21. THURSDAY. Good. This promises to be a productive day. You will probably be in the mood for some hard work, which can be rewarding both personally and financially. If you have new ideas which you would like to suggest, now is a good time to discuss them with a superior. Higher-ups should be willing to hear you out. Demonstrating your own initiative can impress the right people and make you a more valued employee; in turn, this can improve your promotion prospects. If you are retired but still active, consider looking for a part-time job. You may also want to consider volunteer work if making extra money is not your main priority. As the Taurus birthday period for this year comes to a close, make firm resolutions for the future.

22. FRIDAY. Disconcerting. Most of you Taurus workers will probably be gladder than usual to see the end of the week. You may pick up on a lot of tension around you. If you are working to a deadline you may need to remind yourself that you are not the only one who is under pressure. Tempers can flare in stressful moments; your best policy is to try and stay out of the line of fire. Be alert to the fact that someone could be looking for a scapegoat; make sure that it is not you. This is not a good day for making final decisions in your work life; take the weekend to mull something over. Relaxation should be your goal for this evening; steer clear of rowdy parties.

23. SATURDAY. Happy. If you were given some money for a birthday present or if you have had a windfall this can be a good day for spending it. This is a time for treating yourself rather than letting extra cash get eaten up by general living expenses. New clothes or jewelery may be a priority. But take some time to browse around book or record stores too. If you owe someone a thank you or if you want to return a favor this can be a good time for taking them out. A first date is likely to be successful; your efforts to impress should hit the right note. This evening can be the perfect time for celebrating special occasions of all kinds.

24. SUNDAY. Satisfactory. Enjoy a lazy morning. Thoroughly read the newspapers to catch up with what is happening all around the world. Reading or doing the crossword puzzle can be relaxing. This is a good time for starting a personal journal; writing down your thoughts or recent experiences can be therapeutic. You may also want to commit some happy memories to paper just for the sake of posterity. Later in the day you are apt to be in a sociable mood. If you have not made definite plans, arrange an impromptu get-together for your family or a few close friends. Games can be modified to suit all age levels; play for fun, not just to win.

25. MONDAY. Sensitive. Money, or the lack of it, can be a main preoccupation. If you do not get paid until the end of the month but are already overdrawn, now is the time to plan your way back to solvency. One way to do this is to agree to reduce your debt by a certain amount each month. Some immediate economies or sacrifices may also have to be made. Discussing your financial situation with your mate or another loved one can lead to some heated exchanges. It is important not to apportion blame, even if you feel that they have been overspending. Reach an agreement on what you can and cannot afford to do. Fresh starts of all kinds are under very favorable auspices.

26. TUESDAY. Fair. On this busy day the key to success lies in being well organized. Make a list of the day's tasks, then put them in order of priority. Try to avoid spending too much time on any one task. You could easily get bogged down. Variety makes the day more interesting. If you are going out shopping, pay for your purchases in cash so that you are more realistic about what you are spending. Hold on to your receipts and product guarantees. If someone at work is leaving or has a special occasion to celebrate, this is a good time for organizing a collection for a group gift. You should be able to coax most people into giving generously.

27. WEDNESDAY. Disquieting. You have a tendency to be absentminded or vague now. Keep a close watch on your personal belongings when you are out; there is greater risk of losing something or even having your pocket picked. Avoid lending money or possessions to a friend unless sure that they can be trusted. If you owe money to a friend, make a point of settling your debt as soon as possible. Keep in mind your own abilities and strengths. A certain individual may be set on undermining your self-esteem. Although you may guess that this behavior springs from their own insecurity, you still need to stand up for yourself and protect your reputation.

28. THURSDAY. Unsettling. A problem in a personal relationship may seem all too familiar. There is a chance that you are repeating patterns which you learned unconsciously some time ago, maybe as a child. It can be difficult to discuss sensitive or complicated subjects even with your closest friend at the moment. A helpful alternative could be to seek some counseling; an objective, professional interpretation could be just what you need. Do not be too hard on yourself if you are not currently meeting your aims in your work or personal life. It is most important now to learn from your mistakes, then put them behind you and be ready to move on.

29. FRIDAY. Demanding. The morning is the more demanding part of the day. In the workplace you may have to deal with a backlog of paperwork. Bring your correspondence up to date and return telephone calls from earlier in the week. If you have a written work to complete, such as a report, try to get it out of the way by lunchtime. Later in the day is favorable for group effort of all kinds. Open discussions can elicit some interesting ideas regarding current work projects that have bogged down. Accept an invitation to go out this evening even if you feel tired. Once you are in a social atmosphere you should soon get your second wind.

30. SATURDAY. Mixed. If you are looking for property to rent or buy this is a good day for attending open houses. Do not rely just on a real estate agent; your own efforts are likely to be more productive as well as cheaper. Scan the local newspaper for private advertisements. Also let friends and colleagues know what you are looking for; you could hear of a place through word of mouth. This is a good time for painting and decorating. You may be able to do much of the work yourself rather than paying a professional. This evening is a good time for a party, but be on the lookout for gate-crashers who could stir up trouble.

31. SUNDAY. Deceptive. It can be difficult to shake off the effects of a late night or too much carousing. Avoid any tasks which are mentally or physically demanding; you may only make yourself feel worse. This is a day for taking things as easy as possible. There may be an occasion when you are tempted to lie because it appears to be the easy option at the time. However, there is a greater risk of your lie being exposed, which could cause you considerable embarrassment. If you recently exaggerated the truth, get it off your conscience now rather than later. A loved one is apt to be in an uncommunicative mood. It is probably best to leave them alone until they are ready to talk.

JUNE

1. MONDAY. Disquieting. If you feel exhausted as the new workweek begins it can be difficult to muster enthusiasm for work matters. Try hard to avoid situations which require you to be in top form. Even with the best intentions in the world, you may not be able to rise to the occasion. If you are a parent at home, young children can be more of a handful than usual, probably because they are bored. If the weekend has been exciting there may be a sense of anticlimax. Guard against allowing your irritation to escalate to the point where your temper snaps; take a walk or a nap to relieve stress. A new romance which started recently may not lead to the long-term relationship you really want.

2. TUESDAY. Difficult. Just when you think that you have your finances under control, something unexpected can come along to upset the balance. It can be difficult not to become concerned about a specific money problem, but remind yourself that it will not last forever. A friend who is better off than you may be willing to help you out with a loan. For once you should accept their offer, but make sure that the repayment terms are clear. Do not let pride keep you from accepting help of any kind. You can always return favors at a later date. In your personal life make a greater effort to accept and even enjoy the differences between you and your loved one; opposites attract, and for good reason.

3. WEDNESDAY. Easygoing. If you have had a tough week so far, you should find life getting easier today. Your efforts with a difficult project should finally begin to pay off; you may now be in line for the recognition that you deserve. Someone in authority could have earmarked you for a promotion in the not too distant future. Taurus people who work on commission or who rely on bonuses to supplement a basic salary can expect to have a lucrative day. This is a promising time for starting any sort of new treatment to correct a health problem. There is a greater chance that you will respond quickly. A telephone call from someone special can highlight the day and make you feel special.

4. THURSDAY. Variable. In business dealings this is a time when bold strokes can pay off. You cannot expect to obtain the results you want by sitting comfortably on the fence; be prepared to stick your neck out. However, risks should be well calculated, especially if a large sum of money is involved. Throwing more cash at a certain problem may not be the answer; it might be better to cut your losses now. Avoid signing any binding document just yet. You need more time to read and consider the small print. Be sure to question any points which seem unclear. Discussions in regard to controversial issues should be kept low-key when you are around people who have old-fashioned views.

5. FRIDAY. Disconcerting. This is a demanding end to the working week. You may have to skip taking a lunch break; there could be time only for a sandwich on the go. Someone in authority may be delegating more than you can comfortably cope with. Ask for time to clear your desk before you are loaded down with any new responsibilities. Stress can manifest itself physically, such as a persistent headache or extreme tiredness. However, a dogged determination can keep you going until the end of the day as the

Taurus stubbornness stops you from admitting defeat before trying your best. Arrangements for this evening could become complicated. A night at home may be more relaxed and also cheaper.

6. SATURDAY. Demanding. Friction between you and your loved one or an older family member can make this a difficult start to the weekend. At least one of you needs more personal space. If the other person clearly wants to pursue their own interests or see their own friends, realize that there is no requirement for you to tag along. Living in someone's pocket can be a surefire way of creating boredom or killing romance. A friend of yours may be glad for the chance to see you alone rather than as a couple. If you are embarking upon a new relationship, stay alert for early signs of tension. Ignoring them is not going to make them go away.

7. SUNDAY. Exciting. This promises to be the fun day of the weekend. Whatever pressures were weighing on you or a loved one yesterday have lifted. Someone who has been morose or just distant for a while should now be all smiles again. You may also reach a deeper understanding of their nature, which can make difficult moments easier to cope with. This is a good day for browsing at an outdoor market or secondhand shop. You could pick up all sorts of bargain-priced odds and ends for your home. A certain object could turn out to be worth a lot more than you pay for it. Accept an invitation to lunch or dinner at a friend's; their hospitality can be a real treat.

8. MONDAY. Mixed. If you have been contemplating making changes in your work life for some time, now is the right moment to start. Bear in mind, however, that most people are resistant to change, preferring to stick to tried-and-trusted methods which feel safe. Offer suggestions for discussion rather than presenting them as absolutes or directives. A certain individual could quickly come to resent you if they feel that you are assuming too much power. Avoid situations which are sure to end up in a battle of wills. Taurus people who work in the caring professions may be exhausted at the end of the day, but there can be many rewarding moments that compensate.

9. TUESDAY. Stressful. You could become involved in a situation where you find yourself tangled in red tape or up against ridiculous rules. Avoid venting your frustration on someone who is only carrying out orders and just trying to do their job. Take complaints to a much higher level in order to have any effect at all. For the time being try to play the system to your own advantage. In meetings of all kinds you need to be extra well prepared. Someone in a position of authority expects you to have all the answers at your fingertips. A social event this evening could be a disappointment; it can be difficult to stay awake even in a crowd.

10. WEDNESDAY. Cautious. If you have been mulling over a personal dilemma, seek advice from someone who knows you well. Do not bare your soul to a casual acquaintance just for the sake of having someone to talk to; their reaction could leave you feeling dissatisfied. Work matters are likely to get more interesting as the day goes on. You may get a chance to be involved in a totally new area of your job; learning new skills can be satisfying. Taurus students who are preparing for examinations should find it easier to study; your powers of concentration are at their best. A movie or a best-selling book can give you food for thought this evening.

11. THURSDAY. Fortunate. This is an excellent day for long-distance traveling, especially if you are setting off on a vacation. You are unlikely to encounter any prolonged delays. This is also a lucky day for booking a trip at the last moment; there is a greater chance of finding a real bargain. If you cannot get time off, consider a weekend break just for a change of scenery. Passport or visa applications made at this time could be processed more quickly than usual. If you are involved in any kind of litigation, push ahead with the relevant paperwork. A court decision is likely to go in your favor. A settlement could be finalized at long last, making your lengthy effort seem worthwhile.

12. FRIDAY. Good. If you are on vacation this could be a memorable day. Sightseeing or learning about local culture can be stimulating. There is a greater possibility of making new friends while traveling. A friend who lives abroad may get in touch and urge you to come for a visit. At work this promises to be an enjoyable day. If you work in a managerial capacity you should be able to enthuse your staff. Decisions you take can boost your popularity and reputation. This evening lends itself to a group night out, mixing colleagues and friends. Choose foreign food if you are eating at a restaurant.

13. SATURDAY. Inactive. It can be difficult to get going today. If you were out late last night or are feeling the ill effects of a strenuous week, try to catch up on some sleep. Morning dreams are likely to be graphic but confusing. It could be useful to write down what you can remember; later you could make sense of a scenario which seems nonsensical at first. You may be in an unusual antisocial mood; someone's efforts at conversation can be irritating. Do not allow yourself to be pressed into going out if you would really rather stay home, especially if it means mixing with strangers. Making small talk can be tiring.

14. SUNDAY. Fair. If you are unemployed at the moment, go through the help-wanted section in the Sunday newspaper. Draft a standard letter of application; be sure that your work history is complete and up to date. Give careful thought to personal and business references; seek permission from someone you intend to use. A family get-together can be successful on the whole. However, an older relative who assumes the right to criticize your lifestyle or the way you dress can get on your nerves. Do not tolerate comments which border on rudeness. This is a good time for going through your wardrobe and giving away anything which you have not worn for the past year or two.

15. MONDAY. Fruitful. It is an excellent day for teamwork of all kinds. Being able to pool ideas and resources enables you to race through certain tasks much quicker than expected. Be quick to offer assistance to a busy colleague if your own workload is minimal at the moment. If you are taking an examination or going on an interview your last-minute review is sure to pay off. If you have to prepare a speech or presentation of any kind, a practice run with a colleague as your audience can lessen any stage fright you might feel. A friend may welcome your company this evening. You may be able to offer a solution to a problem with which they have been tussling.

16. TUESDAY. Changeable. In both your professional and personal life you may need to attach less importance to what other people think. Keep in mind that you cannot please all of the people all of the time no matter how hard you try, so you might as well at least please yourself. Be willing to accept your own limitations, but acknowledge your own special Taurus strengths as well. This way you have the confidence to ignore someone who is trying to diminish your self-esteem. Do not share your personal ambitions and wishes with someone who is prone to pessimism or envy. If you go out shopping, treat yourself to a new pair of shoes. Jewelry can make the perfect gift for a special occasion.

17. WEDNESDAY. Disquieting. The day gets off to a busy start. If you do not take the trouble to set clear aims and goals you could soon find that time slips through your fingers. Have a definite plan for what you want to achieve by the end of the day. In your business dealings it may prove impossible to contact the right people. If someone is not returning your calls, putting your request to them in a formal letter or memo is more likely to solicit an answer. Taurus people who are unattached could be attracted to someone new, but you have to create an opportunity to ask them out rather than relying on chance.

18. THURSDAY. Good. If you were expecting a difficult day at work you are in for a pleasant surprise. Decisions made at a higher level can bring about changes for the better. You could even find that you have been let off the hook with regard to a project that was beginning to prove burdensome. Someone who has been avoiding you may now get in touch. An honest conversation should clear up any misunderstandings existing between you. Do not be tempted to hold a grudge toward anyone at this time; be willing to accept the ups and downs of human nature. If you show tolerance and compassion now you can expect the same in return on another occasion.

19. FRIDAY. Tricky. The morning is the more productive part of the day. In the workplace you should be left mostly to your own devices; a superior may be absent or too busy to breathe down your neck. Work which requires close concentration is best done before lunchtime. A crisis may erupt later in the day. Trying to unravel mistakes which are not necessarily yours can take a lot of time and effort. If your work requires dealing with the general public, you will need all of your Taurus tact and diplomacy in order to keep customers happy. If you feel a little downhearted this evening, avoid staying alone. Friends or family members are sure to cheer you.

20. SATURDAY. Unsettling. If you are short of money and considering taking on a part-time extra job, weigh the financial gains against the effect on your personal life, especially if your family counts on having you around. Temporary work may be the best option for now. Avoid being extravagant with money if you are out shopping. Do not buy on credit unless it is interest-free; even then, be careful not to overextend yourself. If you are in the mood for a night out, opt for a favorite restaurant; a new place could be expensive as well as a disappointment. A blind date is likely to fall flat.

21. SUNDAY. Excellent. If you are at the beginning of a new relationship this should be an especially happy day. Being able to spend time together away from the pressures of work or other responsibilities can be a real joy. This is also a favorable time for introducing a new partner to your own social circle; they are sure to hit it off together. Find time for your outside interests. A hobby could now be turned into a money-maker, allowing you to soon earn a living from something you love doing. Parties or celebrations of any kind are sure to be a resounding success, with you a focus of attention.

22. MONDAY. Lucky. In the workplace associates are apt to turn to you for leadership and guidance. Someone who is new to the job can benefit from your experience; take them under your wing for a while until they feel comfortable. If you are self-employed this is a favorable time for teaming up with someone whose skills complement your own. The arrangement should work out well for both of you. A new contact could steer a lot of business your way. Outstanding invoices can now be settled in full. With your loved ones you can afford to be more open in discussing your personal feelings and wishes. One relative in particular may prove more supportive than you had hoped.

23. TUESDAY. Fair. You may be feeling lazy this morning. If you have little to do, enjoy taking life at a slower pace today. However, if you are in danger of falling behind with work matters you need to find a way to motivate yourself. Keep in mind that what you do not accomplish today will have to be done tomorrow. Set achievable goals, breaking a big project into manageable chunks. If you feel that your work does not stretch you enough, this is a good time for taking on extra responsibilities or new challenges. As a Taurus you are quick to learn new skills at this time. Self-discipline comes more naturally once your interest and curiosity are aroused.

24. WEDNESDAY. Calm. This promises to be an enjoyable day. In the workplace you should be allowed to proceed at your own pace. A deadline of any kind can be met with time to spare. This is also a good time to handle administrative paperwork. You can achieve good results by conducting business over the telephone. There are many odds and ends to tie up which do not require a face-to-face meeting. You should be able to complete a lot of personal errands during your lunch break. A new neighbor may soon become a friend; you could discover that you have many interests in common. Relax at home this evening, reading, watching television, or chatting on the phone.

25. THURSDAY. Deceptive. If you have written work of any kind to do make sure that you first check the exact requirements. There is a danger of spending a lot of time on details which eventually prove to be irrelevant. If work is delegated to you without clear instructions, do not make a start on it immediately. Guesswork could let you down; insist on a thorough explanation. Someone who repeatedly disappoints you, apparently without good reason, should now be given less importance in your life. If you allow yourself to be taken for granted in a new relationship you could be setting a bad precedent for the future. Do not sacrifice your principles for instant popularity.

26. FRIDAY. Variable. If you are house or apartment hunting you could get lucky today. Obtain a written agreement before parting with any cash; your security could depend on it. Renting with an option to buy is worth investigating. The pressure is apt to be on at work. Be prepared for some last-minute problems which have to be resolved before the weekend break. Use your Taurus earthy common sense to keep from getting flustered. Simple logic can be the key to problem solving of all kinds. This evening favors entertaining in the comfort of your own home. Prepare food which can easily be kept for latecomers, and be sure to have plenty of beverages on hand.

27. SATURDAY. Good. This is a good time to start painting and decorating work at home. You should be able to get a lot of preparatory work done, such as stripping old paint or wallpaper. If you have an older property you may uncover some original features. Give careful thought to a color scheme; you will be living with your choices for a long time. This is also a good day for working in the garden. If the weather is fine, consider having a barbeque rather than eating indoors. Invite friends or neighbors to join in and make a party of it. Spending time with your family this evening may appeal more than going out on the town.

28. SUNDAY. Unsettling. If you are out and about with small children or a pet in tow, be extra vigilant. They could wander off the moment your attention is distracted. Children can cause extra expense, forcing you to do some careful juggling with your finances in order to meet their desires. This is a good time for encouraging older children to save some of their pocket money so that they can buy things for themselves. They need to learn that you are not a bottomless pit when it comes to financial hand-outs. Taurus parents need to present a united front with each other in regard to discipline and setting limits.

29. MONDAY. Lively. The new workweek gets off to a pleasant start. There may be news of a birth or a baby on the way for someone close to you. Creative work of all kinds is favored. You should find that inspiration strikes just when you need it most. If you are single, someone you admire and like may now be showing particular interest in you. It is likely that you are past the stage of instant romance with this person, but friendship could be a solid foundation to build upon for the future. You have nothing to lose by agreeing to go out. If you have just been paid, work out a budget now for the coming month. Do not forget the money for savings as a definite budget category.

30. TUESDAY. Fair. At work you could find yourself stretched to the limit. Try to get an earlier start than usual. Ignore someone who seems determined to find fault with whatever you do. If you allow yourself to be goaded by them you could end up in a full-scale shouting match. An outburst of anger can help you let off steam, but it is unlikely to be helpful in the long run. Remind yourself that you can win the battle but lose the war; think ahead. Sports of all kinds are a good way of channeling your more aggressive feelings, although you need to guard against overdoing. This is unlikely to be a lucky day for any kind of gambling or betting; do not risk more than you can afford to lose.

JULY

1. WEDNESDAY. Misleading. There should be some exciting developments with regard to a deal that you have been nursing along. However, do not get too excited too quickly. This is a day when you cannot rely on anything until it is signed and sealed. Written work of all kinds need extra care and attention. Do not be tempted to dash off an important letter; think carefully about your words. You may not be able to get a straight answer to a direct question. In your personal life it can be difficult to bring up a sensitive subject; wait for a better time when tempers have cooled down and you have some perspective about the matter.

2. THURSDAY. Frustrating. Work matters may be slow or just downright boring. Vary your tasks as much as possible rather than getting bogged down with only one. It may be increasingly clear that a certain individual is holding you back through their own laziness or inefficiency. If they do not respond to your subtle hints ask them directly to get their act together. A friend who has been causing you a lot of anxiety may again come to you with their problems. By all means be sympathetic, but do not fall into the trap of telling them only what you know they want to hear. The best way to be of help is to tell them some home truths.

3. FRIDAY. Deceptive. Nothing is going to be straightforward. Even tasks which should be quick and simple can prove time consuming or complicated. It is likely that you are trying to be too tactful with those around you. In work matters you need to adopt a tougher attitude; keep in mind that you can be assertive without being aggressive. A certain individual needs to be taught that you are a force to be reckoned with. If a personal relationship is going to endure, it is time for you to stop being a doormat or to stop expecting the other person to always agree with what you want. Taking a stand can lead to arguments, but in the long run it earns you the respect that you deserve.

4. SATURDAY. Fortunate. The effort that you have been putting into a certain relationship should now start to produce desired
results. Remind yourself, however, that it is unrealistic to expect
someone to undergo a complete personality change. What matters
is that you both try to meet one another halfway. This is a good
day for shopping. Be alert for bargains for the home, such as a
more efficient dishwasher or air-conditioner. If you have been
waiting for a price drop you may get your chance today. This is a
favorable evening for entertaining at home. A dinner or dessert
party can be especially enjoyable.

5. SUNDAY. Good. You are not likely to be content just with
your own company. If you live alone, call a few friends; there is
a greater chance of being included in an outing or a party of some
kind. You may especially need intellectual stimulation. Seek out
the company of those who share your special interests or who can
always be relied upon for interesting conversation. Unattached
Taurus people may be intrigued by someone at a social gathering.
The attraction is likely to be mutual even if it is as yet unspoken.
A potential partner may need space and time before feeling ready
to make fresh commitments in a new relationship.

6. MONDAY. Demanding. In your business dealings you must
tread very carefully and cautiously. Someone who is on the point
of reaching an agreement with you may still get cold feet if their
confidence in you is shaken in any way. Your best policy is to be
patient and not try to force the pace. Do not overlook the power
of silence in negotiations; avoid talking just for the sake of it. If
you are about to move into new accommodations, prepare well
ahead; obtain terms, conditions, and any restrictions in writing
even if your potential landlord is someone you know. It is always
wise to have proper written documentation. Set this evening aside
for relaxing at home.

7. TUESDAY. Disquieting. Be prepared for some setbacks and
unexpected changes of even the best-laid plans. You may not be
able to finalize a certain matter as quickly as you anticipate. It is
likely that you have underestimated the amount of work you have
to do and could find yourself racing against the clock. Making a
greater effort to be systematic and thorough can pay off. Do not
waste too much time on tasks which are either not urgent or could
easily be delegated. A social engagement this evening may not
live up to your expectations. There is a greater chance of feeling
out of your element when you are in the company of strangers
who all know one another.

8. WEDNESDAY. Unsettling. You have to be extra tolerant of other people. A certain individual whose views are totally opposite yours may take pleasure in goading you. Keep in mind that it is usually impossible to change someone's long-held views. Becoming embroiled in arguments only underlines the fact that you are banging your head against a brick wall. It is wiser not to rise to the bait. In the workplace it can be stressful dealing with a superior whose rules or demands are always changing. Try to stay in control of your rebellious side. An angry scene can flare up at home over seemingly trivial matters, especially if there is a teenager in your family circle.

9. THURSDAY. Successful. You should be able to put recent arguments or misunderstandings behind you. Even if you cannot agree with someone, they should now be ready and willing to respect your point of view. Make sure that you are also making an effort to meet them halfway. If you allow others in both your personal and professional life to have their say, you can at least reach acceptable compromises. A working relationship which has proved difficult in the past is entering into an easier phase. In a moment of need it can be comforting to find that more than one person comes forward to support you. A brother or sister can be especially generous.

10. FRIDAY. Variable. The morning hours are likely to be the easier part of the day. At work you can take advantage of a superior's good mood if you want to ask for a favor. This is a favorable time for inquiring about a promotion or asking about financial assistance if you want to sign up for a work-related course. All efforts at self-improvement are favored. If you are at home, set aside some time for reading, either for leisure or study purposes; domestic chores can wait a while. You may have to work later than usual and be forced to postpone a social arrangement so that you have time to get ready and enjoy yourself without feeling rushed.

11. SATURDAY. Changeable. Unexpected visitors could disrupt your usual morning routine. Someone who has a habit of dropping by unannounced could be difficult to get rid of. You might have to drop some heavy hints if you are in a hurry to be elsewhere or just not in the mood for idle chitchat. It may be difficult to focus on anything in particular. Matters which require close concentration should be left for another day. This afternoon favors putting your feet up and watching television, maybe a sports event or an old movie. If someone close to you suggests a night out, enjoy being spoiled. Romance is starred after dark.

12. SUNDAY. Fair. Guard against being possessive with your partner. A show of jealousy on your part may only anger or alienate your loved one. Be willing to entertain their friends or colleagues. In a social setting you should make an effort to mingle rather than sticking close to someone you already know. Concentrating on putting someone else at ease can be the best way of forgetting your own shyness or self-consciousness. Extra care with your personal appearance can help boost your confidence. Some forward planning for the week ahead can produce exceptional results, helping you overcome a challenge from a competitor.

13. MONDAY. Quiet. If you are unemployed at the moment, carefully and thoroughly research the job market. There may not be the prospect of an immediate vacancy or interview, but at least you can get a better understanding of what is probably going to be available in the fall. If making money is not too urgent, consider doing some volunteer work. Helping out with an ecological project in your community could be an introduction to useful new contacts. Work matters are unlikely to be hectic. There should be time for a leisurely lunch with a friend or colleague. If you owe someone a letter, write or phone the person this evening while they are on your mind.

14. TUESDAY. Satisfactory. The day gets off to a busy start, which can be helpful; the sooner your adrenaline starts pumping, the more you can get done. Avoid taking on additional responsibilities if your workload already has you at full stretch. In your eagerness to help someone you run the risk of getting behind with your own work; temper your generous impulses with a dose of realism. Donate what you can to a charity. Remember, too, that charity often starts at home. Someone close to you may need some financial assistance, perhaps a small loan to tide them over for a few weeks. It should be satisfying to give rather than to receive.

15. WEDNESDAY. Varied. If you are having problems with neighbors, such as noise late at night or early in the day, things may come to a head. Do not confront them angrily; this could only create more animosity. Wait until you feel calm enough to reason and negotiate. Appealing to someone's social conscience is more likely to achieve the desired effect than threats. If you are traveling, work out your route in advance. There is a greater risk of getting lost, especially in an area which is new to you. This is a good time for joining a road service in case of a breakdown. Keep work worries to yourself rather than getting family members involved.

16. THURSDAY. Tricky. You are apt to get out of bed on the wrong side this morning, with a strong desire to be left alone. If you have to meet other people's demands or needs as soon as the day starts, try to be gracious about it. You only feel worse if you take out a bad mood on someone who does not deserve your anger, especially a child. Your finances are under extra strain. Some careful budgeting now could save you from being overdrawn at the end of the month. In the supermarket look for items which are reduced or are being offered at a special price. A little imagination can go a long way when it comes to planning meals for the rest of the week.

17. FRIDAY. Uncertain. Your creative powers are at their best, but trying to present new ideas to a superior at work can be an uphill struggle. Be sure that you have facts and figures to support your ideas. A half-baked plan will almost certainly be dismissed or ignored. Your own enthusiasm is unlikely to be enough to win someone over to your way of thinking. If frustration is becoming an all too familiar experience at work, it may be time to start looking for a job which offers more of a challenge to your Taurus talents. Try not to let a friend down this evening. A night out may be unappealing to you, but they could be counting on you.

18. SATURDAY. Mixed. Quarreling with someone at home may start the day, but this is unlikely to involve anything serious. Avoid finding fault or being self-righteous. Maintain your earthy sense of humor so that the dispute does not escalate out of proportion. Your ability to get others to laugh can make life easier. Taurus people who work on weekends should have a particularly productive day. If your job involves serving the general public, make a point of being upbeat. You could soon see the benefit in the tips you earn or the referrals from satisfied customers. This evening favors a formal function, such as a dinner party or a dance. Go out of your way to get to know someone new.

19. SUNDAY. Variable. Joint finances require some discussion. If you live with roommates, be sure that you are paying neither more nor less than your fair share of the bills. An itemized telephone bill is the best way to prevent arguments over who made what calls. Try to be extra aware of the needs and feelings of others, especially your nearest and dearest. A casual comment that you make in an offhand manner could be taken the wrong way if someone is in a touchy mood. Making fun of anyone, no matter how lighthearted, could easily backfire on you; it is up to you not to go too far. An unexpected visitor, maybe someone you used to work with, can brighten your day.

20. MONDAY. Exciting. In your business dealings the beginning of the week brings some encouraging news. A meeting may not produce definite or immediate results, but you are successfully paving the way for the future. Thrash out the details of any new project or proposal. You could be presented with new opportunities. Any move designed to expand your current base of operations is worth serious consideration. You can afford to think big. A close friend may be a tower of strength and an inspiration if you have a problem to discuss. Do not worry alone; help and understanding are only a phone call away.

21. TUESDAY. Fair. The day gets off to a cheerful start. A loved one who has recently been difficult to live with is now more kindly disposed toward you. A lighter atmosphere at work and at home can do a lot to lift your spirits. If money is owed to you, there could be a check in today's mail. If you are claiming unemployment or other government benefits you could discover that you are entitled to more than you realize. Allow plenty of time for local travel later in the day. Being late for an appointment or a date could put you at a distinct disadvantage. Snap decisions may cause others to question your judgment; think ahead.

22. WEDNESDAY. Rewarding. Someone you have been trying to contact may finally return your telephone call or drop you a line. Although you may have imagined the worst, the reasons they have been out of touch are probably not too serious. Guard against supposing that someone is trying to avoid you if they turn down an invitation. In the workplace this is a good time for dealing with correspondence and administrative tasks of all kinds. Conducting business over the telephone may be more time efficient than face-to-face meetings. Do not sidestep dealing with touchy issues in a personal relationship. This evening is the perfect time for a heart-to-heart talk.

23. THURSDAY. Deceptive. You may feel that this is the day to make a fresh start with a certain working relationship. Nevertheless, you cannot afford to take anything for granted. Although someone may claim that they are willing to meet you halfway, there may not be much concrete evidence to back up their words. You have to distinguish between what someone says and what they do; the two could be far apart. In your personal life insist that someone honor a promise made to you. You can damage your own self-esteem by letting them off the hook too easily. Do not give in even if you are accused of being inflexible or uncaring. Get to bed early tonight.

24. FRIDAY. Calm. This promises to be a straightforward end to the week for working Taurus people. If you would like to take the day off in order to have a long weekend, this is the perfect time for doing so. Working from home could also be an option. If you are shopping, look for items which can brighten up your home, such as a wall mirror or metallic flower pots. Or treat yourself to some flowers, either a plant or a bouquet. Someone may try to talk you into going out tonight. However, if you have already decided to spend the evening in the comfort of your own home, stick to your guns. Relaxation should be your priority.

25. SATURDAY. Good. After your busy workweek, make a point of catching up with people in your personal life. Return telephone calls and respond to invitations from earlier in the week. The mail is likely to bring more letters than usual. There is a possibility of receiving an invitation to a formal event, such as a wedding or anniversary celebration. Do not delay sending off your reply. Personalized stationery can be an ideal gift or a treat for yourself. This is a lucky day if you are house hunting, especially if you have to move soon. There is a greater chance of finding a place through word of mouth without having to pay a finder's fee.

26. SUNDAY. Difficult. Taurus parents of young children may find them a greater handful than usual. Avoid being cooped up at home all day. Problem behavior is almost certainly a sign of boredom. Head for the park, or involve your children in sports of some kind. Public places or a formal event not geared to children should be avoided; they could be more stressful than enjoyable. Taurus single parents need to be cautious when it comes to introducing a new partner. A period of adjustment may be needed on both sides. A romance could be reaching the stage where you need to choose between working to improve the relationship or ending it.

27. MONDAY. Uncertain. Your schedule for the day may not go according to plan. Meetings or other arrangements can be canceled at short notice. If you have appointments away from your workplace, confirm them before setting off; in this way you should avoid what may turn out to be a wasted trip. In both your work and your personal life, do not count on other people's promises made today. Although someone may be sincere at the time, they may not be able to keep their word. Keep in mind, the old saying that if you want something done right, it is better to do it yourself. Consider volunteering to correct a situation close to home that is aggravating you.

28. TUESDAY. Starred. If you are unemployed this is a day when your work prospects start looking up. There may be an opportunity to take courses designed to improve your current work skills or to teach you new ones. Do not underestimate your own abilities. The Taurus determination can see you through when it comes to breaking new ground in your professional life. A part-time job could lead to a permanent position once an employer recognizes what a valuable asset you are. You should be feeling physically fit, but do not overlook making routine health appointments to have your eyes tested or to visit the dentist for a checkup.

29. WEDNESDAY. Unsettling. Little things can conspire to irritate you. Although the Taurus temperament is usually placid, you may be on a short fuse. The old adage of counting to ten before acting or speaking could be useful, especially at work. Offending someone in authority can put you in a difficult situation. Try to make allowances for a colleague who is naturally slow or is new to the job. Being critical or impatient is likely to slow them down more. Be extra careful in traffic. You cannot afford to take risks on the road, such as jumping the light or exceeding the speed limit. Neither should you chance parking in an unauthorized place even for a few minutes.

30. THURSDAY. Disconcerting. The morning is the easier part of the day. Try not to let time slip through your fingers. You may have regrets if you do not use the morning hours productively. You are apt to find yourself under increasing pressure this afternoon. Bring work records and reports up to date; an employer could be on the prowl later on. If certain matters are in dispute, be sure to be armed with reasons and not excuses; you need to cover your own back. Avoid taking on more than you can comfortably cope with in an attempt to impress a higher-up. You could all too soon find yourself having to acknowledge your own limitations. Avoid socializing this evening with work associates.

31. FRIDAY. Disquieting. There is a greater risk of feeling at odds with the world. Try not to let negative feelings get the better of you. Upheavals going on around you can be difficult to cope with, but it appears that change is definitely in the air. There is no point trying to fight against the inevitable. Strive to accept the fact that enforced changes in your work or home life could be a way of getting out of a self-imposed rut. Look forward rather than holding on to the past. For Taurus people in a committed relationship, this is a time to pull together; resolve not to let life's ups and downs drive a wedge between you.

AUGUST

1. SATURDAY. Mixed. Start off the new month with fresh resolutions concerning your social life. If you feel that you have become isolated or are all too often bored, now is a good time for action. Contact friends whom you have not seen for a while rather than waiting for them to get in touch with you. Arrange a get-together at a sports field or restaurant. Accept any invitation that comes your way even if it at first sounds unexciting; you never know who you might meet. Taurus singles not actively looking for love are most likely to find it. A family gathering could be more successful if you extend the circle to include close friends as well.

2. SUNDAY. Uncertain. Keeping a certain relationship on a superficial footing is becoming impossible, even if you started out on this basis. This person needs to know how you feel and what makes you happy. You may hesitate to share your deeper thoughts or feelings, but such intimacy is necessary if the relationship is to become really meaningful to you both. If someone is keeping you at arm's length, find out why. You may question the spiritual side of life. Seek out the company of someone who can share such a discussion in an informed, intelligent way. Do not close your heart to any option.

3. MONDAY. Difficult. This is a difficult start to the workweek. Certain personal issues that are weighing on your mind can interfere with your concentration regarding more day-to-day matters. Your Taurus instinct to keep some things to yourself is probably justified. This is not a time for talking to just anyone in order to ease your conscience. Gossip can circulate like wildfire in your neighborhood or workplace. Make a point of not contributing to idle speculation concerning other people. Work which requires accuracy and close attention to detail should be left for another time. Instead, stick to routine tasks which require little or no mental agility.

4. TUESDAY. Variable. What you expect from those closest to you may be unrealistic at this time. Although it is in your Taurus nature to attach great importance to loyalty, avoid stretching this too far. Keep in mind that others have their own lives to lead. Ironically, the more space you make for a loved one the more they will probably want to be with you. Although you may start the day feeling unmotivated, your energy should pick up by the afternoon. Getting down to some hard work can be rewarding. If you have some free time later in the day, read up on a specialized subject which interests you. Academic pursuits of all kinds are favored.

5. WEDNESDAY. Quiet. If you have not already taken your summer vacation, make some definite plans today. Consult a travel agent to fully investigate package options as well as independent travel. You may decide to visit a country you have not been before. Taurus students who are now on a summer break should think about traveling while special rates are available. A travel publication could recommend cheap places to stay. Work is unlikely to be too demanding. There should be time for a shopping trip or lunch with a friend. This evening favors going out to a movie or renting a video for a relaxed night at home.

6. THURSDAY. Changeable. The morning is the more productive part of the day. That is the time to tackle a difficult work project with renewed energy and enthusiasm. Clearing your desk of odds and ends which have been piled up for too long can be therapeutic. You should then find it easier to give your full attention to more interesting matters. Guard against delegating tasks to a colleague unless they can guarantee to complete them on time. If you are up against a late-day deadline of any kind you have to work flat-out to meet it. Putting in overtime on the job can play havoc with your social life; let others know if you are going to be running late.

7. FRIDAY. Stressful. There are times when you have to sacrifice your individual needs in order to fit in with a group. This is a day when finding such a balance can be tricky. In work it is more important than usual to listen to all points of view, especially if you need to make a decision which will affect others. Snap judgments are unlikely to be reliable. Base your actions or decisions on factual and carefully sifted information. You may realize that your personal life is suffering because of work pressures. No matter how busy you are, make a point of taking some time off in the not too distant future.

8. SATURDAY. Inactive. The effects of this busy week could easily catch up with you today. Keep household chores to a minimum. You might decide to shop locally for basic provisions, but overall you will probably be content to stay home. Reading or watching television can provide the sort of relaxation you need at the moment. Avoid the company of people whose self-centered conversation drains you at the best of times. Someone with many personal problems should be kept at arm's length if you do not feel up to the task of playing counselor. If someone does not take the hint that you would rather be left alone, be prepared to be more direct with them.

9. SUNDAY. Disquieting. Your solitary mood continues today. When it comes to making or breaking arrangements, be guided by your conscience. You know instinctively if someone will be upset or indifferent if you want to change your joint plans for the day. A friend may be embarking on a course of action which you consider unwise or ill considered. However, try to keep your opinion to yourself unless expressly asked for advice. Unsolicited opinions may be interpreted as interference and could even lead to a bitter dispute. On the other hand, do not let others pour cold water on your own hopes and wishes for the future.

10. MONDAY. Fortunate. If you had an uneventful weekend you will probably be glad to get back into the swing of work today. You are apt to be offered new challenges which inspire you. The atmosphere among your colleagues is congenial and cooperative. Teamwork of all kinds is favored. Be willing to participate in a social event organized through work. The chance to get to know certain individuals on a more personal level can be advantageous to your career. A brother or sister who has been going through a difficult period may call you with good news. An impromptu celebration could be in the cards for this evening.

11. TUESDAY. Pleasant. Your working life is taking an upward turn. You are likely to receive praise or recognition for your recent efforts and achievements on the job. Enjoy your moment of glory. If you are self-employed, this is a good time for some market research. Anything which helps you stay one step ahead of the competition can be useful. In your business dealings the art of skilled negotiating should come easily to you. Devote this evening to a loved one or close friends. Share an informal meal, either at home or at a favorite local restaurant. Very spicy dishes may not agree with you.

12. WEDNESDAY. Fair. This is an especially productive day for Taurus people who consult or write for a living. You can soon get into your stride, especially if you arrange to be undisturbed. If you work from home, telephone calls can be a source of distraction. Switch on your answering machine, then return all of your calls at one sitting later in the day. If you have a tendency to accumulate clutter, this is a good time for a weeding out. Getting rid of extraneous items can provide you with welcome space. However, guard against being too hasty when it comes to throwing away items of sentimental value. You may later regret being ruthless or hard-hearted, or a family member may get upset about it.

13. THURSDAY. Deceptive. Work responsibilities may be weighing on you more heavily than usual. What started as simple tasks can prove to be more time consuming than you bargained for. Do not let others add to your workload, especially if you are already under more pressure than they are shouldering. A fairer distribution of routine jobs in the workplace or at home may be needed. If you are involved in buying or selling property, this can be a stressful time. Avoid taking shortcuts of any kind; make sure that all transactions are reviewed by an attorney or other knowledgeable person. Read the small print of any document which requires your signature.

14. FRIDAY. Disconcerting. Someone close to you seems intent on picking a quarrel, but accusing them of nagging is not going to solve anything. Take the time to discuss what is at the root of their behavior. You may then be able to clear up some misunderstandings and get back to being friends. Clear communication is the key to problems of all kinds. Someone could soon set your mind at rest if you are willing to bring anxieties or nagging doubts out into the open. Compromise can be essential in romance. If your mate or steady date wants a night out with their own friends, show that you are quite capable of being independent.

15. SATURDAY. Productive. This is a favorable time for a shopping trip, especially if you want to buy summer clothes or other personal items on sale. You may decide to shop in another town where the choice is wider. Take a friend along and make a day of it. Look for bargains in perfume or jewelry. You may find the perfect gift for a friend who has a birthday coming up. Know your budget limit before you start out. There is a danger of getting carried away and overspending. If you feel that your social life is becoming monotonous try something different this evening. Live comedy or a musical performance could be memorable.

16. SUNDAY. Slow. Shaking off the effects of a late night can take a long time. If you can muster the energy, some gentle exercise could make you feel a lot better. Swimming or walking is ideal, but on the whole make a point of taking life easy today. If you are providing lunch for family or friends, rope in some helping hands when it comes to preparing the meal or cleaning up afterward. Make the main meal of the day a leisurely affair. Sitting around the table and chatting can be enjoyable. A feeling of togetherness is important if you and your loved ones are often too busy to share mealtimes during the workweek.

17. MONDAY. Good. This is a promising start to the workweek. Local travel should be easy if you need to be out and about. There is a chance of striking up an interesting conversation with someone you meet on the bus or train, maybe on your way to work. Meetings of all kinds can prove far more straightforward than you imagined. A certain individual who has often been an adversary may now agree with your way of thinking. Life at home should be on an even keel. If you know that you have been difficult to live with recently, let the special person in your life know how much you appreciate their patience and good humor.

18. TUESDAY. Calm. You can achieve as little or as much as you want today. Superiors may be absent from the workplace or just too busy to breathe down your neck. It is up to you to get on with what needs doing. If you are looking for a secondhand car, this is a good time for making a deal. Try your local garage, or respond to an advertisement in the newspaper. If you are not technically minded, take along someone who is; their advice could be useful. This is also be a favorable time for advertising unwanted goods for sale; the extra cash could come in handy. Make a point of calling on a neighbor who is housebound and may be lonely.

19. WEDNESDAY. Misleading. In your business dealings you may need to adopt a tougher attitude. Guard against letting someone take advantage of you. Point out that your time is as valuable as theirs. It is up to you to insist on definite answers or arrangements. If you are single and romantically interested in someone at work, find out more about them before you make your interest obvious. There is a risk that they are already involved. Be wary of putting someone on a pedestal; they are almost sure to fall off it eventually. This is a time to accept human failings, both in yourself and in others.

20. THURSDAY. Deceptive. Career issues may come to a head. Feeling that you are in the wrong job is one thing, but knowing what would be right for you is another. Professional career guidance could point you in a new direction. You may find that there are more options open to you than you realize. Do not be guided by financial considerations alone. Getting into your true vocation may necessitate a drop in salary in the short term. If you have to make a formal presentation or deal with an important client today, it would be wise to devote extra time to your preparations. Concentrate on being concise and to the point.

21. FRIDAY. Unsettling. This is a hectic end to the working week. Trying to stick to a carefully worked out timetable will probably be pointless. You may be asked to abandon set tasks for the day in order to help out with a crisis. Be flexible. This is a time when it is in your own interests to prove that you can be counted on. Keep your cool when all those around you are arguing. In your home life be quick to spot the first symptoms of friction between you and a loved one. If you nip a problem in the bud you can avoid an upsetting clash. Be ready to compromise rather than insisting on having everything your own way.

22. SATURDAY. Variable. Children can be the source of extra expense for their Taurus parents. You may have to make a few sacrifices in order to meet their needs. However, be prepared to say no to requests which are clearly beyond your financial means at the moment. This is a favorable day for sports matches, whether you are participating or just going along as a spectator. If you want to learn a new sport, you could make better progress by paying for some lessons from an expert in the early stages. Lack of funds may prevent you from taking part in a certain social event this evening, but do not be too disappointed; another option which is much cheaper is foreseen.

23. SUNDAY. Disquieting. A friend who is involved in a new romance may not have much time for you at present. Try not to feel too left out, especially if you know that you have been guilty of the same selfishness in the past. This is a day for pursuing your own outside interests, whether or not you have company. If you are feeling a little low, avoid seeking comfort in excessive eating or drinking; this is apt to make you feel worse in the long run. Spend time with people who are able to draw you out. Children can be fun even though you may find their limitless energy exhausting. Their simple view of the world can be an eye-opener.

24. MONDAY. Rewarding. If your work depends on your creative skills this should be a highly productive start to the workweek. You are apt to be brimming with new ideas. Set to work at once while they are fresh in your mind. In the business world the morning is an excellent time for dealing with overseas contacts. Transactions of all kinds can be finalized without further delay. Jump at an opportunity to arrange a trip which combines business with pleasure. If you are now on vacation, today could be one of the highlights of your time away. A holiday romance for single Taurus people could be just what the doctor ordered.

25. TUESDAY. Good. It can be easier to handle run-of-the-mill jobs today. The trick lies in being methodical. Make a list of tasks in order of priority, then cross them off as you go. If you are at home you should be able to race through the usual domestic chores. Listen to talk radio or to some music as you work. Written work of all kinds is also favored. Your powers of concentration are strong. This is an auspicious day for signing a contract, perhaps for a new job or a new home. The evening favors entertaining at home. Ask some friends or workmates to come over for an impromptu dinner or dessert.

26. WEDNESDAY. Mixed. Work matters are mostly straightforward, but you may feel the pressure building as the day goes on. It can be all too easy to lose patience with a project which is not falling into place. Seek assistance from colleagues who are more experienced than you; they could come up with useful suggestions. There is nothing to be gained from struggling on alone. Be extra careful if operating machinery or using sharp instruments; there is a greater risk of an accident if you are in haste. Keep potentially dangerous objects, such as knives or matches, well out of the reach of children.

27. THURSDAY. Sensitive. You could be especially sensitive today. Comments or criticisms which would normally wash over you may hit a raw nerve. Try to be more objective. Avoid any head-to-head confrontation. Also guard against a tendency to brood over imagined slights or hurts. In the workplace you may sense a power struggle going on around you. A new boss or someone who has recently been promoted might be throwing their weight around just for the sake of making their presence felt. Your best policy is to ignore any display of egotism. Some tensions at home are also possible; try to spend most of the evening alone.

28. FRIDAY. Challenging. The placid side of the Taurus nature should be a big help to you. The day does not get off to an easy start; you need to maintain a sense of proportion. A sharp exchange at home, or a squabble over something petty, should be taken in stride. Minor disputes or differences need to be forgotten almost as soon as they happen. Success in work matters at the end of the week depends on your level of cooperation. Make an extra effort to understand how someone else's mind is working. The same applies to your personal life if you hope to put a current relationship on a more intimate footing.

29. SATURDAY. Fair. The earlier part of the day is the best time for an outing with your partner, such as shopping together or visiting relatives. If there are no particular errands to run, have a leisurely breakfast together. This can be a lucky day if you are hunting for a last-minute deal for a late summer vacation. There is a greater chance of finding a travel bargain, especially if you can jet off at short notice. Do not skimp on your travel or medical insurance. Even if you do not use it, you are paying for peace of mind. Before heading for a night out on the town, get a couple of hours of rest first.

30. SUNDAY. Satisfactory. If you are in the process of setting up a new home, some financial assistance could be forthcoming. Either your own family or your partner's relatives may ease your financial burden. This is a good day for a family get-together. If the weather is good you might opt for a barbeque. Eating out at a local restaurant can be a pleasant change to home cooking. If you are mostly townbound, take a drive to the countryside. The fresh air can blow away any cobwebs. The answer to a personal problem is apt to pop into your head once you stop agonizing about it. Trust your Taurus intuition rather than just your logic.

31. MONDAY. Cautious. The working week gets off to a rather frustrating start. Teamwork of any kind is likely to be complicated because of conflicting views or a clash of egos. Someone whose sense of fairness is recognized by all should be asked to arbitrate. Diplomatic solutions can be best, such as putting options to a vote. This is not a time when the person who shouts the loudest should win. In your personal life guard against collecting too many opinions from friends concerning a new venture or relationship. You will only end up with conflicting and confusing advice. Confide only in those who know and love you and are not likely to reveal what you tell them.

SEPTEMBER

1. TUESDAY. Buoyant. The new month is a good time to turn your thoughts to your long-term goals. If you are going to fulfill certain ambitions you may need to acquire some new skills. Find out about weekend or evening courses. Your employer might help out with the fees. If you are looking for last-minute travel accommodations, this can be a lucky day. Telephoning around can produce results. In the important relationships in your life, concentrate more on developing shared interests. Having an academic subject or a hobby in common can bring you closer together. Surprise your loved one with a special food treat, perhaps imported cheese or chocolate.

2. WEDNESDAY. Productive. This can be an especially productive day for Taurus men and women who work in a school or university setting. Preparing for a new term is sure to keep you busy. Meetings are likely to be successful. If you are taking up a new job you should feel that you are in the right place; colleagues can be very welcoming. Any new situation can be nerve-racking at first, but this is a day when you should be able to relax and enjoy the prospect rather than worrying about it. Cultural pursuits of all kinds are favored this evening. Try to get tickets for the ballet or theater. Invite a fellow enthusiast rather than going with someone whose tastes run along different lines.

3. THURSDAY. Unsettling. In the workplace this morning you could be greeted with some unexpected news. A colleague may be leaving, perhaps not of their own free will. Changes at the management level can come as a surprise or even as a shock; it may be hard to see the wisdom of certain decisions. Remind yourself that it is probably pointless to make waves about matters you cannot hope to change. Speak out only if you think you can influence the situation for the better. Work-related complaints should be put through proper channels, such as a union representative. This is not a good time for attempting to take matters into your own hands in any circumstances.

4. FRIDAY. Difficult. It probably seems it has been a particularly long week. It can be hard to muster the energy or enthusiasm for work matters today. You are not in the right frame of mind for making a major decision of any kind. Snap judgments could be misguided, especially if you are anxious to just get someone or something off your hands. It may be best to put certain matters on the back burner until you are more composed and under less stress. In this way you can be more confident of taking the right course of action. Avoid entertaining at home this evening; it could be too much like work. If you want to see friends, a cheerful, inexpensive local restaurant is a good option.

5. SATURDAY. Variable. If you are out shopping keep a careful watch on how much you spend. A friend who is better off than you may encourage you to splurge on items you cannot really afford. Paying cash rather than by credit or check could help you be realistic. For Taurus people who are politically minded, this is a good day for attending a rally or demonstration. Consider working for a candidate whose goals and policies agree with your own views no matter what party they represent. Avoid forcing your beliefs on those around you; a debate can turn hostile. Observe the rule of live and let live.

6. SUNDAY. Mixed. A friend who continually burdens you with problems needs to be discouraged from monopolizing your time and attention. Their neediness could be wearing thin. Try talking about your own difficulties in life and see how long they listen. There is no need to return a telephone call from someone you would prefer to see less frequently. This is a favorable day for a group outing, the more the merrier. Being part of a crowd fits your mood better than a one-to-one rendezvous. Young children can be great fun but also exceptionally demanding. Taurus single parents may want to join forces with a friend or a family member to keep youngsters occupied.

7. MONDAY. Good. Socially you are in demand at the moment; your calendar should be filling up with a variety of engagements. Take care, however, not to schedule too much; leave a few gaps which represent time just for you. Friends and neighbors are apt to be cooperative and willing to help out. Team efforts are highly favored. In the business world this is a favorable time for arranging meetings or even a large-scale convention. Getting together with others in your line of work can be an eye-opener. Exchange phone numbers with someone who promises to be a useful contact for the future.

8. TUESDAY. Quiet. You can work best if you work alone today. If you have the option to work from home, this is a favorable time for doing so. Plans for the future should be kept private at the moment. The time for discussion will come when you have done more research or given deeper thought to a certain subject. If you recently ended a close relationship, your thoughts may turn to this person. If there is true regret on both sides, this can be a good time for a fresh start. However, you both must be prepared to thrash out the problems which drove you apart in the first place. This could take time and willingness to forgive and forget.

9. WEDNESDAY. Rewarding. Get an early start since your workload is apt to be greater than usual. Plug away at a difficult project until you can see the light at the end of the tunnel. Your problem-solving abilities are at their best. Hard-won achievements can bring you a great deal of satisfaction. This is a good day for a job interview. Although there may be some tricky questions to answer, you are able to think on your feet and impress your listeners. Make sure that you have some questions of your own to ask as well. Catch up with personal telephone calls or letter writing this evening; do not stay up late.

10. THURSDAY. Demanding. Family obligations can be demanding. Someone may be pressuring you to give up an activity that you greatly enjoy. Try to meet them halfway rather than avoiding a commitment. It can be difficult not to take minor irritations out on those closest to you. Fortunately, friends and loved ones appear to be tolerant of your current mood swings. A quick apology for words which you know were rude can defuse a tense moment. In your business dealings this is not a day for being too conventional. Try out a new idea or take a calculated risk. If you are single, be bold enough to ask out someone to whom you are attracted both physically and intellectually.

11. FRIDAY. Pressured. The morning is the easiest part of the day. In the workplace problems can crop up from issues which you thought had been resolved. There may be no choice but to restart a certain project from scratch. Focus on work which requires close concentration before taking a break for lunch. Later it may be difficult to concentrate on one thing at a time. You may find yourself daydreaming in a meeting. Write down information rather than trusting it to memory. The first rumblings of discontent in a new relationship can be alarming, but one stressful evening does not necessarily spell the end. Tiredness can make you feel more vulnerable and rob you of your sense of humor.

12. SATURDAY. Changeable. Do not wander too far from home. Allow yourself to wake up without a blast from your alarm clock if possible. This is a good time for catching up with domestic chores; putting your home in order can have a therapeutic effect. Taurus parents may find that young children are at loose ends. Use your imagination to think up games, or get them involved in what you are doing in the home or garden. If a close relationship is going through a stressful period it may be wise to spend less time together than usual this weekend. Absence can make the heart grow fonder and differences seem unimportant.

13. SUNDAY. Satisfactory. This is a good day for visiting relatives, maybe a brother or sister, who live nearby or a short journey away. People who accept you just as you are can be the best company. Avoid any situation where you may feel that you are out of your depth or have to put on a show for other people's benefit. A change of environment can be helpful if you have a lot to think about. A day trip to the countryside should be worth the effort. Writing your thoughts or recent experiences in a journal can help you find the answers you are seeking, and decisions should then be easier to make. You have many options that are equally attractive. Do not be afraid to break with tradition.

14. MONDAY. Manageable. If you have been waiting to hear from someone special there may be a card or letter in today's mail. A thoughtful gesture from a loved one can put you in a buoyant mood. If you are involved in research of any kind, this promises to be a productive day. Obtaining the right information should be easier than usual. If you are stuck on a work project, enlist the assistance of your colleagues; their input can get the ball rolling again. Creative work of all kinds can bring you a great deal of satisfaction. Devote this evening to a favorite hobby. An evening class can be ideal for learning a new technique.

15. TUESDAY. Stressful. Guard against biting off more than you can chew. Be realistic about your own workload before volunteering to help out others. You could find yourself racing against the clock later in the day. Try not to make promises or give assurances which will be inconvenient to honor. A certain individual may be relying on you more than you realize and could be hurt if you have to let them down. Business dealings with overseas or long-distance contacts can be tricky. A language barrier may cause mix-ups. If you are traveling be prepared for delays. Carry valuable documents or other papers in your hand luggage so that they are with you at all times.

16. WEDNESDAY. Sensitive. If you are house hunting you may find the perfect place today. Be quick to put in your offer; there may be another purchaser hot on your heels. Business negotiations of all kinds require delicate handling. Guard against trying to force someone's hand. Applying too much pressure could result in a deal falling through. Patience can win a client's confidence. Although dramatic changes in the life of someone close to you can have an unsettling effect on you, the most you can do at the moment is offer moral support. Turn down an invitation to go out tonight. You can benefit more from relaxing at home.

17. THURSDAY. Calm. Everything should proceed according to schedule. In work matters you should start to see the fruits of your recent labor. New procedures or systems which you put into place are proving successful. A rival at work may be forced to admit your better judgment. Jealousy can be short-lived. This is the perfect day for taking some time off. Being at home by yourself can seem like a real haven from the usual hustle and bustle of day-to-day life. As a Taurus it is important to you to have a secure and peaceful home. Give some thought to home security measures; you may want to purchase a new smoke or burglar alarm.

18. FRIDAY. Variable. If you have the time to go shopping, treat yourself to something new to wear. Choose one good-quality designer item rather than several cheaper no-name ones. If you want to have your hair cut, stick to a stylist you know and trust; drastic change could be regretted. In work matters it is important not to deviate from tried-and-trusted methods even if they seem long-winded. Thoroughness and attention to detail are the keys to success. Slapdash work will probably be returned to you to do all over again. Put this evening aside to be with that special person in your life. If money is in short supply, eat at home rather than going out.

19. SATURDAY. Rewarding. As far as possible, aim to make this day for fun. You are not likely to be in the mood for housework or other domestic chores; just do the minimum. Family demands should not be pressing. If you have small children, a neighbor or relative may offer to watch them for a while so that you should have time to pursue a hobby or play a sport. A long lunch with a friend can give you the chance to switch off from life's pressures and catch up with the latest gossip. This evening favors inviting friends over for a meal followed by a game of cards or just some good conversation. Include a newcomer in your plans.

20. SUNDAY. Disconcerting. If you have children you may be feeling the weight of parental responsibilities more than usual. Keep in mind when considering disciplinary measures that unruly behavior can be a way of testing you or of establishing their own individuality. This is a favorable time for establishing house or family rules. It is important to arrive at these rules through discussion rather than one person laying down the law. In all of your personal relationships do not shy away from an argument or showdown. Letting off steam can be an effective way of reducing friction and getting to the real root of a recurring problem. However, be prepared to listen as well as talk.

21. MONDAY. Excellent. You should be brimming over with both mental and physical energy. This is an important start to the working week. Meetings and negotiations of all kinds should go in your favor. A certain achievement could be a real feather in your cap. This is also an excellent day for starting a new job or for accepting a promotion or transfer. You could make an impressive start. If the opportunity for advancement comes up, do not be afraid to go for it; colleagues are rooting for you. Do not underestimate your own abilities and strengths or the salary you deserve. You will not be criticized for blowing your own horn.

22. TUESDAY. Starred. If you have an ongoing health problem this can be a fortunate time for starting new treatment. There is no reason to be deterred by any doctor who tells you that you must learn to live with a condition or with constant pain. Keep seeking a remedy for yourself. Alternative medicine may be worth exploring at the moment, perhaps acupuncture or hydrotherapy. If you are unemployed there may be an offer of temporary or part-time work. The opportunity to work overseas can be tempting. Give the matter serious consideration, especially if you have no close ties at present and would enjoy some adventure in your life.

23. WEDNESDAY. Confusing. The working day is unlikely to get off to a productive start. It can take a long time to come to grips with a new work project or to tie up the loose ends of an existing one. If work is delegated to you, insist on clear and concise instructions. Guessing at what is required could create even more problems. Taurus students may be swamped with homework. The key to success lies is structuring your time effectively. Work out a timetable of regular study hours. Do not struggle with a difficult subject alone. Seek some help from other students or from an experienced tutor.

24. THURSDAY. Frustrating. A new romance may not be progressing as fast as you had hoped. This could be due to the fact that one or both of you is genuinely tied up with work or family commitments. The desire to spend time together is likely to be sincere, but finding that time may be the real problem. Try to plan ahead more than usual. Do not rely too much on a colleague to support you regarding a work issue. This person may privately believe that it is your problem and not theirs. You may feel alone in your battle, but stick to your guns when it comes to issues which are bottom-line for you. Your Taurus conscience will not let you compromise your principles.

25. FRIDAY. Lucky. Work matters which have been troublesome during the week can be resolved now. A close working relationship is moving from strength to strength. Because one of you is strong where the other is weak, you make a good team. If you are self-employed this is a favorable time for taking on a partner. Company mergers are also favored. You could get a lucky break if you are negotiating a new contract or to change the terms of an existing one. Self-employed Taurus are more likely to pick up well-paid work. If you have room in your garage at home, now can be a good time for renting it out. Someone you know could be looking for just such a place.

26. SATURDAY. Exciting. In your personal relationships this is a time to establish greater intimacy. If you are in a committed relationship you may now decide to set up home together or even talk about marriage. New romance can quickly show signs of being really special, particularly if your spiritual beliefs are in close harmony. There might be a surprise visit from a friend or former neighbor whom you have not seen in a while. Be welcoming even if you had made other plans for the day. Do not miss the chance to catch up with their news. Celebrations of all kinds are favored tonight.

27. SUNDAY. Productive. If you are in the process of moving do not take on too much alone. If you cannot afford the services of a professional moving company, seek assistance from your friends or family members. Remind yourself that there is always more to do than you think. This is a good time for home decorating, but again, do not underestimate how long certain jobs can take. Entertaining at home can be fun as long as you have the right mix of people. Be sensitive when it comes to whom you invited. One unmarried person, for example, could feel out in the cold if everyone else is in couples. Some useful advice regarding a personal matter can crop up in the course of general conversation.

28. MONDAY. Manageable. Long-distance travel is favored, especially if you are returning from vacation or from a weekend break or leaving on a work-related trip. Make allowances for jet lag, which may catch up with you later in the day. A health worry is probably not as serious as you imagine. Anxiety may be playing tricks with your imagination. Do not ignore the worry; make an appointment to see your doctor to put your mind at ease. Be sure to get some physical exercise today, particularly if you have a sedentary job. Someone you argued with recently may be eager to restore good relations. Do not stand on your dignity; accept an apology with good grace, or offer one if you were in the wrong.

29. TUESDAY. Challenging. Although this is likely to be a busy day and you may find yourself stretched to the limit, you should enjoy the flow of adrenalin. Luck is on your side. Coupling this with hard work means there is very little that you cannot achieve once you put your mind to it. Learning a new skill or subject can be easy; you should have a natural grasp of the ideas put to you. In business dealings others will almost certainly recognize that you are a force to be reckoned with. If you are involved in litigation of any kind, there could be significant progress with your case today. A court decision is likely to go in your favor.

30. WEDNESDAY. Fair. The earlier part of the day is the best time for creative work of all kinds. If you need to implement new ideas in the workplace, make sure that you first research all the facts. Half-baked schemes can be worse than none at all. Turn on the charm with someone you want to impress or win over to your side. You may sense that someone seems interested in you romantically. If the feeling is not mutual, guard against giving out mixed messages just because your ego is flattered. Flirting may seem harmless but could land you in emotional trouble. A long-distance call made or received is apt to be the highlight of this evening.

OCTOBER

1. THURSDAY. Variable. An ongoing drama in the life of another family member, maybe a parent or in-law, can have a direct effect on you. Although you may wish you could distance yourself from it, your Taurus nature includes a strong sense of family duty. This will probably keep you from avoiding any involvement and might mean having to change your own plans for the day. A superior at work may be in a volatile mood. If this person is looking for someone to blame for something which has gone wrong, make sure that you do not become the scapegoat. This is a time when emotional stress is more likely to appear as physical symptoms; treat the mental as well as the bodily ailment.

2. FRIDAY. Demanding. Morning hours are the more demanding part of the day. Jobs which you have been putting off all week now have to be tackled and finished. Remind yourself how virtuous and carefree you will feel once you get them out of the way. If you have scheduled an important meeting or appointment, make a point of clearing your mind of all other issues. Success depends on your ability to focus clearly on the matter at hand. Avoid aggressive tactics in your work, especially with someone who is older or more experienced than you. Listening rather than talking can put you at a distinct advantage.

3. SATURDAY. Relaxing. Whatever work matters are on your mind at the moment, this is a day to make an effort to ignore them. Try to sleep late; recharging your batteries can do a lot to lift your general mood and sense of well-being. Read the morning paper to catch up with what is going on in the world. Consider making a donation to a person or charity that is featured in a news article. Focus on friends as well as family members, especially those you have known for a long time. New friendships made at this time are likely to be lasting. Accept an invitation for this evening to go out as part of a group, although you may pair up later.

4. SUNDAY. Easygoing. The relaxing but sociable mood of the weekend continues today. If you have overnight guests you may want to ask them to stay another day or arrange a return visit in the near future. The quality of your life is linked with the quality of your friendships. Do not neglect close friends if you are caught up in a new romance; look for ways to mix the two. A new partner is sure to be welcomed into your existing social circle. Do your bit for ecology by bringing plastic, glass, paper, and aluminum to a collection point. Try to eliminate or at least reduce your use of chemicals outdoors.

5. MONDAY. Pleasant. If your working life has been increasingly stressful, now is the time to take control of your job rather than letting it control you. Keep in mind that nothing is worth sacrificing your health for, which should encourage you to start taking certain matters or individuals less seriously. Take back your power. Conserve your energy by refusing to get involved in issues which neither concern nor interest you. There could be good news on the financial front, such as a tax rebate or even a legacy. This is a time when you can benefit from other people's generosity. Do not hesitate to enter a competition, even if you have never done so before.

6. TUESDAY. Deceptive. You might have to tap into extra reserves of energy to see you through the day. Other people's demands can be exhausting, especially if they are looking to you for solutions to problems which are unclear. Focus on facts rather than opinions or hearsay. If you are traveling a long distance to pick up someone at the airport, call ahead to check departure or arrival times; there is a greater risk of delays. If you are planning a trip for business or pleasure, be sure to confirm flight or hotel reservations. This evening favors staying home and enjoying a good book.

7. WEDNESDAY. Useful. You are apt to have a lot of nervous energy, which can be beneficial if you put it to good use. You should find it easier to inspire others if you work in a teaching or managerial capacity. Do not sit on the fence in discussions of any kind. Come out and say exactly what you think even if you raise a few eyebrows. You might even decide to deliberately play devil's advocate in order to liven up the proceedings; someone is sure to rise to the bait. Socially, this is a time for breaking with old habits and patterns of behavior. Try something new to you, even if it seems frightening at first.

8. THURSDAY. Variable. If you are studying, writing, or holding meetings, the morning is the best part of the day for getting down to hard work. You could surprise yourself with how much you achieve before lunch. A shopping trip for personal items should be successful, especially if you need clothes for a special occasion. Consider treating yourself to a new cologne or to some jewelry. A good wine can make the perfect gift for someone whose personal tastes are unknown to you. A night out could end up costing you a lot more than you expect. Do not pick up the tab for someone who often does not pay their fair share.

9. FRIDAY. Good. You may get a chance to earn some extra cash. This is a favorable time for finding part-time work or a weekend job, especially if you have to fit your hours around family commitments. Self-employed Taurus people should have a very productive end to the workweek. Extra customers may come your way by referral. Your cash flow situation should be positive. Invoices which have been outstanding for some time could now be settled in full. As a Taurus you are known for a love of good food. This evening favors hosting or attending a dinner party. Have fun trying out food that is new to you or is served in a new way.

10. SATURDAY. Fortunate. This is a fine time for making new resolutions concerning your health. You might decide to start eating more sensibly, either to lose weight or just to improve your overall sense of well-being. It can be easier now to kick a habit that you know is bad for you, such as smoking or even biting your nails. A regular exercise schedule can be difficult to stick to, especially if your life is usually very busy. Try walking short distances rather than taking the car or bus, or walk up stairs instead of waiting for an elevator; this can keep you in trim. If you are wondering how to get to know someone better, do not hesitate to enlist the help of a mutual friend.

11. SUNDAY. Misleading. Someone may break a date with you, possibly because of ill health. If the same person seems to be in the habit of letting you down, you may suspect the given reason is an excuse. However, give the benefit of the doubt on this occasion, but be wary about relying on this individual again. At home arguments can flare up over little things, but there could be deeper issues at stake. If someone is showing their anger in an indirect fashion, try to find out what their real grievance is. Go slowly if embarking upon a new romance. Expecting too much too soon could be a mistake.

12. MONDAY. Frustrating. This is apt to be a frustrating start to the workweek. Taurus commuters may be faced with delays this morning. There is a greater risk of train cancellations or of traffic being heavier than usual. Try to avoid routes where you know there are road repairs in progress. A letter you are expecting is unlikely to turn up in today's mail. You may wonder if someone has forgotten you. A recent argument or painful episode with a loved one could be weighing on you, but try not to brood over it. The time is not yet right for a reconciliation; you could even make matters worse by trying to force the issue.

13. TUESDAY. Mixed. If you are in the process of buying or selling property there could be some delays ahead. Administrative errors may be the cause. The wording of a contract may have to be changed to protect your interests. If you are hoping to buy a place with your partner or with a friend, do not assume that you both have the same tastes. Be prepared to compromise so that you are both happy. This is a good time for updating your household insurance. Make sure that you are covered for accidental damage as well as fire or theft. A family squabble may cast a cloud over an evening at home. Avoid taking sides in a dispute between loved ones.

14. WEDNESDAY. Good. A work project may have been hampered by other people's mistakes or their slowness in providing you with information. Now, however, you should be able to go full steam ahead. Obstacles which have been frustrating work of all kinds can now be removed or overcome. Putting pressure on those with influence can work in your favor; do not be afraid to make a nuisance of yourself in order to get what you want. At home this is a favorable time for embarking upon decorating or building. This evening favors a family night out, perhaps to eat out and see a movie. Children will enjoy being included in your plans.

15. THURSDAY. Changeable. Push ahead with your own plans and ambitions, especially if your work is of a creative nature. Do not wait for others to inspire you; self-motivation is what counts. Avoid comparing yourself with others in your line of work. There will always be those who are better than you are and those who are not quite as successful. Professional jealousy is a waste of time and energy. What you achieve in your own right is likely to bring you the most satisfaction. In a personal relationship the time has come to bring up a sensitive issue. Stay calm and consider any criticism which is leveled at you; it could be justified.

16. FRIDAY. Quiet. This should be a pleasant end to the working week. Deals of all kinds can be finalized more easily and with mutual satisfaction. This can be a favorable time for taking a valued client or a potential customer out to lunch. Working relationships can be improved by socializing outside the office. Do not hesitate to join in on after-hours social or sporting events. Taurus singles could find new romance just a few doors or desks away. Do whatever you find relaxing this evening, whether this is staying home or going out to meet up with friends.

17. SATURDAY. Challenging. The Taurus nature sometimes chooses the line of least resistance in order to avoid conflicts. Today, however, your bid for the quiet life is unlikely to be successful. Your nearest and dearest may hound you over minor issues or insist on your company at an event which does not appeal to you. Try to find the balance between meeting their needs as well as your own, so that they in turn will meet you halfway. Obstinate refusal or an unwillingness to compromise could lead to an angry scene. Harsh words can be difficult to forget or forgive. If you are out on the town tonight, steer clear of nightspots which have a reputation for trouble.

18. SUNDAY. Rewarding. Do not let time slip through your fingers. Even if you were out late you may still wake up earlier than usual. Restlessness can drive you to get up. An early morning walk or workout can boost you physically and mentally. This is a good time for tackling odd jobs around the house. If a personal relationship has been causing you some heartache recently, things should take a turn for the better today. You should get the feeling that you are regaining control, especially of your own feelings. It can be easier to make a clean break from a relationship which you know is going nowhere.

19. MONDAY. Successful. If you are unemployed you are likely to pick up some work today. Someone who has promised to find a position for you may now come up with a solid offer. Promises or assurances of all kinds should be honored, restoring your faith in human nature. If you want to say a special thank you to someone, the traditional gift of flowers is sure to be appreciated. Your partner may go to great lengths to make you feel special; enjoy being spoiled. This is also a good time for pampering yourself with a massage or a manicure. You may want to splurge on tickets to a concert, play, or sporting event.

20. TUESDAY. Unsettling. The easy start to the working week may have lulled you into a false sense of security. Difficulties which you encounter today remind you of the dangers of becoming complacent. Someone's motives could be suspect; keep up your guard until you know each other better and feel that you are on solid ground. There is a greater risk that a certain individual is not being totally truthful for reasons which are yet to be revealed. A health problem may prove difficult to diagnose. Try not to attach too much importance to an initial opinion. Treat the symptoms while continuing to seek a cure for the cause.

21. WEDNESDAY. Productive. The middle of the week is once again a busy time. Negotiations of all kinds are almost certainly to involve long meetings or constant communication with someone at a distance. For Taurus employers this can be a favorable time to advertise for new staff. If you are conducting interviews today aim for an informal atmosphere. Make sure, however, to follow up references. Sales work, either over the telephone or face-to-face, can be highly rewarding. Verbal agreements are likely to be honored to the letter. If you are single, accept a blind date; there is a greater chance of finding that you have a lot in common.

22. THURSDAY. Tricky. Keep in mind that you cannot please all of the people all of the time. Decisions which have to be made are undoubtedly not going to be welcomed by all, but the wishes of the majority now have to take precedence. Dealings with overseas contacts can be especially troublesome. A misunderstanding from a previous conversation may come to light. If you are traveling a long distance, make sure that all of your luggage is clearly labeled; there is a greater risk of something going astray. Do not ignore travel insurance. If you are renting a car, obtain a copy of the agreement and check it over.

23. FRIDAY. Challenging. In work matters you can be more influential than you think. Attempts from others to undermine you should be ignored or sidestepped. Do not sabotage your own career opportunities in an attempt to avoid professional jealousy. If a certain individual has the ability to intimidate you, it is important not to let this show. Present a calm and controlled front even if you are trembling inside. This evening you may have to put duty before pleasure. Family responsibilities can be especially demanding or restrictive. A personal arrangement may have to be postponed until a less stressful time.

24. SATURDAY. Confusing. There is a lot being asked of you. As you try to plan and organize you are apt to encounter unforeseen complications. Consider whether you are trying to deal with too much all at once. This is a time for reducing your commitments rather than taking on more. Be prepared to say no to someone who is often difficult to refuse. Your expectations of others at this time may be too high. A romance which is just beginning may not be plain sailing. You might have to come right out and ask if you have the same ideas of where the relationship is heading. Guard against playing second fiddle to anyone.

25. SUNDAY. Sensitive. Tread carefully around your loved ones. The temptation to offer advice when you have not been asked for it is strong, but there is a greater risk that your well-intentioned words can be mistaken for interference. You also run the risk of being patronizing without realizing it. If you are worried about someone, find a natural way to open up a discussion. Take the role of listener more than talker. Cultural or intellectual pursuits of all kinds are favored. It can be worth giving up some of your free time to go to a lecture or take part in a workshop on a subject which interests you.

26. MONDAY. Good. You should now be well into the swing of new responsibility that you took on after the summer lull. Today you can make significant progress with written work. Despite your busy schedule, do not be tempted to skip a lecture or meeting; you could miss out on some valuable information. Find a way to get involved in charitable activities. You can make excellent friendships through any sort of group interaction. If you are involved in a legal case, this is a favorable time for pushing ahead. A court decision made today is likely to go in your favor. Be on hand to help a child who may need assistance with homework this evening.

27. TUESDAY. Stressful. A close relationship is going through a stressful period. Someone may not be revealing as much as you would like to know. However, many of your fears are unfounded. Try not to let your imagination take over; force yourself to look at the facts. In a new romance it is unwise to dwell too much on past ties on either side. What matters is the here and now; look forward rather than back. At work this is a day for keeping a low profile. Your own areas of responsibility should take priority. Seek the advice of someone you trust if a particular project has you stumped. A totally new approach could be the best solution.

28. WEDNESDAY. Variable. You may not be able to stick to your usual routine. In the workplace there could be some changes going on at the management level which have a direct effect on you. A crisis could mean that you have to abandon whatever you are doing at the time. Do not let a sense of urgency panic you. Problems which arise today demand calm, objective handling. A positive approach can ultimately produce positive results. For Taurus people going through the process of court proceedings, this can be a trying time. Practical details must be sorted out, and this can be done more amicably than you may think.

29. THURSDAY. Frustrating. Your powers of concentration are not at their best. Make a point of not relying on your memory. Write down important information or telephone messages which have to be passed on. Being efficient is likely to cost you extra effort but is sure to be appreciated by those with whom you work or live. If you have had more than your fair share of disappointment lately, this is a time when you discover who your true friends are. A close friend of the opposite sex could prove especially supportive and sympathetic. Others will rally around if you ask for help; there is no need to carry a heavy burden alone.

30. FRIDAY. Useful. The working week is likely to end on a high note. A project which you have been nursing along for some time could now draw to a satisfying conclusion. Your recent achievements may be formally recognized, perhaps with a bonus or letter of commendation. An upset with a friend should be forgiven and forgotten; it can be a relief to let a difficult subject drop. Romance is high on the agenda for Taurus people who are unattached at the moment. Someone new coming into your life at this time may be the right person for you. The evening favors a group night out, perhaps to a nightclub or open house. Enjoy putting on your finest clothes and getting into a party mood.

31. SATURDAY. Deceptive. Although you may start the day in an optimistic mood, a certain individual seems set on pouring cold water on your high spirits or downplaying your suggestions for the day. Criticisms can catch you off guard. You may feel that you cannot do or say anything right. The Taurus nature is usually placid, but you can explode if pushed too far. Do not feel guilty if someone goads you to the point of losing your temper. A full-scale argument might actually be the way to clear the air. Plans for this evening may be difficult to finalize until the last minute. Try not to rely on any one person for a night out. It is important to keep all your options open.

NOVEMBER

1. SUNDAY. Mixed. On this sociable day even if you live alone people are likely to drop by or call to suggest going out together. Someone may go to great lengths to persuade you to join them, in part because they need some moral support. Overcome your initial impulse to stay home. The more adventurous you are, the more fun you will have. There is a risk of running into someone you would prefer to avoid, but you should be able to sidestep getting trapped into a one-on-one conversation. A family get-together can be a lively affair. Minor friction or squabbles should not be taken too seriously. Have a camera on hand so that you can update the family photograph album.

2. MONDAY. Quiet. If you are owed some time off, this is the perfect time for taking a day to yourself, especially if those you live with are out for the day. You are sure to benefit from time alone; your need for company or conversation is minimal. Solitude gives you the space you need to think through any personal issues. The time is not right for gathering other people's opinions; decisions need to be made independently and irrespective of what others might think. In your business dealings this is a day for playing a lone hand. Draw upon your past experience. Keep more ambitious plans a secret for a little while longer.

3. TUESDAY. Uncertain. A health problem may require consulting a doctor. If you have an appointment with a specialist, be sure to get answers to all your questions. Writing them down in advance can be helpful. If a friend or colleague is hospitalized, try to find time to visit, or at least send some flowers if time is at a premium. You may not feel very energetic. It can be difficult to arouse enthusiasm for routine tasks. However, force yourself to deal with at least the most pressing matters. In your working life guard against using up too many favors. Spontaneous offers of help could have strings attached; it may be better to struggle through as best you can on your own.

4. WEDNESDAY. Good. Taurus people are recognized for a high degree of ambition. This is a favorable time for pushing yourself forward in the workplace. Do not be afraid to draw attention to your recent achievements if you sense that they have been overlooked by those in power; sometimes you need to blow your own horn. Taking on more responsibility without being asked, or putting in some overtime, should impress the right people. This is a good time for shopping for clothes. Try out new colors or styles. Seek advice from someone whose taste you admire. Feeling good about the way you look can boost your self-confidence. For Taurus singles, this evening is a propitious time for a first date.

5. THURSDAY. Disquieting. Take a close look at your financial position. If you have just been paid, now is the time to work out a budget for the rest of the month; do this with your partner if you have a joint account. There is a chance that you may not be as well off as you think. Your current expenses may be greater than your income, but efforts to economize in little things could soon even the balance. For instance, in the supermarket be alert for special sales and resist imported delicacies. Also give some thought to your long-term finances. If your employer does not provide you with a pension, now is a good time to start one of your own.

6. FRIDAY. Frustrating. Creative work of all kinds can be frustrating. What at first seemed to be a good idea may now prove impractical or too expensive to pursue. In any of your dealings, a problem is unlikely to be resolved just by throwing more money at it. It may be best to just cut your losses now. Someone close to you could break a promise; find out their reasons before going on the attack. They are probably facing problems and deadlines of their own. A new love interest might not live up to your expectations. If someone is not as free and unattached as they had led you to believe, now is the time to bow out with your dignity intact.

7. SATURDAY. Difficult. You may feel very much on your own at the moment, especially if you have just ended a relationship. Guard against patching up a friendship or romance in the belief that someone is better than no one at all. It should be more productive to concentrate on the advantages of being free to come and go as you please. This is a time for some self-questioning. You can learn a lot about yourself if you put your own behavior under the microscope. Acknowledge your faults while at the same time reminding yourself of your many strengths. Looking at childhood experiences can give you clues to your current behavior patterns. A brother or sister may be able to shed more light on certain events that are only hazy memories to you.

8. SUNDAY. Excellent. Recent efforts in a personal relationship should start to pay off. Your own soul-searching may have provided you with a new insight and a fresh approach. A deeper understanding of a significant person in your life can bring you a great deal of contentment and reassurance. This is a starred day for celebrations of all kinds, including a wedding or engagement. Different friends and all generations should mix easily. This is also a good time for introducing a new partner to your family or social circle. Forging closer bonds with a child can be rewarding. Be lavish with love and praise when they seek your approval.

9. MONDAY. Lucky. This is a busy start to the workweek. Plan your time carefully so that you can get through all that awaits you. If you are starting a new job or taking on new responsibility, you may wonder what you have let yourself in for at first. Enthusiasm and a willingness to learn can carry you through. By the end of the day you should feel that you have made an impressive start. If you are house hunting at the moment there is a greater chance of finding the place of your dreams. An owner who is in a hurry to sell may accept an offer much lower than the asking price. A gamble could pay off, but do not risk more than you can afford to lose.

10. TUESDAY. Rewarding. If you are at home, race through the usual domestic chores so that you have some time for yourself. If you have children make sure that they are pulling their weight at home according to their age and ability. Encouraging more self-reliance can be healthy for both them and you. On the job this is a good day for teamwork of all kinds. Be willing to lend your time and expertise to those who are less experienced than you. A certain working relationship is going from strength to strength. If you are looking for work at the moment, do not hesitate to get in touch with someone who could pull some strings on your behalf.

11. WEDNESDAY. Successful. For Taurus professionals this is a good day for being office-based. You should be able to tie loose ends and clear out your in basket. If you have to arrange meetings, ask others to come to you rather than the other way around. This is a favorable time for off-the-record discussions. If you have a grievance at work, you may be able to resolve it yourself without involving a superior or going through official channels. If a loved one is more withdrawn than usual, take the trouble to find out what is wrong. Offering sympathy or true interest could be all that is needed to lift their spirits and clear the air.

12. THURSDAY. Stressful. At work you are apt to be under more pressure than usual. If you are racing against the clock in order to reach a deadline, you may have to skip a lunch break or reschedule less urgent matters. Stress can show up as physical symptoms, such as a nagging headache or an aching back. Consider whether you are taking on too much all at once or are making unnecessary work for yourself. If it is a case of being overburdened, ask a superior to lighten your load. In a personal relationship be quick to spot undercurrents of discontent. People are unlikely to volunteer information; you will have to come right out and ask them what is wrong.

13. FRIDAY. Fair. Working with children should be especially rewarding today, although you may have to tap into extra reserves of patience from time to time. Keep in mind that you may have to exert your own authority. In work matters guard against a tendency to rush headlong into a new project without sufficient advance preparation. Do not brush off advice from a colleague; it could get you over a hump. Enthusiasm alone is not sufficient when it comes to selling others on a new idea. They expect you to back up your claims with facts and figures. Socializing after work could develop into a late night out. Dancing or playing a team match can be excellent for working off stress.

14. SATURDAY. Satisfactory. Even if you do not normally work on the weekends you might choose to put in some extra hours today at home or in the office. A particular project that has fired up your imagination can make you impatient to push ahead with it. If your working life has become boring, now is a favorable time to begin planning a change. Look at the help-wanted section in quality newspapers. Send off application for jobs that appeal to you. Later in the day the emphasis is on having fun. Opt for the company of those people who are positive and exciting companions. This evening favors seeking the unusual rather than the commonplace.

15. SUNDAY. Good. This is an active day. Do not waste too much time sleeping in or lazing around the house. The morning is the best time for physical exercise of all kinds, with the emphasis on fitness rather than competition. If you are playing in a team match, have fun as well as just trying to win. This is a good time for eating out rather than cooking at home. Choose a favorite restaurant, or accept an invitation to a friend's house. Social gatherings of all kinds are likely to be successful. You may get the chance to play matchmaker between two of your friends or even neighbors.

16. MONDAY. Deceptive. Do not push yourself too hard, especially if you start the day feeling physically under par. Taking a day off could actually nip an illness in the bud. Do not fall into the trap of believing that things will not get done without you; someone else is capable of taking over in your absence. This is a good time for making changes in your diet, whether you want to lose weight or just eat more health-consciously. Boost your system with extra vitamins and more sleep. Traveling could take longer than expected. Keep your timetable flexible so that being delayed does not create a crisis or throw you into a tailspin.

17. TUESDAY. Variable. There may be surprise news from a colleague perhaps announcing a promotion, transfer, or acceptance of a new job. Although you may be sad to see them go, this could be a cloud with a silver lining for you. Changes can create opportunities for you much sooner than expected. A superior is apt to be in a difficult mood. It is probably safer to ignore their irritable outbursts or excess criticism; they may be under more pressure than they are willing to reveal. A personal relationship should bring you a great deal of contentment at the moment. A new romance is likely to progress swiftly, especially if you share a number of outside interests.

18. WEDNESDAY. Fortunate. There is very little to hold you back. It should be easier to tackle difficulties with a positive and determined attitude. Your cheerfulness is bound to rub off on those around you, making work more of a pleasure than a duty. New friendships made at this time are apt to be lasting ones. If a certain relationship has been causing you anxiety lately, this is the perfect time for a fresh start. Try to wipe the slate clean of old grievances and problems. Make some plans for the future together rather than dwelling in the past. Happy news for someone close to you is likely, perhaps inspiring you to plan a surprise party for them.

19. THURSDAY. Fair. If it is difficult to make financial ends meet at the moment, there may be a chance to earn some extra money. Drive a hard bargain if you are selling your services; you cannot afford to take on work for anything less than the recognized fee. Do not offer discounts to anyone unless there is a case of genuine hardship. Keep in mind the importance of putting a proper value on what you do. Taurus employees who are expected to put in overtime should insist on extra pay or compensatory time off. Keep a personal issue to yourself for now. You need to analyze your own feelings before seeking out other opinions.

20. FRIDAY. Unsettling. Administrative work of all kinds can be troublesome. You may be tempted to put off writing letters or returning telephone calls, but at least try to clear away the more urgent ones. If you have forms to fill out, be sure to include all relevant information. Otherwise you could hold up the proceedings. Ask for clarification if there are questions which you do not fully understand; guesswork is likely to be wrong. Business proposals or decisions should be put in writing in order to avoid a possible misunderstanding. Confirm any social arrangement for this evening, especially if it was made some time ago.

21. SATURDAY. Variable. Children can be especially demanding. If you do not feel able to keep up with them, get some extra help. Try to arrange for another parent to swap child care sessions with you. In this way you can be sure of time for yourself. If you are going shopping, head for a mall which provides a good mix of stores. Someone close to you may make you angry. If you keep your negative feelings bottled up you will succeed only in creating an even more tense atmosphere. No matter how painful a subject may be, this is a time when open, frank discussion could be profitable. Just be sure you are talking together, not lecturing or preaching at someone.

22. SUNDAY. Buoyant. This is the perfect time for a day away from home, especially if the weather is unusually good. Make an early start. Drive or take the train to revisit a place which has special memories for you. Traveling is likely to be not only trouble-free but enjoyable. Cultural activities of all kinds are also favored, such as visiting a museum or art gallery. An exhibition related to a special interest should be well worth a visit. If a loved one now lives abroad or will be away for some time, treat yourself to a long-distance telephone call. Talking together can lift your spirits and make them seem closer. Give free rein to your Taurus creativity this evening.

23. MONDAY. Disquieting. This is unlikely to be an easy start to the workweek. Legal matters of all kinds need to be handled with extreme caution. An adversary could have several surprises in store for you. If you are embarking upon litigation of any kind, be prepared for a long battle. Ask yourself if the issue at stake is worth long-term stress. It may be better to cut your losses. Seek professional advice. If you are taking an examination today or interviewing for a job you may feel that you have not done yourself justice. Others, however, are likely to have the same feelings. Avoid carrying a large amount of cash; there is a danger of losing it or of spending too freely.

24. TUESDAY. Fair. The morning is the easier part of the day. If you have written work of any kind to do, aim to complete it by lunchtime. You should also find studying easier in the morning, when there are likely to be fewer distractions. Get some extra help with a subject that is a struggle for you. Later in the day there can be some unforeseen problems in the workplace. You may have to think fast on your feet, but try to avoid making a major decision without first consulting those who will be affected most. Joint finances may require some discussion this evening. Be honest with your partner if you know that you have been overspending recently.

25. WEDNESDAY. Good. It is a fortunate day for an interview. Although some questions may come as a surprise to you, it should be easy to talk with a potential employer. Competition is unlikely to be as intense as you fear. You may be offered a position on the spot. Meetings of all kinds should be successful, and they should run on time as well. In the workplace this is a favorable day for dealing with financial matters such as departmental budgets or filling out expense forms. If you are self-employed, find time to confer with your accountant. Some ingenuity by a financial professional can mean a lower tax bill for you at the end of the year.

26. THURSDAY. Mixed. An upset among family members may not be as serious as you at first believe. An older relative may go to great lengths to ensure that you are not blamed for events which are out of your control. Let this person know how much you appreciate their support. If you are unemployed do not hesitate to use contacts you already have, perhaps from a former job. A certain individual is willing to put in a good word for you if you ask. Later in the day you need to handle a proposition with great care, especially if a large sum of money is at stake. Do not give financial backing to any venture which appears risky.

27. FRIDAY. Disconcerting. In your working life you may sense that there is a great deal going on behind closed doors at the moment. It is probably best to ignore any rumors which are flying around; they are unlikely to be based on fact. Make a point of distinguishing between hearsay and actual evidence. In this way anyone who is bent on making trouble will soon have the wind knocked out of their sails. If someone close to you is acting out of character, do not question them too closely. Trust that they will confide in you when the time is right. Single Taurus people could strike up an immediate bond with a stranger this evening.

28. SATURDAY. Fair. With the holiday season less than a month away, it is not too soon to make a start on your Christmas shopping. Careful budgeting could pay off. Work out what you can afford to spend on gifts, especially if you are buying for a lot of people. It may be helpful to agree to a price limit with family members if money is tight. If your plans involve a break with tradition, do not postpone letting your family know. It can be hurtful to spring sudden changes on them at the last minute. If you need to discuss a sensitive subject with a loved one, pick a good moment today. Tact and delicacy are essential to reaching a compromise solution.

29. SUNDAY. Exciting. Your plans for a quiet day are unlikely to come to anything. This is a time when you may be asked out unexpectedly. Someone may refuse to take no for an answer, so you might as well go along with their plans right from the start. You will be glad that you did. Meeting an old flame, or friends from your past, can lead to a fun occasion. In romance this is a time for following your heart rather than your head. Too much analyzing could lead you in the wrong direction. You can afford to follow your good Taurus instincts, even if others accuse you of being headstrong. If you are married, treat your partner to a special day out; they are sure to welcome some loving spoiling.

30. MONDAY. Difficult. Taurus people who work full time are likely to suffer from Monday morning blahs today. An attack of the blues can be difficult to shake off. You need to exert greater self-discipline to get through the day's tasks. A personal problem could be weighing on your mind, making it almost impossible to concentrate fully on other matters. Try to take the pressure off yourself wherever possible. Someone could be playing mind games with you. It may be time to get angry rather than depressed, forcing them to acknowledge that they have pushed you too far. When others see that you are not going to back down you are apt to get your way.

DECEMBER

1. TUESDAY. Productive. This is a busy day and not the time for sitting on the fence. The more enterprising you can be, the more likely you are to succeed. Test out unusual or unconventional ideas and approaches; they could serve you better than traditional methods. Proving that you can lead as well as follow is the way to impress a superior. Do not take for granted a possible promotion at work. You need to stand out from the crowd. An older relative, perhaps a parent, may surprise you by sharing exciting plans of their own. Be sure to give them your enthusiastic support. Do not put off purchasing airline tickets or making other travel arrangements.

2. WEDNESDAY. Uncertain. If you are starting your holiday shopping, guard against a tendency toward extravagance. Do not spend as if money grows on trees. You are apt to regret your impulsiveness when it comes to balancing your checkbook later. Try to pay in cash rather than using a credit card. Avoid taking on new credit unless it is interest-free and with affordable repayments. If you are looking for a place to hold an office party, be prepared to shop around; prices could vary considerably. Socially you are apt to be in demand. However, guard against booking up too many evenings and leaving no free time for yourself.

3. THURSDAY. Variable. If you are unemployed or struggling to make ends meet, be sure that you are claiming all the benefits to which you are entitled. There may be extra help available for fuel bills during the winter months, or a group ready and willing to provide extra food. Taurus business people approaching the busiest time of year may decide to boost advertising or launch special offers. The extra sales that publicity produces could soon cover the initial layout. For Taurus men and women who are weight conscious, now is a good time to start a diet. Although you may not be able to shed surplus pounds during the festive season, at least you can avoid putting on more weight.

4. FRIDAY. Easygoing. This quiet end to the week should come as a relief if you have been especially busy. Deal with a backlog of smaller tasks which were put aside during busier times; in this way you can start next week with an uncluttered desk. If you need more insurance coverage, be sure to shop around for the best deal. This is not a lucky time for buying a secondhand car; mechanical problems may only come to light after you have bought it. Pinning someone down to a definite arrangement for this evening or the weekend could be difficult. Have other options up your sleeve so that you are not left high and dry.

5. SATURDAY. Mixed. Make a list of people to whom you want to send Christmas cards. If you are buying your cards today, consider buying from a charity as a way of making a donation. Taurus people who are artistically inclined may decide to make cards or gifts. This is also a good way of keeping children occupied. Household chores are likely to take up more time than usual. Pace yourself when it comes to work which is physically demanding; there is a greater risk of overdoing. Opt for a quiet evening at home rather than a night out on the town. You need extra sleep before holiday parties fill your weekends.

6. SUNDAY. Disquieting. This day may not go according to plan. There is a greater possibility of arrangements being canceled on short notice. Someone's excuse for letting you down could sound somewhat lame. Taurus people who are unattached should not invest too much hope in a new romance. There are reasons a new relationship will not get past the starting gate. Do not sit at home and wait for a telephone call. Either make the call yourself to find out what is going on, or keep busy with your own interests. This is a favorable time for broadening your social horizons in order to create more romantic opportunities for yourself.

7. MONDAY. Fair If you are in the process of buying or selling property, this is a good time for putting pressure on the right people. Try to complete a contract before Christmas. Your concerns can get ignored if you do not make enough of a fuss. Shop around for the best mortgage. The atmosphere at work is apt to be tense at times. Make allowances for a colleague who is clearly under a lot of pressure; offer a helping hand if your own workload is lighter than theirs. Guard against being too possessive with your partner or another close family member. They may need some extra time to themselves.

8. TUESDAY. Satisfactory. This is an especially productive day for Taurus people who work from home. You should find it easier to settle down to tasks which require close concentration. If you can take some time off, this can be the perfect day to catch up with domestic chores or just laze around in the comfort of your own home. Meeting a friend for lunch can be fun. This is a propitious time to apply for a loan if you want to make home improvements of any kind. If you are going shopping, be alert for unadvertised bargains. Treat yourself to flowers or a flowering plant for your home or place of work. You may also want to send flowers to a friend.

9. WEDNESDAY. Rewarding. Your worries about someone close to you may be unnecessary. If you step back you should see that they are far more capable than you are giving them credit for. There is probably no need for you to run to their assistance unless you are specifically asked for help. If you are looking for Christmas presents for children, you may be dismayed by the prices. Remind yourself that a little imagination can go a long way; be prepared to shop around as well. The chance to earn some extra money may come along. Married Taurus people may benefit financially from the good fortune of a close family member or in-law.

10. THURSDAY. Disquieting. You may have cause for concern about a child, especially a teenager. You need to find a way of drawing them out if they are being uncommunicative. Do not make light of a problem they disclose to you. It may seem trivial to you but could be very serious to them. A short-term romance may not be working out as you had hoped. It may be best to tactfully stop seeing each other if you know in your heart that you are simply not compatible. Do not fall into the trap of finding the hat and then making it fit; you deserve better. Do not dwell on disappointments of any kind; chalk them up to experience and move on with your life.

11. FRIDAY. Misleading. Do not attach too much importance to other people's promises. Although they may be sincere at the time, they could soon be sidetracked by other matters. If you need to guarantee that something will be done or delivered on time, take personal responsibility for it. Nor should you entrust an important message to a third party. Think twice before lending money to a friend or colleague; it may be some time before you are repaid. The same warning applies to your possessions; there is a greater risk that they will not be returned in good condition. In any business dealings all agreements should be confirmed in writing.

12. SATURDAY. Successful. If you have not already started your Christmas shopping, this is a good day for doing so. If you know what you are looking for before you set out, you should be able to get a lot done in a short time. Ideas can come to you as you browse around. Place orders now for flowers or other fragile gifts. You should have lots of energy today. Physical exercise, such as a workout or a swim, may appeal. This evening is favorable for a formal occasion. It should be easier to break the conversational ice with people you meet for the first time. Look your best; first impressions are likely to be lasting.

13. SUNDAY. Mixed. In contrast to yesterday, take life at a slower pace today. Tiredness can creep up on you; sleep late this morning if you get the chance. Later in the day seek out the company of people who always accept you just as you are. Avoid a social occasion where you have to put on a bright face or make superficial conversation; you could end up feeling drained. If you are entertaining at home, try to do most of the preparation before guests arrive. In a new relationship this is a day when you can establish deeper intimacy. Spend time together away from friends or family members. A candlelight dinner can set the stage for asking that all-important question.

14. MONDAY. Changeable. If you have cards or packages to send, do not delay mailing them off. In this way you can be sure that they will arrive in plenty of time. A card from someone in your past may be delivered to you. Taurus business people should make a point of sending a card or gift to valued customers. This is also a favorable time for arranging a festive get-together with colleagues or associates. If your work involves serving the general public, this is sure to be a busy day. You need extra patience when it comes to dealing with a difficult customer; do not risk your good business reputation.

15. TUESDAY. Exciting. Career issues need some attention. Think more about long-term opportunities. This is a good time to sign up for a course which will start next year; learning a new skill could improve your job prospects as well as being fun. This is an excellent day for an office party or a Christmas lunch with others in your line of work. Make sure, however, that important tasks are finished in the morning; you may not get back to your place of work until late in the day, if at all. You are probably in the mood for a night out and should not be short of offers. Friends make the best social companions, allowing you to relax and be yourself.

16. WEDNESDAY. Rewarding. This is one of those days when people are apt to bring their problems to you. Even if an answer is not required, your sympathetic ear is sure to be appreciated. If someone asks for advice, your best policy is to be bold; do not say just what you think they want to hear. In your business dealings this is a favorable time for off-the-record discussions. You can learn far more about someone if you make a meeting unofficial or talk over the lunch table. If you have been somewhat guarded in a new relationship, now is the time to let down your barriers. Exchanging stories from your past or talking about your emotional needs can bring you closer together.

17. THURSDAY. Fair. If you have not yet decided on Christmas plans you could be tempted to take a trip. Even if your financial position is not as good as you would like, a special offer may be difficult to refuse. Do not forget to budget for hidden extras when away from home. If you are unemployed at the moment there is a chance of picking up some last-minute seasonal work. Many charities are busy at this time of year and may be looking for volunteers. Doing some unpaid work for them for a while could lead to paid job opportunities. If you have money in the bank, make a point of donating a sum to your favorite charity.

18. FRIDAY. Sensitive. If you are finding it hard to meet the expenses of Christmas you may receive an offer of financial assistance, perhaps from a friend or relative who is better off than you are. The offer is likely to be sincere, so there is no reason not to accept it. If you are paid today you could find more than you expect in your pay, such as a generous Christmas bonus. If you are buying presents for children, think up an ingenious hiding place so that they are not discovered in advance. Do not allow yourself to be pushed into partying tonight if you are not in the mood. A cozy evening at home could be more to your liking.

19. SATURDAY. Manageable. You probably cannot escape the crowds on this last shopping weekend before Christmas. Go to a mall close to home. Finding the right gift for someone who is usually difficult to buy for can be easier than you expect. A gift certificate for tapes or tickets to a concert can be a good idea for teenagers, especially if you are not sure of their tastes. If you are going out of town for the Christmas break, this is the perfect time to depart. Long-distance traveling should be problem-free. Later in the day pay special attention to children. Make reservations now for an event coming up next week. A small gathering at home is favored this evening.

20. SUNDAY. Variable. Tread carefully if you become involved in a discussion about religion. Someone who holds views that are very different from yours could take exception to an opinion you express. Make it clear that you respect their beliefs even if you do not agree with them. If you intend to host holiday festivities at home this year, do some forward planning now. Decide on menus which cater for everyone's tastes or special needs, especially for a guest who is a vegetarian or on a low-fat diet. Stock up on snacks and drinks. A friend or neighbor who is at loose ends would probably welcome an invitation to be included in your festive plans.

21. MONDAY. Confusing. If you are at work this week you may have to cover for colleagues who have already started their holiday vacation. Parts of their job could be a mystery to you, but if you keep good records of what you have done or decided you will not go wrong. Someone in authority may ask you to take on extra work or responsibilities. Guard against accepting too much at this late date. Family commitments have to come first, especially for Taurus parents of young children. Do not risk drinking and driving under any circumstances this evening. Arrange to use public transportation or to travel with a designated driver who will not drink.

22. TUESDAY. Difficult. It is pointless to try to maintain your usual routine. Work matters are apt to be chaotic; it may be impossible to get in touch with the right people. Some matters have to be put on the back burner until after the Christmas break. At home there may still be a lot to be done. The more organized you are, the more efficient you will be. Make a list of tasks or shopping; delegate as much as possible. Pick up extra wrapping paper and decorations to be on the safe side. Last-minute travel plans can be time consuming. Purchase tickets in advance rather than trusting luck to get you aboard on a standby basis.

23. WEDNESDAY. Good. Even if this is not your favorite time of year, you should feel the festive spirit rubbing off on you. At work the pace is likely to slow down. Colleagues can be in high spirits and very much in a holiday mood. You should be able to take a long lunch break or finish early. If you are at home, try to finish all of your preparations so that you avoid a last-minute panic tomorrow. Neighbors or friends are likely to drop by unannounced; have food and drink in plentiful supply. This evening is a good time for hosting a party of your own or accepting an invitation to somebody else's home. A card in today's mail may remind you to send return greetings right away.

24. THURSDAY. Fair. You are unlikely to be short of social invitations, but lack of money could be a drawback. Although you expect to overspend at this time of year, a check on your finances could tell you that the situation is getting out of control. You might need to avoid an occasion which you know will prove expensive. If you are at work, try to clear your desk by lunchtime, especially if you are leaving early to go out of town. Checkout lines in the stores or bank could be long; allow plenty of time. Plan an informal supper at home if you have guests arriving sometime this evening. An early night may be welcomed by everyone.

25. FRIDAY. Merry Christmas! If you have young children you can expect an early start to the day. Their delight should soon rub off on you. Festive cheer and goodwill should be in abundance. Let the day's events flow at their own pace rather than sticking to a timetable. Even though this is traditionally a family day, the more people you include in your celebrations the more fun you are likely to have. Invite a neighbor who may be alone to come for dinner or dessert. Other people's generosity can be overwhelming. The special person in your life may have gone to great lengths to spoil you. Your own gifts should also be well received.

26. SATURDAY. Easygoing. This is likely to be a slow day. If you have guests, allow everyone to sleep late and then serve brunch. You and your family may want to relax in front of the television this afternoon. A gift related to a hobby or a new book can be absorbing. Also be willing to play with children who are impatient to try out new toys or games. You may not be in the mood for strenuous exercise; but a gentle walk can blow away the cobwebs and work off a few calories. You are apt to feel the absence of a loved one acutely. Do not shrink duty calls to relatives who live at a distance.

27. SUNDAY. Mixed. A desire to withdraw for a while may have to be put on hold while you visit in-laws or other relatives today. Try to be gracious even if it is a visit you would prefer to avoid. A family get-together may not go as smoothly as you hope. Remind yourself that it is not always possible to get through a holiday period without some people arguing or bickering. Avoid taking sides in any dispute which does not directly concern you; in this way you can stay out of the line of fire. Playing host can start to wear thin. Find some time for yourself this afternoon and let others entertain themselves.

28. MONDAY. Demanding. You may experience a letdown now that Christmas is over, but there is still New Year's Eve to come. Make definite plans for this occasion if they have not yet been finalized. It can be hard to muster enthusiasm if you are back at work. Do not expect too much of yourself; it will take a while to get back into the swing of things. Someone who is already trying to pile on the pressure should be kept at arm's length if possible. If you are at home tackle clearing up and putting your domestic affairs in order. Find time to write thank-you letters for gifts or hospitality that you received.

29. TUESDAY. Pleasant. If you were given money or a gift certificate it could be burning a hole in your pocket. This is a good day for a shopping trip, especially to stores that have already started their sales. Good bargains can be found if you are looking for clothes; treat yourself to a new outfit for a forthcoming party or other special event. In the workplace this should be an easy day; you only need to keep things moving along at a steady pace. Exchanging news or late gifts with colleagues can be fun. A friend who has been away is eager to get together with you soon. Lend your support to a charity that is holding a fund-raising event or soliciting donations.

30. WEDNESDAY. Sensitive. Try to avoid arguments over money. If you have a joint account with your partner, point out that you can always start economizing again in the New Year. If your love of good food means that you have piled on the pounds, this is a good time for planning a diet, although it may be easier to start in the New Year rather than now; in this way you are more likely to stick to it. Someone close to you may not have had an enjoyable Christmas. Be alert to the signs even if they are not saying much; a shoulder to cry on may be just what they need. Be willing to go along with the wishes of a loved one this evening; they may be relying on your cooperation.

31. THURSDAY. Challenging. Take time to reflect on your achievements over the past year. Consider whether you have accomplished all or most of what you wanted, both in your personal affairs and in your professional life. You may realize that some of your goals were overly ambitious. However, aiming too high is better than aiming low. If you are hosting a party tonight make preparations well in advance. If you have a choice of events for this evening, opt for the one where you will know the most people; do not risk feeling out of place and uncomfortable. Be with your partner or special someone when the clock strikes midnight and you welcome in 1999.

TAURUS
NOVEMBER–DECEMBER 1997

November 1997

1. SATURDAY. Easygoing. There may be contact this morning from friends who now live out of town. Arranging a reunion could be fun. Taurus people will probably not want to spend the entire day alone. Call your friends to see what is going on. You can be invited to join an outing or be invited to meet someone for dinner. This is a favorable time for being bold and asking someone out. The challenge of being more socially aggressive than usual may be far more effortless than you anticipate. There is a good chance of being able to buy last-minute tickets for a play, concert, or sports contest. Even if tickets are expensive, the event should be well worth the cost.

2. SUNDAY. Variable. Joint finances need to be discussed. There could be less to go around at the moment than you thought. If you earn more than your partner, you might have to make a larger contribution than usual toward household expenses. If you have just been paid, now is the time to work out a budget for the month. A pay raise at work could be in the pipeline, but do not spend on the strength of a rumor unless it is definite. You are likely to be sensitive to careless comments from others. Try to be forgiving if someone is clearly being tactless rather than deliberately hurtful. However, do not let an insult pass without some form of mild protest.

3. MONDAY. Calm. The workweek starts off with a minimum of pressure. This is a day when others are willing to let you get on with your own job undisturbed and in your own way. This is a good time for addressing any problem in a working relationship. Discuss what has gone wrong rather than entering into an exchange of recriminations and blame casting. If you have some leave due consider extending your weekend by taking the day off, especially if you have the house to yourself. Some time alone can be therapeutic when it comes to thinking through personal issues and deciding on a new course of action.

4. TUESDAY. Pleasant. This should be a productive day for Taurus men and women who work with money, either your own or someone else's. Stocks and property bought today are likely to prove lucrative. This is a favorable time for new investments of all kinds. Consider taking out an endowment policy or annuity, or just opening a high-interest savings account. Older children can be better taught how to value money if you arrange for them to have their own bank account. Some professional counseling could be an answer to solving problems in a close relationship. An objective counselor can help restore the harmony between you and reduce the possibility of future friction.

5. WEDNESDAY. Mixed. This is a demanding day for Taurus people in the field of education. Students are likely to be the least of your troubles. Your administrative workload or battles concerning changes in the curriculum can be surprisingly stressful. If you are teaching or lecturing today, aim for maximum student involvement. You may want to organize work in pairs or groups. Results should be of a much higher quality if you concentrate on boosting enthusiasm. Dealing with the red tape enveloping a legal matter can be frustrating, but your patience is likely to pay off. It is in your own best interests to read through the small print of a contract or other legally binding document in detail.

6. THURSDAY. Fair. Long-distance traveling should be enjoyable, but expect delays if you have to cross a bridge or take a ferry. If you have to pick up someone from the airport, check on their arrival time before you set off; in this way you can avoid waiting around if the flight is delayed. This can be a good time for beginning to learn a foreign language, especially if there is a particular country where you have friends or business contacts. The possibility of a promotion at work may not come to anything just yet because there is someone else ahead of you in seniority. However, you may still be given a pay raise to reward your extra effort.

7. FRIDAY. Useful. Your career prospects take a turn for the better today. Someone with influence in the right places can pull strings for you if you let them know what you want. Taurus people who are looking for work might consider a commission-only position until something more secure turns up; it could be lucrative enough to tide you over for now. Starting your own business could be a sound alternative to seeking salaried work. Do some research into entrepreneurial opportunities. A formal occasion requires the correct dress. You may want to rent a suit or gown rather than buying something you might hardly ever wear.

8. SATURDAY. Changeable. If you have shopping to do, morning is likely to be the best time. You should then be able to avoid the worst of the crowds and find a convenient parking space. This is a lucky time for finding the perfect gift for a friend, probably in a store you do not normally patronize. Bargains can be found if you are looking for clothes or shoes. Keep a close eye on the time if you have arranged to meet someone this afternoon. You are likely to run late or get held up in traffic. A friend may let you down regarding arrangements for this evening. If you have been invited to a party, be prepared to go by yourself rather than miss out.

9. SUNDAY. Good. This is a sociable day for Taurus people. There may be an invitation to join friends for brunch or lunch. This is a good time for participating in a seminar or workshop related to your outside interest. You could learn a lot, and you are almost sure to make new friends in the process. You may get the chance to lend your support to a charity, perhaps by sponsoring someone in a sports event or taking part yourself. Give as generously as you can if you are approached for a donation. If you are unattached at the moment there is a greater chance of being introduced to someone new through your existing social circle.

10. MONDAY. Stressful. At the office, this morning is a good time to meet with other staff members. Certain problems need thrashing out. Meetings later in the day are likely to run over schedule. Although you might find yourself outvoted on a matter close to your heart, you must allow a democratic decision to stand. Someone who likes the sound of their own voice can be boring. Make an extra effort to concentrate on what they are trying to say or you could end up missing the point entirely. A friend who is not returning your telephone calls may be angry with you but not willing to discuss the problem. Drop them a note to let them know you care and are available.

11. TUESDAY. Fair. Hard work is the key to success. This may mean having to postpone a lunch date or putting in some overtime. If you are working efficiently, however, there is no reason for your social or personal life to suffer. Someone may single you out as the person to whom they want to reveal confidences. Do not hesitate to offer advice if it is asked for; this person might be able to reap the benefits of your experience in a similar matter. If you are studying for examinations of any kind, this is a good time for working in the peace and quiet of the library. This evening favors a quiet time at home.

12. WEDNESDAY. Deceptive. A business proposition may come your way if you are seeking to make extra money. Be alert, however, to spot a get-rich-quick scheme. It might sound convincing on paper, but the reality may be quite different. Investigate the matter further if it appeals to you, but do not part with any money unless you are sure that it is a sound investment. This is a good time for seeking legal advice on any matter which you find confusing or odd. If you are planning a major move, put extra money aside to cover unexpected costs. If you are going shopping, realize that cheap goods may not last.

13. THURSDAY. Changeable. If you are planning to vacation during the coming festive season, collect some travel brochures. If you find just what you had in mind it may be wise to put down a deposit right away while the offer is still available. Be sure to clear your vacation dates with your employer; there is a greater risk of clashing with someone else's request. This is a good time for shopping for a major purchase, but make sure that you do not pay over the list price. Be prepared to shop around to compare prices. Keep an eye on the clock if you are out tonight. There is a greater risk of missing the last transportation home once you get engrossed in conversation.

14. FRIDAY. Good. For Taurus business people this is a favorable time for taking on a partner. Being able to share the responsibilities can make it easier for you to take occasional breaks and spend more quality time with your family. Business mergers of all kinds are favored. If you are looking for work there may be a definite offer today. You might have to relocate on short notice. Make sure that your passport and visa are in order. This is a propitious time for romance. Pluck up the courage to let someone know that you are attracted to them. A first date this evening could be a resounding success with the promise of many more happy times to come.

15. SATURDAY. Variable. You may be battling mood swings today. If you are worrying too much about mistakes you made in the past, realize that there is nothing to be gained from punishing yourself when others forgave you a long time ago. Now is the time to let go of fears which are stopping you from enjoying your life to the fullest. If you need to discuss an emotional issue with your partner, carefully pick your best moment. At the end of the evening meal you can be confident of having their complete attention. There is a good chance you will discover that many of your concerns are unfounded once they are brought out into the open.

16. SUNDAY. Quiet. If you are up early this morning, head for a farmer's market. You can buy fresh produce, such as vegetables or eggs, at a fraction of supermarket prices. Stores and shops of all kinds can be fun to browse around if you are looking for antique objects or books. Cooking for others can be far more fun than preparing a meal just for yourself. If you have a large family to feed, cook extra portions to freeze for another time. Later in the day, catch up with odd jobs around the house. Making an item from wood or fabric rather than buying it can be cheaper and should bring you a sense of personal achievement.

17. MONDAY. Fair. A local journey is likely to take longer than usual, probably because of road repairs. If you are driving to work it would be wise to figure out an alternative route in advance. Shortcuts taken on the spur of the moment may cost you more time rather than speeding up your journey. There is a greater risk of breaking down in an inconvenient place. If you are not already a member of a car service, this is a favorable time for joining. If you have a reputation for being always late, you may be able to correct this with a little advance thought. It could be that you always underestimate the time that traveling takes. Try setting your watch ahead.

18. TUESDAY. Calm. Be sure to buy a newspaper this morning, or listen to a news program at home or in the car. Less pressure in the workplace means that you have more time to catch up on current affairs. For Taurus salespeople this is likely to be a particularly productive day, especially if you do most of your work over the telephone. If you are constantly on the go, consider investing in a car telephone so that you can always stay in touch with your office or your clients. A night out with a brother, sister, or other family member can be enjoyable. There are matters to discuss which you need to keep in the confines of the family circle.

19. WEDNESDAY. Mixed. This is a good time for taking out a loan or extending your mortgage if you want to carry out home improvements of any kind. If you need extra space, consider adding a loft or building an extension. This could prove to be far cheaper than moving to a larger place. Use the services of an expert if there is plumbing or electrical work to be done; otherwise you could end up making the job more complicated or expensive. Friends or business contacts traveling from out of town are likely to be delayed. If you are making any arrangements on their behalf, avoid a tight schedule; keep plans as flexible as possible.

20. THURSDAY. Changeable. Getting ready in the morning can be increasingly hard work. You can make it easier for yourself if you work out a routine. Make sure that school bags are packed and lunches prepared the night before. A new alarm clock may be a necessary purchase if you keep oversleeping. Guard against taking on too many new commitments, both in your professional and personal life. You may have an unrealistic idea about how long it will take to complete certain tasks. Give yourself plenty of leeway if you have to agree to a deadline of any kind. Turn down an invitation to go out tonight; you need extra sleep.

21. FRIDAY. Disquieting. An argument this morning can get the day off to a bad start. You might keep going over and over what was said, which can make you anxious or irritable with other people. If you know that you were at fault, do not wait until evening to offer an apology; make a telephone call and set the record straight. A new romance may get off to a shaky start. Give the relationship more time to develop. There is some risk that you are simply incompatible, but it is far too early to be sure of this. The important thing is not to delude yourself; be honest about your own needs and wishes and about what you can give to the other person.

22. SATURDAY. Variable. Taurus parents may find that young children are more inclined to get underfoot. Trying to confine them or losing your temper will almost certainly make matters worse. Instead, take them out for a few hours. Choose an outing with an educational flavor, such as a trip to a museum or an aquarium. You might have to delay taking up a new hobby because of lack of funds, but this is probably better than starting a project which you will only have to give up halfway through. Guard against overdoing if exercising or playing any kind of sport. Stick to your diet, or begin one now.

23. SUNDAY. Confusing. In a personal relationship you might not be able to say or do the right thing today. If you sense that you are in someone's bad graces, try to find out why. This may necessitate having to point out that displays of hostility are both hurtful and nonproductive. You cannot apologize for something until you know what you are supposed to have done wrong. Different outside interests do not have to become a source of conflict with your mate or partner. In fact, you should guard against a tendency toward being possessive. Give other people the freedom to do what they want without thinking that you always have to be included in their plans.

24. MONDAY. Good. For Taurus people who are looking for employment, this is a time when seasonal work is likely to be available. You may be hired to work in a store which becomes increasingly busy at this time of year. Also consider doing some volunteer work; many charities need extra help during the festive season ahead. Meetings of all kinds should be successful. You may be able to wrap up certain matters far more quickly than you expect. This is a productive day for Taurus people who work directly with the public. New clients or customers can come your way by referral. An existing problem is more likely to respond to a low-key approach.

25. TUESDAY. Unsettling. In the workplace you may have more on your agenda than you can comfortably cope with. Try not to let someone delegate any additional work to you until you have caught up with what you already have to do. A colleague could make your life more difficult than necessary. There is a risk that you have unwittingly made an enemy of them. Find the courage to challenge them; in this way you can show that you are not going to be a passive victim. If you are eating out this evening avoid food which is too rich or spicy; you could have an adverse reaction to it. Do not eat food which is past its sell-by date or does not smell quite right.

26. WEDNESDAY. Confusing. If you have a medical appointment of any kind, write down your questions in advance. This way you are less likely to be intimidated by a doctor or other consultant who is brusque and clearly in a hurry. Keep in mind that you have a right to know exactly what is going on and what their diagnosis is. If someone insists on answering you in medical mumbo-jumbo, ask them to simplify their words so that you can be sure you understood them. Legal matters can be confusing; ask for a document or the small print to be explained. If you are purchasing tickets of any kind by credit card, be sure that you get a verification number.

27. THURSDAY. Unsettling. Single Taurus people are going through an unsettling stretch. You may be attaching too much importance to being involved in a relationship. There is a lot to be said for the single life, such as more freedom, so relax and enjoy the advantages. Someone you are attracted to may be oblivious to the fact that you are interested in them. This is probably not the right time to stick your neck out unless you feel strong enough to cope with the possibility of being rejected. Be extra careful if you are traveling by air on this Thanksgiving holiday;

there is a greater risk of your luggage going to a destination other than where you are going.

28. FRIDAY. Pleasant. This is a much luckier day for romance, especially if you are trying to win the attention of a particular person. There is more natural opportunity to get together. It is up to you capitalize on this turn of good fortune. This is an excellent time for making vacation plans for the holiday season. If you usually stay at home toward the end of the year, consider breaking with tradition and going abroad or to relatives for a change. This evening favors outings with a cultural flavor, such as a theatrical performance or a classical concert. Live music of any kind should appeal to you; dancing can release tension and bring you closer to your partner.

29. SATURDAY. Variable. This is a good time to start your Christmas shopping. In this way you avoid the stress of leaving it all to the last minute. If you cannot get to the mall today, at least make a list of the gifts you need to purchase. If you are not sure what to buy for a certain individual, ask them directly what they would like; this is preferable to making an expensive mistake. If money is tight, come to an agreement with your friends and family members about setting a price limit. Conversation with your partner could take a serious turn. Try to be responsive if they need to discuss a personal issue which they have been keeping to themselves.

30. SUNDAY. Satisfactory. Make a point of visiting a friend or relative who is housebound at the moment. Errands or chores which are too much for them could be quick and easy for you to do. Use your empathy rather than waiting to be asked. News of someone who is hospitalized should be encouraging; a full recovery can be expected. Your mate or partner could receive unexpected financial help, perhaps as a gift from someone in their family. Try not to advise them how to spend it even if their wishes seem frivolous; you are sure to be on the receiving end of their generosity anyway. This is a good time for cleaning closets at home; donate unwanted goods to a charity.

December 1997

1. MONDAY. Rewarding. If you have to send holiday cards or packages abroad, be sure to check on the final mailing deadlines for different parts of the world. Make a list of all the people to whom you need to send cards this year. Buy cards from a favored charity as a way of making a donation. If money is in short supply, consider making your own. This is a propitious day for interviews of any kind; you can make a good impression just by being yourself. In your business dealings, snap decisions are likely to be right. You can afford to trust your own instincts. An evening class or workshop can provide intellectual food for thought.

2. TUESDAY. Challenging. At work it is important to pace yourself. Be methodical when it comes to approaching the day's tasks. Throwing money at a problem is unlikely to be productive; fundamental issues need to be reassessed first. Taurus students have a lot of work to get through by the end of the term. Devise a study schedule for yourself; this way your rate of progress should be easier to monitor. You might need to spend less time and money on your social life, but try not to let someone down over arrangements for this evening. Your mate or date may be relying on you more than you know. Someone who drops by your home this evening may have a secret to share with you.

3. WEDNESDAY. Stressful. You are more likely to be hypersensitive to criticism of any kind. Someone at work may just be trying to help, even if they do come across as tactless. Do not shy away from discussing your feelings with your mate or partner. Taurus people have a tendency toward moodiness when feeling unsettled or vulnerable. Speaking up and saying how you feel can help dispel an attack of the blues. You cannot expect others to read your mind. For Taurus individuals who work as performers, this can be a demanding day. An audition may be more of an ordeal than you had bargained for; let your professionalism shine through.

4. THURSDAY. Fair. Your usual work routine is apt to be in a state of upheaval. Attempt to take changes in stride rather than resisting them. Being open to new ideas can make life easier in the long run. You might find it difficult to settle down to any one task. However, try to bring at least one project to fruition; otherwise you might end up feeling that you have wasted the day. A relative may be demanding more of your time and attention than you can afford to give. Point out that you have a life of your own to live, which means that you cannot always be there for them at the drop of a hat. Shrug off any attempts to make you feel guilty or selfish.

5. FRIDAY. Good. Taurus business people could be facing a calendar filled with lunch engagements for the festive season. This is a good time for arranging dates to entertain your own clients or employees. If you are looking for work, renew your efforts. You should be able to line up something for the start of the coming year. Give careful thought to references so that you have plenty of time to ask the best people. A valued colleague may announce plans to resign or retire. This can open up new opportunities for you. A formal occasion of any kind is likely to be successful this evening if you listen more than you talk.

6. SATURDAY. Disquieting. If you want to go shopping it is probably best to go alone. In this way you can spend a little or as much time as you want hunting for presents. An early start is advisable to avoid the worst of the crowds. Keep your money in a safe place; there is a greater risk of having your pocket picked or your wallet stolen. The problems of a close friend could be giving you cause for concern, but they are more likely to ignore your advice than act on it. Sometimes you just have to let others make their own mistakes; try not to get too involved. A party this evening may be a disappointment because a certain guest does not show up.

7. SUNDAY. Pleasant. This is a good day for gathering your friends and family members around you. You might decide to go out for lunch rather than cooking at home, giving everybody a day off. Social occasions can be great fun today. Accept any invitation which comes your way, even if you have to go alone. New friendships made now are likely to be lasting. If you are single you may be introduced to someone who is obviously attracted to you; chances are you share the same sense of humor. Act naturally rather than putting on any airs and dropping names of important people you know. Conversation which centers on political or religious issues can be enlightening.

8. MONDAY. Deceptive. If you are sending cards or packages make sure that your own address is clearly shown. In this way an undeliverable parcel is more likely to be returned to you if it does not reach its proper destination. Use a trustworthy delivery service for important documents or packages. Do not treat any rumors as gospel truth without checking out the facts for yourself; they may just be the result of idle gossip. Being caught in a lie can be embarrassing; your best policy is to stick to the whole truth. Do not be tempted to discuss someone behind their back. There is a greater risk that your words can be distorted and passed on, which may do a lot of damage.

9. TUESDAY. Fair. The festive season is the time for goodwill to all. This is the right moment for burying the hatchet if you are caught up in a feud with a former lover or friend. Even if you cannot forget the incident which brought about the rift in the first place, make an extra effort to forgive. Everyone has faults; you may not be entirely blameless. This is a lucrative day for Taurus people who work on commission. If your work involves serving the general public, you could earn a healthy sum in tips and other gratuities. Do not be tempted to skip a meeting today; you could miss out on important information.

10. WEDNESDAY. Variable. If you are at home this is a good time for writing your greeting cards. This might take a lot longer than you anticipate, especially if there are several people to whom you write only at this time of year. It may amaze you to realize how much has happened in the last twelve months. Today's mail may include a card or an invitation from someone in your past; you do not have to reply unless you really want to do so. Taurus business people should establish a company policy about giving and receiving gifts. The time difference can account for difficulties with business abroad; you may have to work late waiting for an important fax or phone call.

11. THURSDAY. Mixed. You are unlikely to win sympathy if you exaggerate your problems. Resist the temptation to make a mountain out of a molehill. People are far more willing to come to the rescue if they believe that you are genuinely in need of a helping hand. Keep a sense of proportion. If you are trying to lose weight before the festive season gets into full swing you have to be more disciplined than ever. The temptation to eat and drink too much at a social event may be hard to resist, but try to keep your limits in mind. Treat yourself to new clothes when you have reached your target weight, but not before then.

12. FRIDAY. Unpredictable. Try to keep your spending under control. Make a point of paying household bills before you go Christmas shopping. In this way you will have a clearer idea of what you can afford to spend. This is not a favorable time for buying on credit, no matter how tempting special offers or terms may be. There is a greater risk of overcommitting yourself; meeting repayments in the future can become burdensome. In the office this is a good time for putting up decorations; a festive spirit can do wonders for morale. An office party this evening is sure to be enjoyed by all. Be prepared for a late night.

13. SATURDAY. Satisfactory. You have the time and intuition now to look for unusual gifts. If you cannot find exactly what you have in mind for a certain someone, there is still enough time to place an order. If you are entertaining guests at home over the Christmas period, begin to plan the menus. You may be able to do the bulk of the shopping in advance, saving you a lot of last-minute rushing around. Do not forget to make allowances for someone who is a vegetarian or who has other special dietary needs. If you feel restless later in the day, arrange to meet up with friends who are also at loose ends. Choose a cheap and cheerful restaurant that does not require a long commute.

14. SUNDAY. Frustrating. This is not a favorable time for lending out money. If someone comes to you for a loan, make your terms absolutely clear. Also remember that you have a right to say no without explaining why. Someone who often wants to borrow things from you may not be so good at returning them. Now is the time to ask for items on loan to be brought back. You might finally be realizing that a certain individual often exaggerates. Learn to take their promises with a grain of salt and some healthy skepticism. Above all, do not place your trust in those people who have let you down in the past; you could be just asking for more trouble.

15. MONDAY. Slow. If there are any shows or movies you want to see over the festive period, purchase your tickets now. Do not trust to luck at the last moment; you could be disappointed. If you are making reservations for others, ask them to pay you in advance; otherwise you could wait a long time to be reimbursed. Administrative tasks at work can be more time consuming than usual. Someone else's errors could slow you down. Take extra care with written work; sloppy grammar or spelling mistakes can make a poor impression. If you are using a word processor, take the time to make a backup disk for all your work in order to be on the safe side.

16. TUESDAY. Misleading. Short journeys on public transportation can end up costing a lot. This is a good time for buying a weekly or monthly travel pass, which could reduce your traveling costs more than you realize. Be sure that you have enough money in your wallet for cab fare if you are going to an appointment; it might be the only way in which you can arrive on time. Ask for any telephone messages if you are away from the office for any length of time. Someone may forget to pass them on unless you remind them. Enter any social or professional arrangement on your calendar before they slip your mind. Do not reverse the charges on a long-distance telephone call this evening.

17. WEDNESDAY. Changeable. Plans for your holiday vacation may still be up in the air. This is a good day for finalizing your arrangements. This might mean having to pin down certain members of your family for a definite yes or no. At work it is important not to let the festivities interfere too much with your responsibilities; someone has to make sure that the work gets done. A superior could be evaluating your abilities from behind the scenes. Make sure that they have every reason to think highly of you. A night out may be canceled. Putting up the tree or other decorations at home can be a fun option. Do not forget a sprig of mistletoe.

18. THURSDAY. Variable. This is a busy day as small jobs mount up. Try to delegate where possible rather than putting yourself under unnecessary pressure. In the workplace you cannot be all things to all people without your own work suffering as a result. Someone will just have to wait their turn if they need your undivided attention. This is a good time to shop for intimate gifts for those closest to you. Make sure that you find a safe and secure hiding place at home. If you are entertaining this evening the number of guests is likely to escalate. Opt for a menu which can easily be stretched to accommodate extra people.

19. FRIDAY. Disquieting. Buying presents for children can turn out to be even more expensive than you had bargained for. A little imagination can go a long way, however, when it comes to choosing stocking fillers. Shop for inexpensive wrapping paper, ribbon, and tags; there is no need to spend a fortune on what will be ripped off. Single Taurus people might have high hopes of a new romance, but the reassurance you need may not yet be forthcoming. This is not a time to be demanding or impatient; you run the risk of frightening someone away before they get to know you. Avoid serious or soul-searching conversations. Instead, concentrate on having fun together.

20. SATURDAY. Unsettling. Taurus people who have postponed Christmas shopping until the last moment may now be regretting it. But if you are well organized you should be able to catch up today. Ask friends and family members what they want rather than guessing; this could save you a lot of time. Find out about activities in your local neighborhood for children. This is a better option than having them underfoot at home if you have a lot to do. Squabbles with a loved one are foreseen, but these are unlikely to develop into serious arguments. This is a time when there are no problems which cannot be solved if you show that you are willing to talk and listen.

21. SUNDAY. Fair. You can afford a leisurely start to the day. If you spent yesterday rushing around, or if you had a late night, you need some time to recharge your batteries. Treat yourself to breakfast in bed if possible. Tensions in a close relationship can melt away simply by spending some quality time together; suggest going out for lunch or a long walk. If household chores have been neglected recently, this afternoon is a good time for catching up with tasks such as ironing and cleaning. If you have been invited to a social gathering, check what time you are expected; someone may have given you the wrong information.

22. MONDAY. Demanding. For Taurus employees who have to work right up to Christmas, this can be a stressful day. You may have to cover for colleagues who have already begun their vacation. Try not to defer too many decisions in the absence of a superior; some matters are just a question of using your common sense. There could be generous rewards in your pay; a bonus may be higher than you expect. If your business depends on the Christmas trade, you are in for a spectacularly productive day. Revenue from last-minute shoppers should be substantial. If you are going to be away from home this evening, double-check all your home security measures.

23. TUESDAY. Optimistic. Taurus business people should be able to wrap up an important project before taking off for a Christmas break. Attending a social function can lead to making new contacts in your own field. You may get a chance to talk with someone who has often been unavailable in the past. If you are unemployed you may get a lucky break today. An offer of work in the coming year is probably sincere and should be followed up. Getting to know a colleague or business associate on a social basis may lead to romance for Taurus singles. This evening is a good time for going to a party or hosting one of your own. Relax and have fun; do not try to impress anyone.

24. WEDNESDAY. Variable. If you are going away for the holidays, this is a good day for traveling. You may need to make an extra effort to switch off from work problems. Whatever the work issue is, it will wait until you get back. The important thing now is to relax and enjoy yourself. If you have to work today, a family member or friend may be willing to make last-minute purchases for you. If you are staying at home this week, stock up on food and favorite drinks. A family gathering this Hanukkah and Christmas Eve may have its tense moments. Do your best to avoid arguments of any kind, even if someone seems intent on provoking you. To be on the safe side, get to bed early.

25. THURSDAY. MERRY CHRISTMAS! This day of the year is often noted for excesses, and this is no exception. If you are someone's guest, sit back and enjoy being thoroughly spoiled. Food and drinks are likely to be flowing throughout the day. However, you will probably enjoy the day more if you pace yourself. If you are entertaining at home you might wonder if you have taken on too much. Make sure that you rope in others to help out with serving food or washing dishes. Exchanging gifts should be the highlight of the day; the generosity of a loved one could be overwhelming. Your own gifts are sure to be well received.

26. FRIDAY. Fair. This promises to be a pleasant day even it is more low-key than yesterday. A call from someone far away can be cheering. If you have guests, just serve a simple meal and enjoy chatting. Make a point of getting some physical exercise later on, even if it is just a walk around the block. Some fresh air can be revitalizing. Keep arrangements flexible. There is a greater chance of visitors dropping by unannounced, including someone you would be disappointed to miss. If you have to work you are unlikely to be under pressure and should be able to finish earlier than usual. Do not put off writing thank-you notes.

27. SATURDAY. Happy. The Christmas vacation provides a chance to get closer to family members. Today you might want to talk about the past. Recalling shared memories can strengthen bonds. A reunion with a loved one is sure to be a special occasion. This is not a time for repressing your feelings. Let that special person in your life know just how much you have missed them. Taurus singles may choose today to discuss wedding plans. And for Taurus who tied the knot years ago, the relationship can benefit from a second honeymoon. An intimate gathering of friends at home is the perfect way to enjoy this evening.

28. SUNDAY. Good. This is a good day for visiting family members you have not yet seen during this holiday period. Someone may have a special gift for you which comes as a wonderful surprise. This is a day when other people seem more considerate and kindly disposed toward you. If you have to put in an appearance at work tomorrow, make the most of this day of leisure. Do what appeals to you most, whether it is relaxing in front of the television or focusing on a creative hobby. Weekend guests can be a delight to have around and should extend the festive spirit. You might have forgotten just how much you enjoy the company of a certain individual.

29. MONDAY. Disconcerting. For Taurus people who are back at work this can be a tiring day. You will probably find it hard to get back into the swing of things. Higher-ups are unlikely to expect great things of you; they are probably in the same mood themselves. It might be helpful to spend some time thinking about your work-related goals for the coming year; this could help motivate you. Someone who has been away may not get in touch as soon as you had hoped. There is a chance that they have come home to a stack of problems, so give them time. The possibility of a new job might not be as glamorous as it sounds; research it thoroughly before deciding.

30. TUESDAY. Deceptive. Returning from a trip can be tedious. There is a greater risk of delays in your journey. If you have been abroad, it is not worth the risk of bringing in goods undeclared. Allow extra time for all traveling; the roads are apt to be busier than you expected. Your powers of concentration are not at their best. If you are at work, postpone important matters until after the New Year. Someone who is usually helpful may not be available or may not understand your problem. Make an extra effort to be clear about arrangements for tomorrow evening; there is a greater risk of creating confusion around you. Guard against strenuous physical exercise.

31. WEDNESDAY. Exciting. The end of the year finds Taurus people in an optimistic mood. Take some time to review what you have achieved in the past twelve months, both personally and professionally. Focus your New Year resolutions on career issues and the quality of your more meaningful personal relationships. Finding the balance between work and play is a challenge well worth taking up. This evening's celebration should go with a swing, whether you are attending a formal function or have arranged an impromptu gathering of friends and loved ones. The company of those you appreciate is sure to get 1998 off to a joyful start.

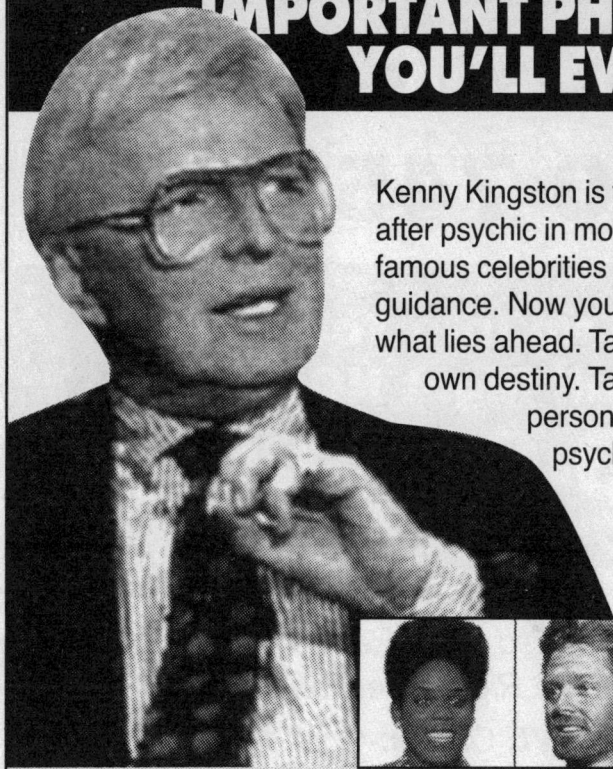

Let The Stars
Guide You To
The Future...
Where,
Love,
Money and
Success
are waiting
for you!
Get A FREE Sample Psychic
Reading Today!!!
1-800-841-7648
18+. For Ent. Purposes Only.